MAPPING THE PATH TO MATURITY

MAPPING THE PATH TO MATURITY

A Connected History of Bengal and the North-East

Edited by
BIPASHA RAHA
SUBHAYU CHATTOPADHYAY

MANOHAR
2018

First published 2018

ISBN 978-93-5098-180-1

Published by
Ajay Jain *for*
Manohar Publishers & Distributors
4753/23 Ansari Road, Daryaganj
New Delhi 110002

Typeset by
Ravi Shaker
Delhi 110095

Printed at
Shri Ganpati Enterprises
Delhi 110052

For

all our students, past and present

with whom we had shared our ideas

Contents

Acknowledgements

This book has travelled a long way. An edited volume is never an easy task. This book would never have seen the light of the day without the support of our friends and long-suffering families. The idea of the book was first conceived during a seminar which was organized in the Department of History, Visva-Bharati, in January 2011. It is time to acknowledge the intellectual and moral debt that we have incurred as we journeyed to India's modernity.

We must first thank all the contributors who sent in their essays in time and helped to enrich this volume. All our colleagues in the Department of History, Visva-Bharati, have been ever supportive. They have generously shared ideas and been patient listeners. We are greatly indebted to our postgraduate students with whom we have discussed many of our thoughts.

Our debt to our families is too great to be enumerated. They have been with us all the way. They have been very patient and supportive and tolerated the long hours that we devoted to the book.

EDITORS

Introduction

Bipasha Raha and Subhayu Chattopadhyay

Well into the twenty-first century, India has made its place in the contemporary world. While it holds out great hope for the future, its long history offers interesting read and helps understand much of its greatness as it traversed an arduous route to maintain its uniqueness. Freedom from two centuries of colonial rule came at a price that has been heavy. Her journey into the present has been a rough one, plagued by difficulties at every step. This book is, however, not intended to trace this journey.

This book delves into varied aspects of the history of Bengal and the North-East, situated within a time frame of more than a hundred years. There are fourteen essays in this book which throw light on hitherto unexplored aspects of these two regions, highlighting the richness and varied nature of Indian history and tradition. The book begins its journey in India's colonial past and walks into the present. The essays deal with ideas, sociology, literary texts, politics, gender, industries, culture, health, tribal issues, as also science and technology.

Achintya Kumar Dutta has addressed a significant issue. In the essay titled 'Colonialism and Public Health in Rarh Bengal: Development and Underdevelopment', he shows how underdevelopment may be seen as a product or by-product of development. He argues that underdevelopment in the subcontinent during British rule derived inevitably from the colonial forms of economic exploitation. He has focussed on the Rarh region in Bengal encompassing the districts of Burdwan, Birbhum and Bankura. The author argues that while colonial authorities developed 'colonial (modern)' infrastructure with the intention of extracting resources of Rarh Bengal to fulfil their requirements, this in turn created an environment which adversely affected public health, which may be perceived as a manifestation of underdevelopment. There was reluctance among the colonial rulers in adopting adequate measures to improve public health and develop health care services. The author has tried to explain this reluctance as he attempts to understand why the agriculturally and minerally rich Rarh region, that was so crucial to the British, presented a sorry picture of public health lacking basic health care facilities and was home to some of the fatal/worst communicable diseases. Rarh Bengal witnessed the prevalence of several lethal diseases, viz., malaria, *kala-azar*, cholera, small pox, influenza, tuberculosis and leprosy that occurred epidemically and continued to act upon as endemic during colonial rule. The author holds colonial infrastructure intervention, suited to support economic exploitation, responsible for playing havoc with public health. Colonial infrastructure in the form of expansion of irrigation canals, and construction of railway embankments and bridges led to ecological changes which had far-reaching and enduring effects on public health. They became veritable breeding grounds for mosquitoes, the carriers of most dreaded diseases. These developments shut out flood water of rivers like Damodar and Ajay and acted as impediments to natural irrigation and drainage, thus leading to proliferation of Burdwan fever that devastated south-west Bengal extensively. Rice cultivation was adversely affected causing economic hardships to a large majority of cultivating classes. Insanitary conditions from stagnant flood waters led to further diffusion of diseases. The poor were the worst hit by epidemic diseases, the author observes. He relates the economic decline of the region under study to the ravages caused by the various diseases that were so widespread. The last quarter of the nineteenth century witnessed periodic outbreak of epidemics which continued in the first half of twentieth century. Communicable diseases like cholera became rampant in newly-developed industrial and urban areas. Immigration of labourers to coal mining areas led to further spread of unhygienic conditions. The author thus draws attention to the relationship between disease and urbanization and between industrialization and disease-prone environment or living working conditions. If the developmental works, argues the author, could be seen as instances of success of colonial government, lack of health care facilities were indeed areas of failure. Underdevelopment or low level of public health could be easily ascertained from the repeated inroads of communicable diseases in epidemic forms, prevalence of these diseases for a long time and the high mortality rate caused by them. Measures adopted by the colonial government to fight diseases and protect public health were inadequate. Similarly, investment in this sphere was meagre. So was the number of hospitals and trained workforce. Low salary of the latter further hindered work. Sanitary reforms were far from satisfactory. The author concludes that while development of public health system as well as medical science in Britain was 'organic', it was not so in India.

Bipasha Raha's article titled 'Ladies' Parliament: Literary Representation of a Site of Female Interaction in Colonial Rural Bengal', examines female relationships in late nineteenth and early twentieth century family, cutting across class and caste barriers particularly in the countryside. She selects one particular site of social exchange for women as she argues historians have failed to explore this aspect. Written texts fill in the gaps in our knowledge of social practices and customs. Literature recorded people's past and sustained their cultural identity. The author claims that literary sources of the colonial period that include novels, short stories, personal narratives, poems and plays, give a glimpse into sites of social interaction. These bring to light how such sites of interaction were witness to social power plays, internal bickering, forging of relationships and other aspects of social life in colonial Bengal.

Continuous social interaction helped to keep the villages a vibrant entity. There were many sites of such interaction as is evident from contemporary literature. Raha too uses one such site, the bathing *ghats*, where the 'ladies parliament' was held daily. It was the only public space allowed to the country women. Although it was prevalent among women in rural Bengal to pay social visits, nowhere did so many women meet together and talk on so many different subjects as at the bathing *ghats* to which they resorted for their daily ablutions. Even colonial authorities acknowledged the significance of these *ghats* in the social sphere. The interactions at these congregations furnish a picture of the social life of these women and their take on the indigenous and colonial power structure.

The coal industry in Bengal, its growth and development in the colonial period is a domain where relatively little research has been undertaken. Naina Banerjee's article is a welcome addition in this uncharted territory. In 'Indians and Europeans in Coal Business: Conflict of Interest in the Bengal Coalfield, 1900-1947', she focuses on the development of Indian enterprise in the coal industry. As she traces the growth and development of the coal industry in Raniganj and Jharia region, Banerjee argues that pressure from British capitalists dwarfed growth of this industry. It was the expansion of the railways that gave a fillip to the industry. She analyses the role of the agency houses and managing agencies in this regard. Indigenous entrepreneurial involvement was initiated by Dwarkanath Tagore. This created a sharp rift between European managing agencies and the Indian colliery owners and coal traders. The author traced this confrontation over ownership rights of collieries back to the 1840s. She claims that at the turn of the century the conflict took the form of a confrontation between the Indian Mining Association (IMA) affiliated to the Bengal Chamber of Commerce, which had long represented the interests of the bigger European coal companies, and the Indian Mining Federation (IMF), organized in 1913 to promote unity among Indian colliery owners and was affiliated to Bengal National Chamber of Commerce. The expansion of the railways into the Jharia field encouraged Bengali entrepreneurs to enter the coal mining industry since the 1890s and the interest continued well into the first quarter of twentieth century. Banerjee discusses the activities of some of these entrepreneurs. Since the middle of the 1920s new immigrant trading communities from Marwar, Kutch, Sindh and Punjab gained foothold in the coal industry. The economic depression in the 1920s gave a blow to Bengali concerns. Their entrepreneurial activities in coal industry declined and this vacuum was filled by the Marwaris, Kutchis and Sindhis. They later went on to become major players in coal mining. But the indigenous coal sector, argues the author, faced serious difficulties from the beginning. There was the problem of raising loans from the organized and the unorganized money market of Calcutta. They did not possess sufficient economic muscle to counter the railways, which preferred European colliery owners, as far as supply of wagons was concerned. It was difficult, says the author, to reconcile the conflicting interests although on occasions Indians joined hands with European colliery owners to curb the menace of labour unrest. Such instances, however, were rare as indigenous colliery entrepreneurs held a position subordinate to European corporate concerns. The latter always enjoyed the capital, greater resources in personnel, support of a strong political lobby which ensured almost total European hegemony. This, observes the author, continued for some years even after India attained Independence.

'Potter's Craft: A Traditional Sector in Colonial Bengal' is a refreshingly new research that studies the unorganized pottery industry. Sourcing a wide range of primary data, author Supti Raha has made a study of producers and production till mid-nineteenth century, techniques of production, principal variants of pottery in late colonial Bengal and the problems and prospects of the potters' craft. She argues that while traditional industries were impacted by the long colonial rule, pottery in Bengal did not face an untimely death. There were generally two types of potter-artisans, one who produced unglazed earthen pottery and those who made artistic wares, often glazed, fulfilling both ritualistic and household need of the people. Raha discusses the pottery of Bankura and Krishnanagar, and the image-making industry in the potters' colony at Kumartuli, in Calcutta. While the Bankura pottery was important for its cultural significance and was an example of achievement in the history of clay-modelling; Krishnanagar pottery set a new tradition in modelling realistic subjects in naturalistic style. Image-making too acquired new heights at the hands of the Kumartuli potters due to the fact that a conspicuous social phenomenon of the colonial period, according to the author, was the steady rise in idolatry by the Bengalee community as a whole, also known as *barowari pujo*. Factors like patronage of the landed aristocracy and contact with Europeans impacted the pattern of clay and terracotta goods produced by potters. But from the close of the nineteenth century, admits the author, the potters began to face certain problems. She lists among them technological backwardness, laborious and time consuming nature of manufacturing, problems of marketing and changing values. While adoption of cooperative methods could have been a possible way out, such societies did not exist prior to Independence. Import of earthenware and porcelain added to the problems. The author examines how the beginning of the twentieth century saw efforts made by the *swadeshi* entrepreneurs to organize the traditional pottery industry on modern lines. While the upper and the middle classes started using steel, bell metal, porcelain and enamelled iron wares, potters continued to find a market in the rural areas for their products. It was the continuity of tradition and the link between the craft and the social and religious life of people that led to its survival in Bengal. Consequently, even at the close of the colonial rule, Bengal potters retained their profession to a large extent.

Amitava Chatterjee's 'Genealogies of Sports Associations in Bengal: Historicising the Institutionalization of European Clubs with Native *Akharas*' is a significant addition to the steadily growing research work on the issue of health, sports and colonial masculinity. Sports began to acquire relevance in the middle-class cultural world of Bengal by the close of the nineteenth century as a leisure and health option, moulded by ideas imported from Europe. With the advent of colonialism, says the author, Bengali society witnessed the diffusion of modern sports which had colonial origins. The sporting clubs, an European prerogative in India, had a distinctive identity of 'colonial public sphere'. They allowed for a relatively greater degree of openness. The author claims that the Western sports slowly caught the fancy of Bengali society and attracted the rich and middle-class sections. He attempts to show how the sporting clubs and associations that emerged as an institutional novelty in the sporting arena in the course of the nineteenth century made the public sphere critically important for a modern sporting culture. Here, public patronage and public viewing of sport replaced the older connection with patrician patronage. The growth of physical culture in an institutionalized form, thus according to Chatterjee, became integrally linked with this club culture. The patronage of indigenous sporting associations came mostly from relatively affluent men, whose ambition to achieve fame in the public sphere accounted for their interest in promotion of traditional games. In the process, says the author, a distinct locus of sporting activity was created, in which the involvement of the public mattered. The significant issue concerning the sporting culture in Bengal in the late colonial period relates to the transformation of traditional sporting activities from leisurely practice to the larger process of institutionalization and as aspects of a public culture. In this essay, the author seeks to explore the history of institutionalization of traditional sporting *akharas* of colonial Bengal from its marginality as a counterpart of European sporting clubs.

Arpita Sen's 'The Missionary among the Khasi' emphasizes that the British Empire did not use military and physical force alone to rule. She argues that it endured by getting both colonizing and the colonized people to see their world and themselves in a particular way, 'internalizing the language of Empire' as representing the natural, true order of life. She takes as a case study the Khasis, a matrilineal tribe of Meghalaya in the north-east of India. She examines the process of conversion of the Khasis to Christianity in the nineteenth century by the Welsh missionaries. The author argues that though British colonialism and Christian missionary activities 'cannot be put together within one register to employ the Khasi story of conversion', in the long run it eased the work of the British by helping to subdue the Khasis. It made it easier to reconcile the war-like Khasis, renowned for their prowess in archery, to colonial rule. This process of conversion in the second half of the nineteenth century was never at any stage entangled with British colonial rulership. However, it had their tacit support and protection. The missionary, 'with his supremacist instinct', was instrumental in the West's 'spiritual, physical and intellectual conquest' of the Khasis. Sen observes that conversion was made possible by the denigration of Khasi religion, culture and tradition through factors such as education, medicine and natural calamity like the earthquake of 1897 that devastated the Khasi hills. She concludes that in spite of the initial difficulties that the Welsh missionaries encountered in evangelization, by the turn of the century there were considerable number of converts among the Khasis. Christianity was accepted for various reasons. It was the religion of the rulers and accepting it implied obvious advantages. Admission to educational institutions, hospitals, jobs, help in cash or kind were offered generously to the Khasis by the missionaries and Christians were given preference over others. Yet at the same time, the author feels, one cannot ignore the fact that the Welsh missionaries were on their part very gifted, devoted and selfless people and their constructive humanitarian work, particularly in imparting education and providing medical care, drew the Khasis towards Christianity.

Madhumita Mondol's 'Swarnakumari Devi: A Trend Setter in Colonial Bengal' seeks to explore the changing perception of a woman towards her own condition, gender issues, the home and the nationalist movement. The daughter of Debendranath Tagore and the elder sister of Rabindranath Tagore Swarnakumari Devi's (1856-1932), activities spanned a period of more than half a century which co-incided with a crucial phase of the country's history. Swarnakumari was one of the most outstanding women who made a place for herself in the literate society of Bengal in the late nineteenth and early twentieth century. This essay seeks to highlight her significant contribution to the cause of women. She emerged on the social scene of Bengal at a time when a handful of reformers were attempting to redress some of the social atrocities against women. She talked of equal opportunities for women and the author attempts to portray how she epitomized the 'new' woman. She claims that the way Swarnakumari brought up her daughters and educated them bears testimony to her perception of what the position of women should be in society. The author argues that Swarnakumari skilfully used her pen to address pertinent issues relevant to contemporary times and attempted to popularize scientific knowledge among the common people. She flourished and blossomed, observes the author, in the newly-found freedom which literacy brought. It was access to the male preserve of learning which helped some women give expression to their feelings. The author argues that Swarnakumari received recognition from her contemporaries for her work and was widely acclaimed for her literary pursuits. She focussed upon education and self dependence for women. She was an achiever who, according to the author, not only attempted changes in the condition of her hapless sisters but also struggled to influence how society at large perceived them. In terms of education, culture, dress reform that made it possible for women to cross the inner confines of their household, vocational guidance, initiating women's organization, social service and political involvement, Swarnakumari set an example of 'progress' for other women of Bengal. Mondol's article throws light on the achievements of a woman who gave a new meaning, a new dimension to woman's position in society and in the work of nation-building but is dwarfed by the giant like personality of her more illustrious brother.

Sujata Mukherjee's 'Family Health and Dissemination of Medical Knowledge in Nineteenth-Century India' attempts to trace the growth of a new genre of Bengali writings, viz., manuals and books addressed to both men and women on health, hygiene and rearing of children and; analyse the context, content and impact of these writings to highlight certain aspects of medicalization of society in colonial India. She analyses the significance of the health advices in these writings which became part of a new ideal of indigenous domesticity through which, indigenous reformers sought to negotiate and reformulate the received notion of colonial modernity. The author refers to some of the pedagogical texts written in her period, which produced a normative discourse on family and included guidelines for an ideal housewife for proper home management, scientific nurturing of children, regulation of dietary habits, creation of hygienic environment. She claims that one feature of medical advices for women contained in these manuals and periodicals was their heterogeneous nature. Women were expected to know a bit of all available forms of treatment, including folk medicine, allopathy, homoeopathy, *kabiraji* and *hakimi*. The author examines why such emphasis was put on medical advice and women were advised to acquire skills in new medical knowledge as also indigenous therapies. She claims that the educated middle class, including both men and women, tried to blend indigenous tradition with modern or Western medicine in reformulation of Western ideal of domesticity. The author concludes by saying that the new, modern, educated women by simultaneously absorbing new health guidelines and knowledge of hygiene and treatment, and also acting as repository of traditional knowledge would create the possibility of facilitation of women's empowerment. This article, based on some significant primary literature, adds to the steadily growing research on the medical world in colonial India.

In the article 'His Nest and his Sky: Rabindranath Tagore, Women and the Idea of the Feminine', Swati Ganguly analyses the influence of some of the women in Rabindranath's life and on his creations. Some of the letters he wrote to them bear testimony to Rabindranath revealing his thoughts and ideas to his women companions, not only of his inner self, but the public persona that he had cultivated over years. They were crucial to his styling as a creative artist and an ethical philosopher. To suggest, however, that Tagore's entire oeuvre can be understood on the basis of inspiration and influence of individual women, to establish one-to-one equations, is to do injustice to a very complex process of creativity. This is particularly misleading in the case of Rabindranath who, argues the author, inherited an ethical-philosophical tradition of the monotheistic Brahmo religion, a spirituality whose basis was the worship of God-the-Father. However, it is also true that the stern patriarchal nature of the inheritance underwent transformations through Rabindranath's deep reading and imbibing of alternative literary and philosophical traditions. The most important of these are the erotic devotional Vaishnava poetry in which the poet often assumes the persona of a women desiring her lover. Indeed, the emotion of *biraha*, a deep longing filled with melancholy (a leitmotif of many of Tagore's poems and lyrics), is traditionally regarded as a feminine expression. He was also influenced by the *bauls* of Bengal, whose thinking radically reformulates the patriarchal understanding of gender relations. The photo archives of Rabindra Bhavana, says the author, have a photograph of the girl perched on the branches of a tree, absorbed in reading a book. This photograph, she argues, seems a perfect visualization of Rabindranath Tagore's dream of the nest, not so much as a closed cocoon but a resting place which was open to the embrace of the sky.

Subhayu Chattopadhyay's 'Too Long a Prelude?: The Formative Century of Bengali Theatre' argues that Western influence played a pivotal role behind the evolution of modern theatre in India. The experiments with modern theatre in tune with Western concept and technique were first felt in two opposite parts of India, i.e. Bombay and Bengal. But it was a slightly different story in Bengal than Bombay. Apart from the private theatre of the wealthy Bengalis, there developed slowly but surely a new stronger trend where a conscious effort had been taken to make a perfect blending of latest Western techniques with that of a new genre of scripts addressing the issues of contemporary political and social life and practices. The conservative reaction during post-1857 era, evidently made the empire more autocratic and denied the socio-politico-cultural aspirations of the educated Indians for sharing equal space. The offshoot was the rise of a feeling of frustration among the educated middle class, which finally led to the formation of different political associations in different parts of the country to voice their grievances. In Bengal, during this time, parallel to the formation of political associations, one of the dominant cultural expressions, apart from literature, the theatre activity, initially started in the region under the European influence, was also undergoing some fundamental changes, including that of incorporation of the theme of patriotism through glorious portrayal of former heroes of the country as well as exposing the rampant atrocities of the indigo planters in the countryside of Bengal and thereby, making a charge directly against the British authority, the allies of the planters. This made the British apprehensive of consolidation of an alternative front, through which the colonized mind could have sought to assert their voice. The dominant trends during the second half of the nineteenth century included a definite shift in Bengali plays towards maturity in form and content, based on individual talents like Madhusudan Dutta or Dinabandhu Mitra; social plays occupying the centre stage, attempts to organize public theatre on the financial support of the common people, the British apprehension of Bengali 'social plays that gradually slipped into making political statements through theatrical means', new shift in production of theatre under the leadership of Girish Chandra Ghosh, and last but not the least, an unmistakable reflection of middle class mentality of cynicism, ensuring their class interest and choosing a safe option of criticizing their own society began reflecting in the theatre productions towards the end of the century.

Arabinda Samanta has written on the bone-setters of Bengal. In 'Revisiting a Marginalized Community: The Bone-setters of Bengal' he subscribes to the view that under the compulsion of maintaining the health of the troop, a new medical market was created in the nineteenth and twentieth centuries which impelled the colonial government to restructure the variety of 'indigenous' medical practices that prevailed in the country. He observes that while there has been some research on principal medical 'systems', the study of 'folk' practices like bone-setting, particularly in Bengal, has been neglected. He focuses on the socio-cultural trajectory of the bone-setters. While they were all farmers by profession, they were bone-setters by vocation and thus, maintained a fractured identity. The author traces the origin of the practice of bone-setting in India and admits that when the British came they found a well-reinforced orthopaedic system in perfect practice. Bone setting, he contends, was an indigenous 'popular cultural therapy' practised in India since time immemorial. In the first section, the author examines the science of bone-setting as addressed by the *Ayurveda* and *Sushruta*. He discusses the technique of the bone-setters, prognosis, use of practical physiotherapy as laid down by them. The author then goes on to elaborate how traditional orthopaedic practices were to be found predominantly in rural areas. They included a wide spectrum of practices that involved a special understanding of the anatomy and constituted a crucial domain of local health knowledge. The author goes on to examine the work and social position of the bone-setters in contemporary society of Bengal. In the last section he takes up Basipur, in Burdwan district, as a case study. He argues that the bone-setters were neglected in official health-care programme for different reasons. Based on a field study, he concludes, their treatment process was a very simple one. Their speciality rested not much with the medicinal herbs used but with the expertise in manipulating bones. The author goes on to study how their class, belonging primarily to the Bagdi community, struggled to hold on to their craft in changed circumstances of contemporary times.

Sajal Nag 'On Identity, State and Conflict in North-East India', addresses a very pertinent issue, that is, the question of evolution of an identity which has assumed considerable significance in the present political scenario. He argues that social inheritance facilitates the 'formation' of an identity which may not be politically relevant. To make it so, this identity has to be re-fabricated, altered and even reshaped, which according to the author is 'construction'. While identities do not create conflict, their construction and use for political ends could lead to conflict situations. The author makes a study of two tribes, Naga and Mizo. He begins with a study of their pre-colonial identity and states that it was exogenous to them. Most Nagas or Mizos identified themselves by their village/sub-tribal names and the Naga name was given to them by their neighbours. This name was popularized and enforced by the British. The author asserts that the construction of identity of the tribals started with the latter and the nature of construction shifted according to political exigencies. The logical conclusion of this construction was to advocate a separate, sovereign state for the tribals of north-east India. When the British were about to withdraw from India, Nag observes, they wanted to separate the tribals from India and continue to keep them under their authority. When the tribals themselves constructed their identity, argues the author, they borrowed from colonial construction. This construction underwent several shifts according to the phases of their struggle. In the phase during which the Naga 'nationalist' movement had been launched from the 1950s, the thrust was on the consolidation of a regional identity by including all the tribes who were willing to adopt and accept the generic Naga identity. The Naga 'nation-making process', argues the author, apparently unified various tribes into a strong Naga identity and presented this identity as a viable national formation. However, he emphasizes, the Naga identity only constructed an enumerable and presentable national identity for a political objective of 'Naga nation state' that was separate and independent from the Indian nation. On account of its unstable structure, according to him, it also rendered itself fragile and dependent on favourable historical conditions for its sustainability. Arguing within a significant theoretical framework, the author examines the origin of conflict between the Nagas and the Mizos and the Indian State. He says it was a conflict not between the Indian nation and the Nagas or Mizos on the issue of identity but one between modernity and its adversaries, medieval order and its opponents who wanted to make a transition to modern times. The crisis was an internal one where the nationalist discourse was used as an instrument, says the author, to achieve that goal. India's involvement in the crisis was an attempt to negotiate it. The author concludes his essay with a discussion on the autonomy movements among the tribes. He explains that the demands for autonomy, among the tribes included in his study, arose because they were wary of the nationalist discourses and the nationalists' power of submerging smaller and marginal communities. He argues that the Indian State could not afford it and the conflict developed into a secessionist movement. Autonomy demands were seen as threats to national integration.

Atig Ghosh's article, interestingly titled, '"What, Drawn, and Talk of Peace!": Security, Development and the Autonomy Question in the Indian North-East' once again highlights the importance of the need to address the issue of autonomy movements in the Indian north-east. The author argues that the earlier, possibly more clear-cut opposition between the state and the groups seeking autonomy has given way to a 'more complicated template where increasingly the market has come to play a pivotal role'. He observes that the shift from state-orchestrated to market mechanisms of distribution overlapped with new forms of social movement-based struggles in which the old autonomy question was merely reformulated, not abandoned. He discusses the exact contours of this reformulated autonomy question. He asserts that the security-development complex of social governance can produce very different consequences in different geopolitical contexts. The forces of globalization and concurrent social governance that affect class relations are experienced and resisted through a variety of locally relevant 'identities' that include ethnicity and gender. Ghosh examines these two identities in succession and how social governance and the entwined peace building efforts interact with them in the context of the north-east.

The last essay, in the volume articulates the varied dimensions of India's journey to maturity, how her womanhood has evolved. The cue to a nation's progress is to be mapped by the status her women are accorded. So the uncharted path that Swarnakumari treaded, the dream that her famous brother, the country's greatest litterateur, had for the women of his country have not been in vain. Indian women have not let any opportunity to establish their identity go in vain. Manjima Chatterjee in '*Parama*: A Journey from Society to "Self" argues that films of colonial India as well as those produced after Independence portrayed women through the same sociological mirror. However, this stereotype portrayal of women characters in films was reviewed during the 1980s by a galaxy of women directors like Sai Paranjpye, Kalpana Lajmi, Aruna Raje, Prema Karanth, Mira Nair and others who were all educated, urban and progressive and were ready to deal with issues which were so long considered a taboo in Indian films. Their women take their identity from the position they occupy in relation to certain commonly held attitudes about love, marriage or motherhood. Even if they are rarely allowed any possibility of personal transcendence, argues the author, one often finds characters whose deviance from a gender determined norm so pronounced, that they have the effect of denying and challenging their supposed or desired norm. Moreover, once the matters of women's sexuality and women's role have been brought into prominence, they acted as a potential threat to destabilize the position of their male counterpart. Aparna Sen's *Parama* perfectly fits into this genre of films, where the societal notions of a woman's role were revisited to finally initiate her on a journey to her own 'self'. The film released in 1985 was a much discussed one not only for its quite unusual depiction of a sexual relationship between a married woman and a younger man at that time but also because the director actually addresses a whole gamut of feminist concerns like marriage, sexuality, motherhood, etc. Yet the film does not overtly stamp the female protagonist as a celluloid feminist in the sense of taking an active part in women's movement or belonging to some women's welfare organization. Initially one finds Parama, the central character of the film, blissfully oblivious about her specific needs as a woman and stays cocooned in an apparently happy marriage. As the film unravels one finds her reacting against the life of twentieth century with acute sensitivity which is infinitely adaptable and supple to catch the tones, the light and shade of experience of a so-called urban, upper middle-class married woman. From a tiny, marginalized shell Parama emerges as a person dignified and empowered, ready to make her own choice.

All the essays included in this volume give a glimpse into the varied dimensions, rich traditions of the country that is India.

CHAPTER 1

Colonialism and Public Health in Rarh Bengal

Development and Underdevelopment

Achintya Kumar Dutta

Underdevelopment is a term often used to refer to economic underdevelopment, symptoms of which include lack of access to job opportunities, health care, potable water, food, education and housing. Underdevelopment takes place when resources are not used to their full socio-economic potential, with the result that local or regional development is slower in most cases than it should be. Underdevelopment is not only lack of or insufficient development, as many people tend to think. It can also be seen as a product as well as by-product of development. Underdevelopment in the Indian subcontinent during the British rule derived inevitably from the colonial forms of economic exploitation. What I intend to focus upon in this paper is that the colonial rulers decidedly developed colonial (modern) infrastructure, with a view to extracting the resources of Rarh Bengal for colonial purposes. This in turn created an environment, affecting public health, which was in a bad shape during the colonial rule and this can be seen as a mark of underdevelopment. The colonial rulers seemed to have been very reluctant to take proper measures for the improvement of public health and development of health care services. The question, therefore, arise as to why did they do so? This paper addresses this issue. My intention in selecting Rarh Bengal as a case study lies in the fact that this productive region of Bengal allowed the British to extract agricultural and mineral resources for colonial purpose.

This area, which paid the colonial rulers huge dividend, called for amenities for health protection and other allied facilities, but this was also the area which demonstrated a shameful picture of public health, being worst affected by some lethal communicable diseases.

Rarh has a unique geographical identity and cultural significance.[1] But here I will restrain myself from going into its details. Rarh is situated on the south-western part of Bengal. Its eastern side is surrounded by the Ganga-Bhagirathi while the Chhotanagpur plateau extends on the west. According to the present administrative division, the region consists of Birbhum, Burdwan, Bankura and the western part of Midnapore district. The borders of the Rarh region has been stretched both geographically and politically. In a wider sense, Rarh comprises the entire south-western Bengal, excluding only the eastern part of Midnapore district.[2] It is difficult to mark the geographical location of Rarh owing to a raging debate on it.[3] In this context, it is not necessary to deal with that debate. The present essay is confined to the discussion on the districts of Birbhum, Bankura and Burdwan of southern Rarh or south-western Bengal.

Colonialism and Outbreak of Diseases

The colonial government concerned itself mainly with the maintenance of law and order, and collection of revenue and extraction of agricultural and mineral wealth, and showed little interest in resolving public health issues. While modern infrastructure developed, public health suffered. A network of modern means of communication spread over the districts of Rarh Bengal—mainly Burdwan, Birbhum and Bankura. Railways were introduced and expanded, metalled roads were laid and bridges were constructed. But these were chiefly built for their economic importance, the motive was to connect this region to the metropolis or the port with a view to tapping its resources. New railway lines of the East Indian Railway were opened in the 1850s and extended subsequently through the districts of Rarh Bengal. In fact, all sub-divisional headquarters, rich agricultural tracts and principal centres of trade were connected to the port by a wide network of railways. Coal and rice were the two main items of export from the districts of Rarh Bengal. Most of the important marts enjoyed ample facilities for export of surplus crop and import of European goods by rail, road or river. An official report on public health of Bengal reveals that the intention of the development works was to give full facilities for trade and transit by railways and roads.[4]

Similarly, colonial and modern administrative network, consisting of land revenue, judicial and police administration was set up. With the development of communication facilities and extension of administrative network, the colonial rulers got an easy access to the resources of this region and multiplied the quantum of extraction. Railways further influenced industrialization and urbanization in this region, and this can also be seen as the symbol of development.

The other side of the story was that, Rarh Bengal districts witnessed the prevalence of several lethal diseases which occurred epidemically and continued to act upon as endemic during the colonial rule. Diseases like malaria, *kala-azar*, cholera, smallpox, leprosy, tuberculosis, and influenza broke out repeatedly in epidemic form, causing devastation to people's life. Public health in this area was in a bad shape. Colonial intervention was held responsible for this situation. Colonialism itself was regarded as a major health hazard for indigenous people and responsible for the outbreak of epidemics. It is argued that European commercial and political penetration in the nineteenth century, and the creation of colonial infrastructure, viz., roads, railways and system of labour migration, facilitated the spread of disease vectors—the mosquitoes, flees and lice by which epidemics were communicated—and dissemination of diseases.[5] Blaming the common people for their ignorance of sanitary considerations is pointless when it was the apathy and negligence of the government that need to be underlined. There seems no doubt that the nature of colonial infrastructure established mainly for economic exploitation and the consequent ecological changes it brought about have had far-reaching and enduring effects on public health. For instance, the expansion of irrigation canals and the construction of railway embankments created favourable habitats for malaria carrying mosquitoes in India.[6]

Railway Network, Diseases and Public Health

The indiscriminate embanking of vast tracts in lower Bengal for protecting railways and roads from the ravages of the floods had caused serious damage to agriculture and public health.[7] Scholars have identified it as a primary factor behind the economic degeneration and declining status of public health of lower Bengal for about six decades since the 1860s, delineating the fact that obstruction to drainage owing to embankment and culverts was responsible for the malarial environment that prevailed over this region between 1850 and 1874.[8] Before the advent of railways, there were few roads and although river embankments existed in certain districts they were rarely efficient in preventing inundation, because breaches were common and more often than not the embankments were deliberately cut to let river water into the *bils* and on to the fields. As there were few roads to impede the free passage of the floods across the surface of the country, the water flowed from field to field, choosing the natural lines of drainage and eventually, made its escape through the network of *khals* and channels that existed in every part of the delta. But this natural process of flood and flush was destroyed by the advent of railways, which required embankments for their tracks and a system of feeder roads to convey passengers and produce to their stations.[9] The periodic inundation of the country naturally tended on occasions to destroy the continuity of road and railway communications and it became necessary, therefore, to make the river embankments secure against breaching; and as a consequence flood water was shut out, the natural system of deltaic irrigation was interrupted, drainage was impeded and the network of channels, which used formerly to be fed by the spill water from the great rivers, became silted up and in many cases entirely destroyed, rendering boat traffic difficult and in many cases impossible. The embanking of the country and the shutting out of river water from the surface of the delta was further marked by the simultaneous occurrence of appalling epidemics of malaria, a serious decline of agriculture and the progressive depopulation of the affected areas.[10]

The advance of railway network led to the proliferation of 'Burdwan Fever' which devastated numerous promising villages and struck a hard blow to the agricultural potential and public health in south-west Bengal. The embankments for railway tracks and bridges shut out the flood-water of the Damodar, the Ajay and other minor rivers which acted as spill channels for the distribution of silt-laden red water. These were the impediments to the natural irrigation and drainage, and caused the silting up of channels, including the streams and rivers.[11] William Willcocks, an irrigation engineer, has also pointed out that the embankment on the east bank of the Damodar for protecting railways from flood entirely destroyed the already declining system of natural irrigation, and caused famines and fever, because it had deprived Burdwan and Hooghly districts of their natural overflow irrigation and choked many tanks, artificial lakes and even streams.[12] Medical men like Dr French and Lt. Col. Campbell, and engineers of Public Works Department like Mr Adley were also of the opinion that it was the fundamental cause of the epidemic fever and the calamity that had devastated those localities.[13] Willcocks believed that the rivers flowing south from the Ganges through Bengal were originally artificial canals dug by ancient Indians to provide for the adequate irrigation and drainage of the province, and that in allowing these to become silted up, the province had been turned in the course of hundred years from a place then considered to be a health resort to a hotbed of the worst diseases in the world.[14] Above all, embankments creating water-logging condition facilitated the germination of anopheles mosquitoes and these were followed by disastrous consequences to health and agriculture.[15] The loss of silt-laden red water resulted in the alarming decline of quality and quantity of yield. On the other hand, malaria caused rural depopulation and devitalized the Rarh region. The district of Burdwan, the most productive district of Bengal in the early nineteenth century, was in the grip of this disease from the 1860s, which accounted for the mortality of thousands of people, led to a reduction in the area under cultivation and reduced the district almost to ruins.[16] In other words, railways, embankments and closure of the rivers, all combined effectively in producing an environment that was not at all congenial and conducive to rural growth and prosperity in Rarh Bengal. The inhibition of agricultural activities was a normal outcome of stoppage of overflow irrigation, bad drainage and malarial atmosphere, which in turn were the results of the closure of the rivers and construction of embankments.

Colonial intervention for economic exploitation in Rarh Bengal altered the ecological set up which had its corresponding adverse effects on the economy and, thereby, public health. Railway embankment had destroyed the navigability of important rivers like the Damodar, and the building of railways along the natural lines of drainage had aggravated the problems of flooding followed by epidemic diseases. The repeated occurrences of natural calamities in the form of droughts, floods and famines were to a great extent due to colonial intervention. This had brought in its wake poverty to the people. These had also affected the environment that in turn brought in diseases. The districts of Burdwan, Birbhum and Bankura faced a number of famines and floods followed by diseases like malaria and cholera during colonial rule and these compounded the misery of the poor masses.[17] The embankment on the Damodar and the Ajay caused uneven distribution of flood water. The floods of the Damodar caused severe damages to the crops and habitations of the common people in the areas lying to the unprotected right side of the Damodar. The economic condition of the cultivators, particularly in the trans-Damodar region, had been miserable, causing damage to the rice cultivation. On the other hand, it created insanitary conditions leading to the spread of diseases like cholera and malaria. Under such circumstances, these poor people were the worst sufferers of the epidemic diseases.[18] Harry G. Timbers, a medical man, who made a survey on the medical condition in Birbhum district in 1930, has aptly observed that poverty and diseases followed each other in a vicious cycle and that the diseases were eating into the vitals of the society and creating a vicious circle of disease and poverty were recognized by Rabindranath Tagore.[19] In fact, the economic decline of the district was related to the ravages caused by various diseases that were widespread in the district.

More importantly, irrigational projects, which may be considered as symbols of developmental work, also created conditions that affected public health. They helped in spreading malaria which caused loss of life and, more important, people's chronic debilitation. This was the case not only in Rarh Bengal but also in other parts of the country. Elizabeth Whitcombe has shown how along the western and eastern Jumna canals 'noisome and pestilent swamps' due to poor drainage had arisen in the 1830s and remedial action was urgently demanded to relieve the local population from marsh fever.[20] In 1843, an outbreak of fever of epidemic proportions struck Karnal and the Ganges canal was held responsible for that.[21] In fact, the influence of irrigational canals on the incidence of malaria, though disputed, cannot be denied. A conference on irrigation and malaria, organized in 1938 by the National Institute of Sciences in India, showed that there was no dearth of instances where irrigation had compounded the felonies of nature in the obstruction of drainage channels, leading to an increase in the incidence of malaria.[22] The construction of the Damodar canal (opened in 1933), which was an improvement in irrigational works, caused further water stagnation and created favourable habitats for malaria carrying mosquitoes and an unhealthy atmosphere in Rarh Bengal. This led to further decay of public health.

Having triumphed over the ravages of the Marathas in the 1740s and the famine of 1770, the district of Burdwan regained prosperity in the first half of the nineteenth century because of its silt-bearing soil and rehabilitated peasantry. Walter Hamilton too mentioned the progressive state of improvement in Burdwan district in 1820.[23] Burdwan in those days was considered one of the prosperous and healthiest places in Bengal. The agricultural prosperity of the district was so impressive that it was regarded as the granary of Bengal. But this prosperity was to last only till 1863 when the dreaded malaria epidemic, commonly called 'Burdwan Fever', broke out over a wide area. The construction of railways and the consequent embankments necessitated by it were held responsible for the outbreak of this epidemic. Similarly, the prosperity of Birbhum district (it was one of the prosperous districts of Bengal in the 1820s) declined in the second half of the nineteenth century owing to lack of drainage and silting up of the Ajay River caused by railroad. In fact, the whole process of impoverishment and disease began after the railroad was built.[24] This assertion has been strongly supported by C.E. Bentley, Director of Public Health, Bengal.

In the last quarter of the nineteenth century, almost all parts of the

Damodar-Bhagirathi region were in the grip of malarial fever. The epidemic made its first appearance in Rarh Bengal in the 1850s, i.e. immediately after the erection of embankment for the introduction of railways, and there was periodic outbreak of this disease till the end of the colonial rule. Rarh Bengal was severely affected by it, causing the death of thousands of people. A fever of an epidemic nature ravaged Bankura district in 1855 and 1864 and also in the famine year of 1866. Since then, Bankura district experienced at least seven epidemics: in 1873-4 measles, cholera and small-pox, in 1881-2 Burdwan fever, in 1890 and 1901-2 smallpox, in 1919-20 influenza, in 1931 malaria and in 1944 the epidemic following the famine of 1943.[25] Birbhum district faced malaria epidemic for the first time in 1871 and since then was affected by a series of epidemic diseases.[26] Harry G. Timbers visited a number of villages in Birbhum district in 1930, and painted a dismal picture of public health. He wrote, 'The people, however, are not in good general physical condition. Their appearance of lack of energy is striking. The pot-bellied child is the rule, the healthy-looking child is the exception.'[27] Malarial fever in severe form broke out in Burdwan several times during the colonial rule. The dreaded malaria epidemic afflicted Burdwan in the early 1860s and devastated its agricultural and commercial prosperity, carrying off not less than three quarters of a million people within a span of twelve years from 1863 to 1874.[28] The disease reappeared in a virulent form in the 1880s, decimated the rural population and left them weak and listless.[29] The *Census of India* asserts, in this connection:

> The ruined houses and abandoned sites were everywhere visible. The people's physique was poor and ever-stricken, and throughout the district they presented the same appearance. In fact, the sickly physique is the ordinary physique, and commanded the ordinary labour rates; the healthy physique is the exceptional one and commands special and very high rates.[30]

Surprisingly, the disease continued to affect public health in around the district, both epidemically and endemically for a long time during the colonial rule.

In fact, the people in this area had faced at least one epidemic disease in each decade during the first half of the twentieth century.

Kala-azar also became widespread in this area during the same time. This followed in the wake of opening up of communication by rail and road in connection with British commercial and military penetration. Roads and railways had undoubtedly afforded excellent facilities for the transport of goods and, especially, for the rapid transit of passengers. But the embankments for protecting roads and railways exerted the most deleterious effect upon public health and agriculture.

Industrialization and Public Health

Railways had undoubtedly brought about profound changes in the economic life of Rarh. It stimulated the growth of industries and urbanization in Rarh Bengal. Raniganj/Asansol subdivision emerged as one of the thriving industrial areas of India as a result of expansion of railroads and growth of coal and other ancillary industries. More importantly, some places were transformed from small villages into busy towns and consequently, new urban settlements emerged in this part of Bengal. It should be noted in this context that the relationship between disease and urbanization or between industrialization and disease-prone environment or living working conditions has been widely accepted. Communicable diseases also raised their heads in the newly developed industrial and urban areas. Immigration of labourers to the coal mining areas increased density of population and accounted for unhygienic conditions. Stagnant cesspools and open drains with foul smell were a common sight. The unhygienic coolie lines, where the labourers were forced to stay, in the mines and factories facilitated diffusion of the epidemic diseases. The physical condition of work inside the mines, particularly inadequate ventilation facilities underground caused the workers to suffer. The bulk of the labourers had to live in very small rooms in the coolie lines or *dhaorahs* under inhuman conditions.[31] The accommodation for the labourers was most insanitary and unsuitable. In Raniganj coalfields the coolies were rarely provided with latrines or alternative arrangements for the disposal of night soil and refuse. In the absence of such amenities, the colliery areas quickly became a veritable breeding ground for all sorts of diseases and source of epidemics.[32]

Excrement could easily be mixed with the water of the adjacent tanks and thus many bowel-complaints originated. The area became a source of illness and communicable diseases like cholera. The latter occurred in an epidemic form in this area for several times since the beginning of the twentieth century.

If the developmental works could be seen as marks of success of the colonial government, there were many failures in the development of health care provisions. Health care service hardly developed in Asansol-Raniganj industrial belt of Bengal. Drinking of polluted water aggravated the recurrence of cholera. This epidemic is alleged to have been due partly to the unusual shrinkage of water supply and partly to imported infection from outside by daily migration of labour. Asansol Mines Board of Health revealed that cholera broke out in epidemic form in 1935, taking a toll on 616 lives.[33] Health care facilities and sanitary measures in the mining area were very scanty. The provision for drinking water was never adequate, and the miners used water accumulated in coal pits for drinking as well as washing purposes. Consequently, every year cholera and smallpox took a heavy toll on lives.[34] The question of public health and sanitation was indeed alarming to the labourers. The insistence of the Asansol Mines Board of Health on the construction of quarters did not lead to any remarkable improvement with regard to the accommodation of the labourers.[35]

Fevers of all kinds, including malaria, were responsible for thousands of deaths in 1934 and 1935 in the coalfields. Topsi and Ballampur were extremely malarious areas.[36] The Board revealed further that there were altogether 8,165 deaths from all causes with a death rate of 21.3 per mile registered in 1935.[37] The *dhaorahs* had the most adverse effects on the health of female workers and their children. Mortality rates among women and children were relatively higher than that among the males. There was hardly any satisfactory arrangement for the treatment of miners' children when they fell ill. Infant mortality rate was very high in the colliery zone of Bengal.[38] Besides, high rate of maternal mortality, particularly in Asansol, was another disturbing fact.

Moreover, the coolie-lines of heterogeneous sexes constantly proved a temptation to laxity of habitants' morals which was injurious to the mental and physical health of the entire labour community. The unsatisfactory housing and foul environment prevented most of the workers from bringing their families along with them in the coalfields and thereby, created sexual disparity there. This sexual disparity led to an increase in prostitution and a subsequent spread of venereal diseases in the mining areas and later to the villages.[39]

More importantly, most of the labourers of the mines were poor because of low wages and consequently, they were not in a position to consume nutritious food. Their diet consisted of very low grade rice and *dal* and was insufficient in quantity. Consequently most of the miners were in a state of weak physique and, therefore, susceptible to occupational and environmental diseases. All these throw light on the fact that there was lack of improvement in public health in the mining settlement area. People in this area had hardly any access to health care opportunities. In other words, very little health care facilities were said to have been provided for them. There was an absence of adequate healing touch indeed.

Disease, Sanitation and Public Health

Underdevelopment of public health can easily be ascertained from the repeated inroads of communicable diseases in epidemic forms, prevalence of these diseases for a long time and the high mortality rate caused by them. Cholera broke out repeatedly in epidemic form in the first half of the twentieth century in many villages of Rarh Bengal districts. The 'native' doctors, who were appointed on special cholera duty during 1909, pointed out that scarcity of food, unsuitability of food, such as raw Indian corn cobs, and scarcity of water were the main causes for the outbreak of cholera in Burdwan.[40] They also added that the water-supplies in the villages were nearly all contaminated. Most of the reservoirs of water dried up and people had to travel long distances to get even muddy water. It took a heavy toll of human lives in these districts. For instance, during six years from 1904 to 1909, cholera caused the death of more than 30,000 people in Burdwan district alone.[41] It also occurred in severe form in Birbhum district in 1906, 1907 and 1908, causing a mortality of 4.66, 5.96 and 10.17 per mile, respectively.[42] A survey report on the medical conditions in Birbhum district (1930) reveals that very few villages were supplied with wells for drinking water.[43] The family got its drinking water from the same tank in which it bathed and did its laundry. A report by G.L. Batra, Assistant Director of Public Health, Calcutta reveals that 360 villages in Burdwan district, 209 villages in Birbhum and 134 in Bankura district were affected by cholera during 1934-5.[44]

Besides fever and cholera, smallpox, influenza, leprosy and tuberculosis caused havoc in these districts during colonial rule. Smallpox was widely prevalent in the districts of Burdwan and Bankura from 1900, increasing the death rate. *Kala-azar* became a serious menace to the people of Burdwan in the 1930s. In 1930-1, the highest mortality from *kala-azar*, i.e. 3.1 per mile was registered in Kalna subdivision.[45] During the same time, outbreak of beri-beri was also reported from Burdwan and Bankura districts. Leprosy was a serious problem in Bankura and Birbhum districts since the beginning of the twentieth century. In 1930, a doctor reported that none of the lepers he saw in Birbhum district were receiving treatment; but most of them would gladly go to a clinic for treatment if such existed.[46] Public health in Birbhum was so bad that the situation prevailing in the district had been characterized as 'veritable museum of every disease known to mankind'.[47] The health-care service was indeed very poor. The civil surgeons of the district were inadequately equipped, and there were less than 75 hospitals beds in the entire district.[48]

In fact, there was hardly any development in the state of people's health alongside industrial development or development of modern administrative infrastructure. The colonial government neither paid adequate attention to it nor tried to prevent health hazards caused by certain development works. There was hardly any sanitary improvement in this region. Sanitary reforms even in Burdwan, which was known as the granary and Rarh of Bengal, were neglected and far from satisfactory. Most of the drains in Burdwan, Birbhum and Bankura districts were defective and in appalling conditions.[49] Though some facilities were provided in the urban areas, they were short of actual requirement. The rural areas had to suffer incessantly for the absence of sanitation. Public health problems, such as want of drinking water, drainage, health centres, dispensaries, and drugs, remained unsolved. The colonial rulers were said to have either overlooked or neglected them.

The supply of pure drinking water was a 'dire necessity' to make the villages healthy. Myriads of people had to drink muddy water during summer months as most of the tanks got dried up, tube wells being few. In 1934-5, Bankura had 86 tube wells in 19 health circles, and Birbhum 140 tube wells in 14 health circles only along with some wells.[50] Compared to the number of villages and their population, these tube wells could hardly meet the requirement of the people. Burdwan district, for instance, had 1,336 tube wells in 16 health circles for about 2,383 villages, covering an area of 2,314 sq. miles and 11,31,217 people excluding Raniganj-Asansol coal-belt.[51] Birbhum and Bankura painted a gloomier picture than Burdwan in this regard. It was reported by a number of leading newspapers that owing chiefly to the acute water distress, cholera raged in an epidemic form in many districts of Bengal.[52] Some provisions were made for supply of drinking water to the towns, even though water supply was very acute in Kalna.[53] The supply of drinking water to the villages, from where the government collected bulk of the revenues, remained unattended. The revenues from various sources which the government realized from the people was mostly spent in maintaining the police and in meeting high salaries and allowances of the foreign bureaucracy, leaving very little for ministering to the needs of the people.[54] It was revealed by the *Calcutta Samachar* in July 1921 that water scarcity was as acute in Bengal as ever.[55]

The government adopted certain measures to fight the diseases and protect the health of the people. Several dispensaries and hospitals were set up in Rarh Bengal districts. But these were not adequate to save the lives of the people. There were only 25 permanent dispensaries for more than 1.4 million people in Burdwan district in 1925.[56] Burdwan and Birbhum districts suffered the worst from malaria. Though anti-malaria measures had been launched, the disease was widely prevalent in these areas in the 1930. Bankura district was also severely affected by it during this time. Fever dispensaries were set up temporarily to tackle the fever. The hospitals lacked proper infrastructure development to tackle several diseases. A number of village dispensaries were set up by the District and Union Boards. But they could hardly provide proper health care facilities to the villagers owing to lack of funds. For example, a little more than 6 per cent of the total income of the District Board was spent on medical relief and sanitation in Burdwan district during 1902-3.[57] Well-equipped hospitals in each district was beyond the medical activities of the district boards. Most of the village dispensaries were devoid of qualified doctors and adequate drugs, and were run by health assistants or native doctors. Hospital and dispensary network was inadequate. There were places where no modern medical aid of any sort was available.

The hospitals in Rarh Bengal districts did not have arrangement for effectively tackling tuberculosis cases. Despite anti-malaria measures, population of many villages in and around Sriniketan (like Islampur and Ballavpur) in Birbhum district was reduced drastically by death and desertions. For example, in 1926, malaria decimated many of the families of Ballavpur village situated near Sriniketan. The ravages of malaria in 1930 took a toll of about 700 and 500 in the villages of Islampur and Bhadurpur, respectively in Birbhum.[58] From 1894 to 1929, fever deaths in the Birbhum district varied from a low of 14.3 per cent (1899) to a high of 52.20 per cent (1911) with several ups and downs in between.[59] Besides, the outbreak of *kala-azar* exacerbated the sufferings of the villagers further. Not surprisingly, perhaps, venereal diseases also were not unknown in Birbhum district. Malaria and *kala-azar* also took a toll on innumerable lives in Bankura district in the first half of the twentieth century and the victims could hardly be offered adequate treatment facilities. A few charitable dispensaries or anti-malaria cooperative society provided treatment for *kala-azar* or malaria cases in Bankura.

The average mortality rate in Bankura district between 1911 and 1920 was 34.63 per 1,000 against the average birth rate of 32.25 per 1,000.[60] Maternal mortality due to childbirth was alarming in these districts. Infant mortality was also quite high. Harry Timbers' survey (1930) estimated infant mortality in Birbhum as being 191.3 per 1,000 and maternal mortality rate was easily 'comparable with the infant mortality rate'.[61] In 1922, infant mortality rate in Bankura district was 178 per 1,000.[62] What is interesting to note was that the kind of diseases from which people suffered from remained more or less similar over a long period of time. In fact, it was due to lack of development of proper health care system that the population (excluding the number of immigrants) of the districts of Rarh Bengal had either a decreasing trend or remained stationary till 1921. In other words, there was serious inadequacy of existing provisions for affording health protection to the community. Only an improved health care system could have checked the huge mortality rate in the villages of Bengal.

Low Financial Investment and Poor Public Health

The health care system remained underdeveloped or undeveloped during the colonial rule mainly because of low financial investment in this field. There was hardly any possibility of making any profit from this field. It did not give any material return to the colonial rulers, who seemed to have been reluctant to make provision for substantial investment in a field where there was no scope of profit-oriented business transaction. Development in health care system and subsequent improvement in public health could have been made only with an altruistic mission, pursuing a welfare policy. This required a large sum of money, which was lacking.

The government realized huge revenues from various sources from the villagers, but that was mostly spent on maintaining the general and police administration.[63] In fact, public health received a meagre amount from it. The poor structure of healthcare service had been exposed on several occasions, particularly after the flood and famine when different diseases broke out in epidemic forms. Unlike other subjects, such as civil and military administration, public health problems did not receive priority and importance in the government agenda. Whenever there was paucity of funds necessitating retrenchment in expenditure, the axe was applied without the least hesitation on the Public Health Department.

The importance of well-planned water supply and sewerage schemes for the health of urban localities needs no elaboration. The amount spent in this field was, again, very small. While the people were dying of epidemic diseases caused directly by drinking polluted water, the authorities were 'merely building Dak-bungalows and constructing motor-car roads'. It was observed by the *Amrita Bazar Patrika* in July 1924 that while the government imposed a special tax, the object of which was to improve water-supply, it definitely undertook the responsibility of water-supply previously shouldered by the zamindars and other rich people. But this duty was afterwards transferred to the district boards, which with their limited income, were unable to cope with the duty of supplying drinking water for rural areas.[64] Sanitary Commissioner's recommendation for supplying drinking water to the people of Burdwan in 1869 was placed before the government in 1912 and the scheme was executed in 1921.[65] A scheme for supply of filtered water in Bankura town was executed only in 1916. With increasing demand, the capacity of the water-works was extended in 1926 and 1941. Even then, the supply of water could meet the requirements of only a small area.[66]

Since 1922, various sanitary improvement and water-supply schemes were taken up by the Sanitary Engineering Department and the Public Health Department, but a few of them were executed. During 1934-5, the Engineering Branch of Public Health Department prepared sketch projects for water supply in different towns of Bengal, including Burdwan, Asansol, Raniganj, Katwa, Bankura and also for sewerage and drainage in Burdwan. Work was also carried on at some towns. The capital expenditure on waterworks and sewerage works in Bengal towns during 1934-5 was Rs. 2.75 lakh and Rs. 2.25 lakh respectively.[67] This amount was inadequate for the solution of the problem. Even then, the inability of the government to provide grants towards the capital cost of municipal schemes resulted in a lack of progress to a considerable degree. Ultimately, certain municipalities financed the schemes by means of loans from the government.[68] Besides, the government contributed a very small amount for the maintenance of public health. During the year 1934, the government contributed only Rs. 45,347, Rs. 24,895 and Rs. 37,616 for the districts of Burdwan, Birbhum and Bankura, respectively, while the district boards spent only Rs. 12,772, Rs. 67,546 (mainly for water supply), and Rs. 44,637.[69] Amazingly, the colonial government hardly spent money for tuberculosis and leprosy works and for maternity and child development in Rarh Bengal.[70]

In fact, the health condition in this area, though unspeakably bad, was not so bad that they could not be remedied. There was lack of sincere attempts to make any improvement in this field by the government. The Department of Public Health carried on work under extremely adverse conditions not only in the districts of Burdwan, Birbhum and Bankura but Bengal as a whole, the main reason was lack of adequate staff and income.

When fever broke out in Burdwan in the 1860s, inhabitants from various villages sent petitions to the government for establishing charitable dispensaries and sending good doctors for their relief. But the government was reluctant to incur the expenditure for such dispensaries and consequently the affected villagers were deprived of any facilities for treatment. Surprisingly, on many occasions the villagers were asked to bear the financial burden for setting up of a fever dispensary.[71] Although some charitable dispensaries were established in some parts of the district by the government, most of them were ramshackle huts devoid of doctors and drugs. Quinine distributed by the government free of cost did not always reach the masses. C.E. Bentley, Director of Public Health, Bengal, reported in his book *Malaria and Agriculture in Bengal* that only a very small proportion of malaria-affected people of Bengal received treatment sufficient to afford them relief, and the vast majority of the sufferers from malaria received either no medical attention whatsoever or were entirely dependent on the treatment of village practitioners.[72] The government could not even check the black-marketing of quinine. Consequently, the poor people could not purchase it from the market because its price never suited their purse.

More importantly, the government contributed, only Rs. 4,500 and 2,000 for anti-malaria work in Burdwan and Birbhum districts, respectively in 1934 when the scourge of malaria was increasing.[73] Ross had pointed out that unlike many diseases, malaria was a local malady and one which haunted more specially the fertile tracts. If Bengal could be made free from malaria not only would the population increase in number because of the absence of premature deaths there would also be a great improvement in the general health and economic condition of the nation.[74] Malaria was interlaced with agricultural and economic condition of the country and, therefore, it was not so easy to tackle as was cholera and smallpox. But the government did not provide adequate funds for its prevention and eradication.

There was hardly any hospital system for the rural population of Bengal. Although, the local government for the rural areas in the form of union boards was made responsible for local health services following the Montagu-Chelmsford Reforms of 1919, no regular hospital services could be established by them for paucity of funds. There were some district board dispensaries and a few scattered private ones established by the zamindars or philanthropic persons in a few rural areas, but such services were insignificant compared to the vast morbidity and mortality conditions prevailing in the areas.

Conclusion

It is revealed from many official and non-official reports that the district boards in Burdwan, Birbhum and Bankura tried their best to spend as much money as possible on medical relief and also on sanitation and vaccination.[75] But their income was not sufficient to tackle the health problems in the best possible way. They had to depend largely on provincial grants, which was not adequate.[76] More government aid and better supervision of these bodies were necessary. As that was lacking, health care services in Rarh Bengal remained underdeveloped.

In 1934, G.L. Batra, Assistant Director of Public Health, Bengal, suggested development of rural public health organization by adoption of certain measures: engagement of one health assistant in each union; improvement in village sanitation; organizing health societies; supervision of health circles by appointing qualified assistant health officers; housing of public health staff and office and so on. All these would entail more funding, but the colonial government was reluctant to incur further expenditure on it.[77]

It may, in this context, be argued that the colonial and modern infrastructure was created with a view to exploiting the colony's resources for colonial purpose and so one could not expect investment of considerable funds by the rulers on civic amenities. The British came to India to trade and make profit. Naturally, they were not supposed to set aside funds from their profit for any material development of the colonized. But it should be noted that from 1858, the British Crown took the responsibility to govern India. Consequently, the British India government was set up and it started governing the subcontinent. So, as the colonial government attained the right to govern Indian subjects, the latter were entitled to some basic amenities, including health care facilities. The government's right to collect revenue could only be justified if it was spent on health and education. If the government was to be considered as trustee, as custodian of the governed, the latter should pay tax so that the government provides health care facilities, opens hospitals, dispensaries and schools. If the government failed to do so, its rights to collect tax and govern the people could be questioned. In British India, it was a one-sided game. The common people had little scope to enjoy health care benefits. Moreover, since the mid-Victorian era, it was propagated in the colonial literature that the British established their rule with a view to undertaking civilizing mission in the colony. Did the denial of civic amenities to the governed indicate civilizing mission? If imperialism meant not only conquest of territories and people but also a civilizing mission, the question arises as to why disease-ridden areas, a consequential development of colonial economic policy, received low priority in health care and the affected people had hardly any access to health care facilities.

The economic condition of large sections of the population showed few signs of improvement even during the late colonial period and that of agriculturists definitely deteriorated in this part of Bengal. In 1935, test relief works were being fully attended in Birbhum and Bankura districts, and 'hunger marches' (as described by the nationalist press) were taking place. Moreover, in the same year, the Damodar River flood caused further damages to the poor agriculturists in these districts. Colonial extraction of surplus and imposition of land tax and other taxes added to their economic distress. Scarcity of food and proper place of living made them physically weak and an easy prey to communicable diseases. Agricultural improvement in Bengal as a whole, depended chiefly upon adequate irrigation and drainage. But progress in this field had been restricted by lack of money for capital expenditure. Canal irrigation was unknown even in Burdwan district until the opening of Eden canal in 1881, but it proved to be unsatisfactory because of certain inherent defects. There were no regular distributaries from this canal, and therefore, the economical distribution of water could not be properly maintained. Though the Damodar canal, opened in 1933, was an improvement in this regard, it could not serve the district of Burdwan up to the expected level. It supplied water only during rains, and remained dry for the rest of the year. Nevertheless, the government imposed a levy at a high rate on its water by the Bengal Development Act, 1935. There was only a marginal development in this field, but the Development Act was passed to impose the levy—another sign of colonial exploitation. More importantly, the construction of the Damodar canal caused further water stagnation, creating favourable conditions for breeding of mosquitoes and unhealthy atmosphere, and contributed to further decay of health. The development of public health system as well as medical science in Britain was 'organic', but in India it was not so. The British sanitary reforms controlled the major health hazards, and for this reason public health had been established as an autonomous sector. But the so-called sanitary reforms in Bengal during the nineteenth and early twentieth centuries were far from satisfactory.

Notes

1. For details, see Hitesh Ranjan Sanyal, *Nirbachita Prabandha* (in Bengali) [Selected Essays], Calcutta, 2004, pp. 82-104.
2. For details, see Nihar Ranjan Ray, *Bangalir Itihas: Adiparba* (in Bengali) [A History of the Bengali People: Early Period], Calcutta: Deys Publishing, 1993, pp. 118-20.
3. Ranjan Gupta, *Rahrer Samaj Arthaniti O Ganabidroha: Birbhum 1740-1871* (in Bengali) [Society, Economy & Civil Rebellions of Rahr], Calcutta: Subarnarekha, 2001, p. 19.
4. C.E. Bentley, *Malaria and Agriculture in Bengal*, Calcutta: Bengal Secretariat Book Depot, 1925, pp. 33-5.
5. David Arnold, ed., *Imperial Medicine and Indigenous Societies*, New York

and Manchester: Manchester University Press, 1988, Introduction, p. 5.

6. Ira Klein, 'Malaria and Mortality in Bengal 1840-1921', *Indian Economic and Social History Review*, vol. IX, no. 2, June 1972, pp. 132-60.
7. Bentley, op. cit., p. 19.
8. Arabinda Biswas and Swapan Bardhan, 'Agrarian Crisis in Damodar-Bhagirathi Region 1850-1925', *Geographical Review of India*, vol. 38, June 1975, pp. 132-50.
9. Bentley, op. cit., p. 20.
10. Ibid.
11. For details, see Radha Kamal Mukherjee, *Changing Face of Bengal: A Study of Riverine Economy*, Calcutta: University of Calcutta, 1938, p. 75; Bentley, op. cit., pp. 19-20, 35-40.
12. William Willcocks, *Lectures on the Ancient System of Irrigation in Bengal and its Application to Modern Problems*, Calcutta: University of Calcutta, 1930, pp. 65-6.
13. Willcocks, op. cit., pp. 24-5.
14. Harry G. Timbers, 'Report on Medical Conditions in the Birbhum District', *Visva-Bharati Quarterly*, January 1930 (Magh 1336 BS), vol. 7, no. 3, pp. 365-74.
15. For details, see Bentley, op. cit., pp. 35-40.
16. Mukherjee, op. cit., p. 74.
17. Drought occurred in 1923, 1927, 1934, 1935 and floods in 1936, 1939 and 1942 in Birbhum; floods took place in 1913, 1916, 1917, and 1943 in Burdwan; and famine occurred in 1866, 1874, 1885 and 1897 in Bankura. For details, see Dikshit Sinha, 'Tagore's Experiment in Health-care: Health and Medicine as an Aid to Rural Reconstruction', *Visva-Bharati Annals*, New Series, vol. 6, April 2004, pp. 28-47; Sashi Bhusan Chaudhuri et al., *West Bengal District Gazetters: Bardhaman*, Calcutta: State Editor, West Bengal Gazetters Education Department Government of West Bengal, 1994, pp. 195-7; *Krisak*, Bhadra 1320 BY (1913), vol. 14, no. 5, p. 142; GB, Rev. Deptt., Agriculture Branch, progs. 45-6, February 1917 and progs. 7-8, 21-2 December 1917; L.S.S. O'Malley, *Bengal District Gazetters: Bankura*, Calcutta, 1908, 1st rpt.: Calcuta Education Department, Government of West Bengal, 1996, pp. 108-13; Rathindramohan Chaudhury, *Bankurajaner Itihas-Sanaskriti* (in Bengali) [History and Culture of the People of Bankura], Bankura, pub. by the author Nutanchata, Bankura, 2006, pp. 336-41.
18. For details, see Achintya Kumar Dutta, *Economy and Ecology in a*

Bengal District: Burdwan 1880-1947, Calcutta, Firma KLM, 2002, pp. 17-18.

19. Sinha, op. cit., pp. 31, 40.
20. Elizabeth Whitcombe, 'Irrigation', in Dharma Kumar, ed., *The Cambridge Economic History of India*, vol. II, New Delhi: Orient Longman, 1982, pp. 677-737.
21. Ibid., p. 690.
22. Ibid., p. 735.
23. Walter Hamilton, *A Geographical, Statistical and Historical Description of Hindoostan and the Adjacent Countries*, vol. I, London 1820, first Indian reprint, 1971, Delhi: Oriental Publishers, p. 157.
24. Timbers, op. cit., pp. 368-9.
25. Amiya Kumar Banerji, *West Bengal District Gazetteers: Bankura*, Calcutta: State Editor, West Bengal District Gazetteers, 1968, p. 476. (hereafter *WBDG: Bankura*).
26. L.S.S. O'Malley, *Bengal District Gazetters: Birbhum*, Calcutta, 1996, (first reprint by Higher Education Department, Government of West Bengal), pp. 48-52 (hereafter *BDG: Birbhum*).
27. Timbers, op. cit., p. 366.
28. A. Mitra, *Census, 1951, West Bengal: Burdwan*, Calcutta, 1953, p. xiii.
29. *Report on the Condition of the Lower Classes of Population in Bengal*, Calcutta, 1888, pp. 4-5.
30. *Census of India, 1891*, vol. III, p. 92.
31. For details, see Dutta, op. cit., p. 190.
32. Pabitra Bhaskar Sinha, 'Condition of Labour in the Coalfields of Bengal and Bihar 1890-1920', in Sabyasachi Bhattacharya, ed., *Essays in Modern Indian Economic History*, New Delhi: Munshiram Manoharlal, 1987, pp. 273-83.
33. *Annual Report of Director of Public Health 1940*, Calcutta, 1941, pp. 114-15.
34. Sinha, op. cit., p. 280.
35. A.Z.M. Iftikar Ul-Awal, *The Industrial Development of Bengal 1900-1939*, New Delhi: Vikas Publishing House, 1982, p. 86.
36. *Annual Report of Director of Public Health 1940*, Calcutta, 1941, pp. 114-15.
37. Ibid.
38. Ibid.
39. Rakhi Raychowdhury, *Gender and Labour in India: The Kamins of Eastern Coalmines, 1900-1940*, Calcutta: Minerva Associates Publications, 1996, p. 93.

40. J.C.K. Peterson, *Bengal District Gazetteers: Burdwan*, Calcutta (reprint by Higher Education Department, Government of West Bengal), 1997, p. 106.
41. Ibid.
42. O'Malley, *BDG: Birbhum*, p. 52.
43. Timbers, op. cit., pp. 355-6.
44. G.L. Batra, *Fourth General Report on 107 Health Circles in the Burdwan Division for 1934-35*, Calcutta, 1936, p. 44.
45. *Report on the Administration of Bengal 1930-31*, Calcutta, 1932, p. 150.
46. Timbers, op. cit., p. 367.
47. Ibid.
48. Ibid., p. 370.
49. Binata Sarkar, 'Malaria and Medical Intervention: Burdwan District 1860-1947', unpublished Ph.D. thesis, The University of Burdwan, 2010, p. 160.
50. Batra, op. cit., p. 25.
51. Ibid.
52. For details, see, Kabita Ray, *Press and Public Health: Bengal 1921-1947*, Kolkata: Corpus Research Institute, 2009, p. 5.
53. Sarkar, op. cit., p. 165.
54. Ray, op. cit., p. 9.
55. Cited in ibid., p. 3.
56. Sarkar, op. cit., pp. 148-9; Mitra, op. cit., p. xiii.
57. Sarkar, op. cit., p. 155.
58. Sinha, op. cit., p. 28.
59. Ibid., p. 37.
60. Ramanuj Kar and Fakirdas Chattopadhyay, *Bankura Jelar Bibaran* (in Bengali) [An Account of Bankura District], ed. Samir Kumar Patra and Shekhar Bhoumik, Calcutta: Indira Prakashani, 2006, p. 73.
61. Timbers, op. cit., p. 367.
62. Kar and Chattopadhyay, op. cit., p. 174.
63. Ray, op. cit., p. 9.
64. Cited in ibid., p. 10.
65. Sarkar, op. cit., p. 183.
66. Banerjee, *WBDG: Bankura*, p. 499.
67. *Report on the Administration of Bengal 1934-35*, Calcutta, 1936, pp. 143-4.
68. Ibid.
69. Batra, op. cit., p. 25.

70. Ibid., pp. 28-9.
71. Sarkar, op. cit., pp. 177-80.
72. Bentley, op. cit., p. 103.
73. Batra, op. cit., p. 28.
74. *Report on the Working of the Anti-malaria Campaign in Rural Areas of Bengal with Quinine and Plasmochin for the first year 1933-34*, Calcutta, 1934, p. 3.
75. *Resolution Reviewing the Reports on the Working of District and Local Boards in Bengal During the year 1930-31*, Calcutta, 1932, p. 5.
76. Ibid., p. 5.
77. Batra, op. cit., pp. 18-19.

CHAPTER 2

Ladies' Parliament

Literary Representation of a Site of Female Interaction in Colonial Rural Bengal

Bipasha Raha

Recent scholarship on social and gender historiography in colonial India has brought to the forefront the centrality of certain venues as sites for articulation of the views and opinions of the womenfolk. These sites of social exchange constituted domains where women attempted an expression of identity. An interaction between women and their neighbours in the rural countryside offers a good opportunity to probe how they constituted their hegemony over their subordinate sisters in the world outside the domestic domain. Again, there were areas within the domestic domain, within the family itself, where varied and complex identities were constructed.

Review of literary creations occurring in the period give a glimpse into a world hitherto little explored by historians as data preserved in the archives failed to document the workings of a vibrant sphere of activity. Written texts fill in the gaps in our knowledge of social practices and customs. Literature recorded people's past and sustained their cultural identity. Literature is undoubtedly a historical archive. It is the reflection of society, culture, economy and religious beliefs and practices. It is indeed a historical document. It draws attention to traditions, heritage, social and human values. The epics are a great source of information as they preach basic moral values on the basis of which human society and civilization are built upon. The *Iliad*, *Odyssey*, *Ramayana* and the *Mahabharata* are cases in point. *History of the Peloponnesian War* by Thucydides is an invaluable record of contemporary history.

This paper examines female relationships in late nineteenth- and early twentieth-century Bengal in a limited domain outside the family home cutting across class and caste barriers particularly in the countryside. A site of social exchange for the womenfolk has been selected as it constituted a frequent zone of female interaction. This period, which was witness to accelerated tightening of the tentacles of colonialism and the indigenous attempts to be free of the stranglehold through the intensification of the nationalist movement, also saw the reordering and refashioning of social life. This exerted consequent pressure on the women to fulfil certain specified roles in the urban upper middle-class families. The rural women too succumbed to the changes ushered in by colonialism and its accompanying effects.

Select Domains of Social Interaction

Contemporary literary sources that include novels, short stories, personal narratives, poems and plays give a glimpse into sites of social interaction. These bring to light how these sites of interaction were witness to social power plays, internal bickering, forging of relationships and certain other aspects of social life in colonial Bengal. Continuous social interaction helped to keep the villages a vibrant entity. There were many sites of such interaction as evident from contemporary literature. The *Chandimandap* was the focal point of village life. Tarashankar's *Ganadevata* emphasizes its importance as a centre where local quarrels were sorted out through arbitration by the elderly and wise men of the village. The *Chandimandap* was adjacent to the temple of the leading village deity, such as Shiva (Mayureswar Shiva in *Ganadevata*) and Vishnu. In *Ganadevata,* when Aniruddha and Girish, blacksmith and carpenter respectively, refused to work for the villagers, the problem was discussed here. Police investigations of village crimes were conducted here. The *majlis* was held here as also the *samkirtans* (community singing of devotional songs). At leisure, villagers played a game of chess and dice. It was the place where discussions, relevant to village life were held. Prenuptial discussions and marriages were arranged. Esteemed relatives were entertained at the *Chandimandap*. Rice eating ceremony (*annaprashana*), marriages, funerary practices (*shraddh*) were also held here. This was, however, a preserve of the members of the Hindu community.

The verandah (*dawa)* was used by householders to entertain friends, neighbours and relatives who were offered betel nut and leaf. It served as the modern drawing room. In the play *Nabanna,* Bijan Bhattacharya refers to the fact that villagers often sat in the verandah of neighbours to discuss serious matters. Women used the compound to meet one another. They interacted with neighbours while performing household chores. The inner courtyard (*uthan*) was the domain of women. It was the centre for gossip.

The common kitchen was yet another site. All kinds of discussions were held as people cooked and feasted. Village issues received precedence. Harvests and wedding matters were discussed. This was also religion specific. The local health centre served as a meeting place, exchange of ideas. People conversed as they waited for medication. Villagers dropped in even when not in need of medicine.

In every village there was a *dharmarajtala,* that is, the place of worship of Yama, the God of death. Here, even pleasantries were exchanged. This place was identified with an ancient *bakul* tree and the sacred grove. Only Hindu villagers frequented this place for worship. Women too came at specific times. Literary texts make frequent references to this place. Tarashankar's *Ganadevata* makes frequent reference to its importance in village socio-religious life.

The local grocery store or *mudikhana* was a favourite haunt frequented by the men in the village. People came here not just to buy their necessities but to sit and chat over the daily happenings in the village. Here, class divides were temporarily forgotten as people met in easy camaraderie. In Manik Bandyopadhyay's *Putul Nacher Itikatha*, the local grocery shop of Srinath constituted the heart of village life. People sat on the cane benches outside the shop to gossip. Topics ranged from local scandals to imaginative tales. People came to collect local news in the absence of the daily newspaper. In many villages the local newspaper was read out by the village elder while the others listened raptly.

The *zamindari cutcherry* was yet another important centre of social interaction. In the *cutcherry* building people met and exchanged tales. In the evenings, board games were played and people smoked the *hookah*. This was quite natural considering the fact that the zamindar constituted the local power centre. In the *natmandir*, annual Durga Puja was held along with other forms of recreation such as the *jatra,* puppet show, bursting of fire crackers. All villagers assembled irrespective of class and caste as there were no other forms of entertainment. However, these were male preserves. Women were hardly present except as a part of the audience in the entertainment venues. There is mention of *jatras* as an important form of rural entertainment in Manik Bandyopadhyay's *Padma Nadir Majhi*. While performers came from the local areas the men and women of the village participated as audience. In fact, the whole village gathered.

Ladies' Parliament

The bathing *ghat* was a favourite meeting place. It was the only public space allowed to rural women:

> But chief do India's simple daughters,
> Assemble in these hallowed waters
> With vase of classic model laden,
> Like Grecian girl or Tuscan maiden,
> Collecting thus their urns to fill
> From gushing fount, or tricking rill.
>
> H.H. Wilson[1]

While the bigger villages in Bengal contained more than one tank, only a couple was frequented by the villagers for their daily use. Drawing a pen picture of the village of Kanchanpur in the district of Burdwan in his acclaimed novel *Bengal Peasant Life*, the Revd. Lal Behari Dey writes:

> To a person coming towards the village, from whatever point of the compass, Kanchanpur presents a most striking view. In addition to the usual topes of mangoes and clumps of bamboo which skirt most villages in the country, our village is nearly encircled with some of the finest and most picturesque tanks. These tanks, often covering forty or fifty acres of land, are surrounded by lofty embankments.[2]

The smaller villages had at least one common tank. Most tanks had two bathing *ghats*, one for men and the other for women. They were at a good distance from one another. Usually in most villages, the zamindar or some benevolent well-to-do villager, sometimes seeking divine favours, had the steps of the landing places bound in marble. Vivid descriptions of these *ghats* abound in contemporary literary creations: 'At the head of the *ghat*, on either side is a sacred *tulasi* plant (*Ocymum sanctum*), placed on a high pedestal of masonry; a little higher up stand on two sides two *sriphal* trees (*AEgle marmelos*), and in front of the ghat is a temple containing a statue of Chaitanya, of the size of life'.[3]

In many villages a separate bathing *ghat* was reserved, either at the same tank or another if available, for people to perform the rites on the 10th or 12th day after a death. This *ghat* was considered a dangerous place, avoided by women and seldom visited by the people even during the day, night being simply out of the question.[4]

The bathing *ghat* was the main site for interaction for the rural women, where the 'ladies' parliament' was held daily. Though the women in the villages of rural Bengal visited one another in their houses paying social calls, nowhere did so many women meet together and talk on so many different subjects as at the bathing *ghats* to which they resorted for their daily ablutions. The importance of these *ghats* in the social life of the countryside was acknowledged by the colonial authorities as points where all congregated when the law makers directed after the introduction of the Permanent Settlement of land revenue that all notices of sale of landed estates be put up there.[5] Where there were separate bathing *ghats* for men and women, they were so situated that men who bathed in one *ghat* could not see the women who bathed in the other. In most villages these *ghats* had flights of steps built of masonry which did not rise above the surface of the water. At the head of the steps there would be a large floor, also of masonry, where the people, after coming out of the water, would wipe their bodies and sometimes even change into dry clothes. The general practice was to go home, however distant, in wet clothes.

The *ghat* was the meeting place for women in the morning. On account of the great noise and the gathering of a large number of women it has been called a 'mart', not that commodities were actually bought or sold there.[6] If any man wished to listen to the conversation of these women, then during the midday, sometime between 11 and 12 o'clock, was the best time to hide among the trees in the vicinity. However, if caught he would be severely abused by the elderly women. The rush at the *ghat* would be greater when the women came to bathe before cooking meals. In fact, as one author so succinctly asserted, if there was a daily newspaper being published in the village, this place would have saved the editor much labour in collecting the news:

He could sit there, with a pencil and a piece of paper, and note down information on matters such as what was cooked last night, what is the menu for today, at what time they went to bed last night, who were bitten by mosquitoes, who were in need of salt, who bought oil on credit, how the daughter-in-law of Rama's mother is very quarrelsome, how she came but yesterday and has started defying her mother-in-law, when Kamali would go to her father-in-law's house, how daughter Saraswati is very good because she cooks very well and is very shy.[7]

A visit to the *ghat* was a daily ritual. It served to provide the rural women an eagerly awaited respite from their daily chores. It was a necessary diversion in a society that allowed little source of entertainment for its women.

Bengali literature provides graphic descriptions of the activities of women at the *ghat*. The women would drop in one by one. Most of them would bring with them brass *kalasis* (water-vases) while a few had earthen ones. These they put down in a row on the steps and later filled them with drinking water to take home. Women of all ages, of all ranks, of all castes, except the very lowest, would assemble at almost the same time. Even the old and feeble would be there, without the usual *kalasi*, as they were unable to carry back one filled with water:

Their faces are all looking glossy, for they have been well rubbed with oil....There are matrons thirty and forty years old, women of twenty, and blooming girls of sweet sixteen—in England they call it 'sweet seventeen'; in Bengal the sixteenth year of a Hindu young lady is thought to be the sweetest and most charming. Some of them you observe, are very handsome in their features, and their complexion is like the whiteness of milk mixed with the redness of the *alakta* (lac) a colour which most Bengalis prefer to the snowy whiteness of the European.[8]

The gossipy scene enacted at the *ghat* offers interesting insight into the female world and social life in colonial Bengal. A pen-portrait of the women can be drawn from their everyday interests and conversations. The conversation at the pond normally revolved around household duties, motherhood and village gossip.

Bathing was never accomplished in a hurried manner. In general, most of the women, shortly after their arrival at the *ghat*, would sit down on the steps of the water's edge, rub their teeth with a black dentifrice called *misi*, which each woman brought with her wrapped in a bit of paper, gargled their mouths for a full quarter of an hour and scoured their feet with their *gamchha* (bathing towels). The older women spent more time over these activities than the young maidens aware as they were of the watchful eyes of their mothers and mothers-in-law:

> They then go down the steps—with their clothes on, of course—and stand in the water up to the chin. In this position the rubbing of the body commences, the object of which is to take off the oil with which every part of the body has been anointed. Then, the rubbing over, they dip their heads in water I know not how many dozens of times, and remain standing there up to their chin for a very long time; for they seem to enjoy bathing very much.[9]

A classic scene at the *ghat* would reveal various parties engaged in different operations. It would be seen that some had already bathed and having filled their *kalasis* were going away while others had just come. There were some who could be seen rinsing their teeth while others would be seen sitting on the steps and rubbing their feet or standing chin-deep in water: 'Some beautiful women were rubbing their faces with one end of their saris to enhance their beauty. Lakshmi had already reddened at the upper part of her nose above the nosering by hard rubbing'.[10]

These descriptions give glimpses into the basic hygienic practices adhered to by the women. Their methods were simple and unsophisticated.

However, what is of greater interest is their constant chatter and gossip that draw images of their social life. While they adhered to the personal rituals associated with the daily bath lively conversation would go on. There would be no lack of either talkers or listeners. At any moment between 11 and 1 o'clock one would be sure to find at the *ghat* at least twenty women. Class and caste made its presence felt. The Brahmin women would be sure to recite prayers as they bathed. The lower caste women kept their distance where bathing time coincided: 'Just at this time Sundari, Badan's wife came to the *ghat* with an earthen *kalasi* at her waist. As most of the women at that time bathing were of higher castes and of superior social standing, she instinctively went to one of the sidesteps and descended into the water.'[11]

Again, the quantity of jewels, most of them of pure gold, with which the persons of many of them were loaded, was proof of the fact that they belonged to the aristocracy of the village. A vivid description of the arrival of the zamindar's daughter for her bath in one of the classic tales of rural Bengal in the nineteenth century bears testimony to this:

> 'Look there! Hemangini, the zamindar's daughter is coming here.' All looked towards the way leading to the *ghat* from the village, when there was seen a very beautiful girl of about sixteen years of age coming up to the bathing place. Her head was uncovered; her body covered in every part with ornaments; she was somewhat stout, and as she walked slowly, like a young elephant, as the old Sanskrit poets would have said, the silver anklets of her feet made a tinkling noise.... She had no kalasi at her waist, was attended by her maid-servants, and looked as proud as to compare small things with great, Pharaoh's daughter might have looked when she went to make her ablution in the Nile. An old woman, who seemed, from a massive gold chain round her neck, to belong to a respectable and wealthy family broke the silence.[12]

Bengali women's love for gold is apparent. Its possession was an indicator of class. The common bathing *ghat* in the village was a place where women displayed their prized possession as at any other social gatherings such as marriage. Each new jewellery acquired was displayed at the *ghat*:

> Another woman who was in the water up to her chin, addressing another woman sitting on the steps says;

'When did you get that ornament, *Sai*?'

'Which do you mean *Sai*? This *jhumko*, you mean, I got it two days ago. Sidhe goldsmith has made it. You like it?'

'Oh, they are exceedingly well made. There is no end to your ornaments.'[13]

Women fortunate in matrimony on a visit to their paternal village, would be sure to frequent the bathing *ghat* decked in their jewellery to display the prosperity of the marital home: 'She [Hemangini] had been married some years since to a young zamindar of another part of the district, and was now on a visit to her parents. All eyes were directed towards her.'[14]

The prosperous families in the villages had their own water tanks, on occasions several, where pisciculture was practised. Yet, seldom were bathing *ghats* segregated. The common bathing *ghats* in the villages were frequented by the upper- and middle-class Hindu families and were popular sites of social exchange. Yet, there existed at the *ghat* a sort of camaraderie among the women cutting across class and caste.

Conversations give clue to family life. Conjugal life was a favourite topic of discussion among women. There are frequent insightful references to the different ways literate and illiterate rural women perceived conjugal love. Lack of material possessions was frequently bemoaned and the husband's failure to provide was seen by some of the less enlightened as the inability to awaken finer feelings:

'You are covered with jewels from head to foot. You are lucky in getting a husband who makes it the chief business of his life to please you.'

'I hope, *Sai*, you have also got a good husband. They also say he loves you very much.'

'My husband loves me very much! Ha! Vidhata! Jackals and dogs weep and howl at my misery.'

'Why? What great misery are you suffering?'

'He gives me clothes, certainly; but they are not half so nice as yours. Food also he gives me, but everyone eats food, even dogs. And as for his loving me, what is the use of *dry love*? But what can I say? All this misery has been written on my forehead. There is no escaping it except by death. I shall be happy when I die.'[15]

Others were more philosophical: 'Ornaments are no sign of a husband's love. A man may load his wife's person with ornaments, and yet may not love her.'[16]

Women shared many confidences and often acted as advisers helping one another to see the brighter side of life, to recognize the virtues of their husbands, even though economically less well-off, and appreciate the real things that mattered in a happy conjugal life:

> 'You are not in want of clothes, of food, or any of the necessities of life; and he loves you very much, they all say.'
>
> ...
>
> 'I have heard many rich people of Calcutta are of this sort. Their wives are adorned in every limb, and have jewels the very names of which I never heard; and yet those rich Babus seldom sleep at home. They sleep at Machhua Bazar. But your husband is very good; after candle night he never goes out of doors; he is very gentle; he never beats you, nor rebukes you. What do you want more? It is true, he has not given you many ornaments. But is it his wish not to give you? He would if he could, give you a handful of ornaments; but Mother Lakshmi [the Goddess of Wealth] has not smiled upon him. Don't grumble *Sai*; you should be thankful that you have got such a dear lord of your soul.'
>
> ...
>
> 'Whatever husband fate has given you, with him you must be content. It is a great sin to be discontented in such a case.'[17]

This illuminating passage throws light on some of the darker sides of conjugal life in Bengal. It hints at the existence of domestic violence, marital discords, infidelity and lack of harmony. It reveals that stories about increasing prostitution that had become a dominant feature of Calcutta's social life were circulated in the countryside. Like other pre-colonial socio-economic formations, the profession of prostitution also underwent a dramatic change in Bengal soon after the British take-over. In the nineteenth century, from the peripheries of pre-colonial Bengali rural society, prostitutes came to dominate the centre stage in Calcutta, the capital of British India—thanks to the emergence of a new clientele brought forth by the colonial order.[18] Gossips were common about the dark world of urban life.[19]

In late colonial Bengal, many of the women were learning to read and write. It is difficult to assess their number as not all went to school.

There are evidences of the fact that often husbands encouraged their womenfolk to become literate. Elementary education was imparted at home with the husband making an attempt to educate the wife. The picture in the countryside was very different from the urban areas. The village women were not under pressure to discharge specific duties expected of their upper- and middle-class urban sisters. They were not required to fulfil the role of 'suitable wife' to their 'liberal' husbands, modeled on the European society. Ignorant country women could not easily disregard the views of their literate neighbours:

'You have become a great Pandit, Bagala! You speak in that manner, only because you know how to read and write....'

'I am no Pandit, *Sai*. It is true my husband has taught me to read and write, but I am as ignorant as you in many things, only I have read a few books from which I have learnt that conjugal happiness does not consist in the abundance of ornaments, but in the union of hearts.'[20]

Conversations of women at the bathing *ghat* reveal conjugal happiness was central to family life in rural Bengal. Women, contented in marriage, enjoyed hegemony in the rural society. It was a source of feminine envy: 'Oh Bagala! ... I wish Prajapati [the God of Love/Cupid] had given me your husband, and mine to you.'[21]

Such admissions of unhappiness over one's fate and another woman's superior marital status were not, however, openly made before all bathers. These were confidences shared by friends referred to as *Sai*. In rural Bengal, friendships were forged, *Sais* (friends) made, with the water God (Varun) made witness to it.

Daily chores were discussed as also the comings and goings in each family. House guests were mentioned as also the food that was to be cooked. Nobody visited or departed from someone's house without the whole village being privy to the fact. Every deviation from the usual practice was commented upon and discussed by fellow bathers:

A woman who is rubbing her feet [at the *ghat*] sees another woman preparing to go, and says to her,

'Sister, why are you going away so soon? You have not to cook; why are you then going so soon?'

'Sister, I shall have to cook to-day. The elder *bou* [daughter-in-law] is not well to-day: she was taken ill last night.'

'But you have not to cook much. You have no feast in your house?'

'No; no feast certainly. But my sister has come from Devagrama with her son. And the fisherman has given us a large *rohita*, which must be cooked.'[22]

We are informed that in the middle-class household it was the daughter-in-law who was responsible for preparing the daily meals. Where there was more than one the burden was shared. It was only in exigencies and on occasions that the mother-in-law took charge.

There are glimpses into culinary habits. While fish was a must at meals in upper- and middle-class households, particular attention being paid to its preparation on occasions when there were guests, certain dietary items were class specific, viz., *badi* (balls prepared from pastes of pulses mixed with spices by the womenfolk, dried in the sun and preserved in dried form for use throughout the year either fried or in curry) and poppy-seeds. On occasions, no meal would be complete without fish being prepared in different varieties:

'Oh! You have guests in your house. And what are you going to cook?'

'I am going to cook *dal* of *mashkalai*, one *tarkari* [an item prepared from vegetables], *badi* fried, fish fried, fish with peppercorns, fish with tamarind, and another dish, of which my sister's son is very fond, namely, *amda* with poppy seeds.'

'The everlasting *badi* and poppy seed. You banias are very fond of these two things. We Brahmans do not like either of them.'

'The reason why you Brahmans do not like *badis* is that you do not know how to make them well. If you once taste our *badi* you will not forget for seven months. You would wish to eat it everyday. As for poppy seed, what excellent curry it makes.'

'Why sister, you are so eloquent in the praise of *badis*, that my mouth is watering. If I were not a Brahmani woman I would have tasted your *badi*.'

'Never mind, though you are a Brahman, once taste my *badi*. *Badi* will not destroy your caste.'

So saying the banker woman went away with then *kalasi* on her waist.[23]

A listener learns that *badi* making is a highly specialized job. It was not an easy task for all women.

Impending marriages and the suitability of proposals for marriages were discussed and debated upon with great enthusiasm. Elderly rural women were free with their advice. Virtues of prospective brides were considered:

An elderly woman noticing her said—'I hear, Malati's mother, that your son Govinda is going to get married to Dhanamani, Padma Pal's eldest daughter. Is that rumour true?'

'Yes, there has been some talk on the subject, but nothing has as yet been settled.'

'It would be a great match. Dhanamani is a very nice girl. She is gentle like the goddess Lakshmi herself.'

'Don't praise her too much, lest the gods take her away from the world. If Prajapati has tied the knot, the marriage will take place; if not, not.'[24]

The women had great faith in the hand of fate in affairs of marriage as in all else.

Village affairs were not ignored. Nothing happened in the village that was not in their know-how. The women were as interested in domestic affairs as in the rural world at large:

Bimali had started abusing some unknown person using words which do not find a place in the lexicon. The subject-matter of her lecture was that somebody's cow had damaged her pumpkin plant last night. Citing instances of the damage done by the cow, the luxuriance of the pumpkin plant and its fruit bearing potentialities, she wished the cow's owner would gift it to a Brahmin.[25]

Village politics was hotly debated upon. Grisly tales of crime came a close second:

An old woman ... broke the silence by asking—'What man was that sitting in the portico of your house with your father? I saw them both as I was coming to the tank.'

'That is the Daroga of Mantresvara.'

'Daroga! Why, what has he come here for? I have not heard of any *dacoity* or murder in the village.'

'No murder! Have you forgotten the case of Yadumani, Padma Pal's second daughter?'

'But that is an old affair. It was all settled long ago.'

It was not settled—it was only hushed up. But it seems it has come to light now.'

'And what has your father [the zamindar] said to the Daroga.'

'I am sure I don't know what he has said to him; but I believe he has given the Daroga hush-money?'[26]

Some of the women would then launch an argument on the merits of the case, some on the practice of giving hush-money while others condemned it. These were samples of the sort of deliberations that took place in the 'parliament of women'.[27]

Other topics of conversation included cruelties of husbands, quarrels of two women over the same man, atrocious conduct of stepmothers and the beauty of the women of the village. Other interesting scenes were enacted that give clues into the mind-set of village women. Quarrels were frequent over trivial matters among rural women. *Ghats* were not spared:

> Jasoda in chest-high water was cleansing her teeth. Markandia, a boy of five, muddied the water by playing in it. As some water splashed on to Jasoda, she stepped angrily out of water and abused the boy in filthy language, wishing him a premature death. Markandia's mother rushed forward and made a fitting retort in a similar tone. Ultimately, the quarrel ended in a defeat for Markandia's mother who slapped her son and returned home carrying a jar-ful of water in her arms, muttering darkly and dragging Markandia behind her, crying loudly.
>
> The sound of thunder reverberates in the sky long after the bolt has fallen. The quarrel has ended, but discussion about it continued for a long time. The middle-aged and the elderly women divided themselves into two groups, one taking up the cause of Markandia's mother and the other that of Jasoda.[28]

Some considered Markandia to be at the root of the trouble. He was entirely to blame and his offence was inexcusable. Everyone drank the water from the *ghat* and some considered it a serious offence to pollute that water. They forgot that four or five scores of women in a village washed themselves at the *ghat*. Everyday, some washed their soiled mattresses and some the bed clothes of their children and other rags. All these activities of the women were nothing compared to the 'crime' committed by Markandia. Yet, the women quarrelled over the activities of Markandia.

In most literary creations, women are presented as quite petty in their everyday interests and conversations. The conversations of the women who came to the *ghat* revolved round household duties, motherhood and village gossip. They give an insight into the characters of women so commonly to be found in the villages of Bengal. Bagala in Lal Behari Dey's *Bengal Peasant Life*, one of the earliest Indian authors to present a realistic pen-portrait of village life, was an educated woman held in esteem by some of the other women. Jasoda was easily angered and was not fond of children as is clear from her intolerance of little Markanda's harmless playfulness.

Conclusion

The open terrace (*chhad*) was yet another zone frequented by the women at large in upper- and middle-class households, both in rural and urban areas. Rural women enjoyed a privilege denied to their urban sisters. They had the freedom to move around the village, outside the home, at certain times of the day. Visits to the *ghat* were a daily ritual. This was denied to the urban women except the poor and the lowly. A holy bath in the Ganges for the upper- and middle-class women involved their being carried in the palanquin and given a dip while seated inside it by the bearers. In the urban areas only a few of the very rich had their own tanks.

The open terrace in big houses was the female domain. It served multifarious purposes. The terrace and the kitchen shared a closed bond. At noon, the women in the house would sit and make *badis* (balls made of grounded pulses) and dry them in the sun.[29] Again, green mangoes would be cut into slices and dried in the sun to be made into *amshi*, the necessary ingredient for mango pickle.[30] Ripe mango juice would be poured into stone bowls of different shapes and sizes to be thickened and made into *amsatta* (dried cakes of mango pulp). Mango, jackfruit, barley and vegetable pickles would be prepared in mustard oil and dried on the terrace. This was the rural tradition that was also preserved in urban Bengal. These food items were an indispensable part of the Bengali diet.

Much of the afternoons and evenings were spent by the women on the terrace. Straw mats would be laid down for the assembled women to sit. The neighbouring women too joined the *majlis* bringing with them the local gossip. In the winter months the terrace was frequented by them after lunch. While drying their wet hair they would cut betel nut and dress betel leaves. Young wives and girls played on the terrace. Many marriages of dolls were held here.

These interactions describe the social world in which the rural women lived, the indigenous and colonial structures of power as they perceived it. One gets a realistic view of the village women, a complex view that allows for subtle differences between women. Relationships between women and with their male members are revealed. Literary sources constitute the main source of information on these aspects of social life.

Notes

1. Cited in Revd. Lal Behari Dey, *Bengal Peasant Life*, London: Macmillan & Co. 1934 (rpt. edn.), p. 174.
2. Ibid., pp. 2-3.
3. Ibid.
4. Fakir Mohan Senapati, *Six Acres and a Half*, tr. B.M. Senapati and A.M. Senapati, from the Oriya novel *Chha Mana Atha Guntha*, Delhi: Sahitya Academy, 1967, p. 49.
5. *Dacca Prakash*, 26 April 1868.
6. Senapati, op. cit., p. 50
7. Ibid.
8. Ibid., p. 176
9. Ibid.
10. Ibid. pp. 50-1.
11. Dey, op. cit., p. 180.
12. Ibid., pp. 180-1.
13. Ibid., p. 178.
14. Ibid.
15. Ibid., pp. 178-9.
16. Ibid., p. 179.
17. Ibid., pp. 178-9.
18. Sumanta Banerjee, *Dangerous Outcast: The Prostitute in Nineteenth Century Bengal*, Calcutta: Seagull Books, 1988.
19. Sumanta Banerjee, *The Wicked City: Crime and Punishment in Colonial Calcutta*, Delhi: Orient BlackSwan, 2009.
20. Dey, op. cit., p. 180.
21. Ibid., p. 179.
22. Ibid., p. 177.

23. Ibid., p. 178.
24. Ibid., p. 180.
25. Senapati, op. cit., p. 51.
26. Dey, op. cit., p. 180.
27. Ibid., p. 182.
28. Senapati, op. cit., p. 51.
29. They are deep fried and generally cooked in fish curries and other vegetable preparations, viz., *shukto*, *mocha chachchari*, *ghunto*, etc., and served hot with rice.
30. No Bengali diet was complete without pickles.

CHAPTER 3

Indians and Europeans in Coal Business Conflict of Interest in the Bengal Coalfield, 1900-1947

NAINA BANERJEE

At the turn of the twentieth century, British imperialism was at its highest in India and the East. The three most profitable industries in eastern India, viz., tea, jute and coal were firmly controlled by the European managing agencies. Calcutta was till then the economic capital of British imperialism. Yet, what was striking was the development of Indian enterprise in the coal industry. It led to sharp conflict between European managing agencies and the Indian colliery owners and coal traders.

Confrontation over rights of ownership of collieries in Raniganj dates back to the 1840s, when Dwarkanath Tagore's Carr, Tagore and Company often clashed with Gilmore Homfrey and Company over the rights of Naraincoory mines. At the turn of the century, the conflict took the form of a confrontation between the Indian Mining Association (IMA) affiliated to the Bengal Chamber of Commerce, which had long represented the collective interests of the bigger European coal companies, and the Indian Mining Federation (IMF) organized in 1913 to promote unity among Indian colliery owners and was affiliated to the Bengal National Chamber of Commerce.

Early Days of the Coal Industry

Raniganj in Bengal was the birth place of the coal mining industry in India. Coal mining like plantations during British rule, fully manifested all the symptoms of colonial experience, viz., private investment, involvement of indigenous capital, import of labour from other parts of the country to build up a reserve of 'capital labour' and a low level of technology. The Raniganj-Jharia-Bokaro region had collieries that began in the colonial times. It was, however, in the late nineteenth century that coal mining gained pace in Bengal and with the expansion of railways the coalfields of Jharia in Bihar were opened up. The necessities of fuelling the industrial-urban engine during the British Raj, encouraged coal mining in Raniganj and Jharia. Suetonius Grant Heatly and John Summer, two employees of the East India Company in 1774, first struck coal here. But coal mining in India continued to be sporadic in nature. The pressure of the British capitalist community led to slow growth of the industry in India. The firm of Heatly and Summer sent 2,500 maunds of coal to the Company's military stores in 1775. It furnished no reports. Another consignment of 2,000 maunds was delivered in 1777. But the report was discouraging. After trial and comparison with British coal and the pressure of British industrialists, it was reported that the Panchet coal was only half as good as the former and it advised them to mine deeper. However, the firm suffered huge losses. Heatly had brought miners from England. But they all died of fever. Later, Heatly and Summer were transferred and Lord Cornwallis did not encourage coal mining in India. However, the contemporary world situation and the realization of economic needs generated much enthusiasm in opening new collieries at random. Three factors provided the initial stimuli for growth of coal mining industry, viz., the abolition of East India Company's trading monopoly in 1813, opening of the Raniganj mine under European supervision and the introduction of railways in 1855 to facilitate coal transport to the market in Calcutta which was the capital of British Empire in South Asia till 1911.[1] Till then, Bihar was an integral part of the Bengal Presidency. The two coal fields of Raniganj and Jharia are geographically closer to each other and, therefore, have common characteristics.

In 1820, mining activities were initiated by some of the large Agency Houses of Calcutta. The Charter Act of 1813 had abolished the Company's monopoly of trading in India. It opened immense opportunities before the British private traders. Taking advantage of it, the number of agency houses in Bengal went up to twenty-five.[2] The new houses that emerged in Calcutta after 1813, were eager to trade in opium in China. They also took interest in export of raw silk, indigo, cotton piece-goods, shipping, banking and insurance. By this time the Company's government took interest in exploring the areas in and around Raniganj as the prospect of having rich coal deposits in the area became brighter. Alexander and Company, one of the largest of the six agency houses of Calcutta, started financing mining activities in Raniganj colliery.[3] Between 1820 and 1830, Jessop & Company, Gilmore Homfrey & Company, Erskine & Company, became active in the Raniganj coal belt. A fierce competition began among the rival companies of Bengal over the exclusivity of rights between 1831 and 1844. However, by this time the bigger agency houses of Calcutta had begun to decline. The principal houses went far beyond the limits of prudence in advancing money to the indigo planters, and were also tempted to invest recklessly huge sums of money in their own indigo concerns. The obvious result was a glut in the home market causing a marked depreciation in prices. The abrupt fall in indigo prices in 1829 had serious repercussions. Other chief causes of the misfortunes of the agency houses were 'over-trading, improvident enterprise, extravagant miscalculation and excessive expanse in living.'[4]

Managing Agencies

The origin of the managing agency system has been attributed to the mercantile 'agency houses' which flourished in Calcutta from 1793 until their failure in the 1830s. In the crisis of 1829-33, all the agency houses failed. Their place was taken by a new set of commercial institutions. They performed many of the same functions, especially that of advancing money to indigo planters, but relied on the hypothecation of goods imported from Britain for the greater part of their capital. In the period 1834-47, this new type of business organization, recognized as a managing agency, took form. A mercantile agency house first assumed the duties of a managing agent in Calcutta in 1836. Other Calcutta agency houses followed their example and undertook the management of joint stock companies in the 1840s.

The managing agency system came into existence when an agency house first promoted and then acquired the management of a joint-stock company. The Carr, Tagore and Company, founded in 1834 was one of the most energetic of these new houses. Between 1836 and 1846, this company promoted and managed six joint-stock companies. They ventured into coal, indigo, steam tug, insurance, etc. In 1836, Carr, Tagore and Company promoted and assumed the management of the Calcutta Steam Tug Association. In this arrangement, this company assumed certain characteristics of the defunct agency houses in the period before 1834. In the course of the four decades from 1880 until the end of the First World War, the managing agencies of Bengal changed their role. In the period between the 1850s and 1870s, the normal pattern of establishing an industrial enterprise was for the investors to form an association. Since the introduction of the Company Law in Bengal, this association became a typical Limited Liability Company. They appointed the directors. The latter in turn found the managers or appointed secretaries to run the business. The control of the company was in the hand of shareholders. In the 1870s and 1880s it became a normal feature to appoint a managing agent for the company, an agent fit to handle the day-to-day business of the company. Some industries in Bengal, viz., tea and jute, developed independent of one another. But coal was needed by all the major industries in Bengal. Therefore, the demand for coal and the price of coal had to coordinate. From 1890 to 1920, the number of public limited companies in coal mining in Bengal grew from six to two hundred and twenty-seven.

The European managing agencies had an overpowering presence in the coalfields of Raniganj and Jharia. But the coal mines which could be run on small capital were never a complete European monopoly like the jute mills. The jute mills required huge capital outlay to run. But indigenous entrepreneurial involvement was not lagging behind in the coal sector. It dates back to the pioneering career of Prince Dwarkanath Tagore.

Emergence of the Indigenous Sector

Dwarkanath Tagore's interest in coal trade was stimulated by the introduction of the steamship into India during the late 1820s. In 1835, the firm of Carr, Tagore and Company purchased the old Raneegunge Colliery from the bankrupted Alexander and Company for Rs. 70,000. In 1837, a Mr Betts was persuaded to sell off his property at Chinakoori for Rs. 40,000.[5] During the later part of 1830 and the early 1840s, a bitter and violent struggle occurred between Carr, Tagore and Company and Gilmore Homfrey and Company, owner of the nearby Naraincoory mine, for the hegemony of the emergent coalfield. After the collapse of Carr, Tagore and Company, in the crash of 1848, the coal mines acquired by Dwarkanath came to form the nucleus of the huge European-owned Bengal Coal Company. This company, the biggest among all the coal companies in India, came under the control of the leading European managing agency of Andrew Yule and Company in 1908.[6] The Bengal Coal Company managed many Indian colliery and landowners in the Raniganj area.

Despite the towering presence of the Bengal Coal Company in Raniganj field, we find the presence of some native entrepreneurs in the nearby areas. From the writings of A.G. Mackenzie of the Bengal Coal Company we come to know about three different natives endeavouring to open up adjacent areas of the Raniganj field.[7] The prominent among them were Gobin Pundit and Shib Kristo Daw. Gobin Pundit was a deputy collector of the 24-Parganas. He successfully commenced mining operations in Searsole, a few miles to the north of Raniganji.[8] Gobin Pundit or Gobinda Prasad Pundit, a north-Indian gentleman entered into coal production after retirement from government service. D.H. Williams, who carried out the first geological survey of the Damodar Valley in the late 1840s, contemplated Gobin Pundit's open-cast mine. He wrote, 'With the system of mining now in operation together with the absence of common intelligence bearing on the subject, no real good can be expected from this mine.' Earlier, Mackenzie too had expressed the same view. Both were wrong. By 1859, Searsole was producing

18 lakh maunds of coal a year. It was second only to the Bengal Coal Company, which was producing 34 lakh maunds.[9]

It was traditionally believed that Bengali capital and enterprise was 'proverbially shy' of industrial ventures. But the coal mining sector was a marked exception. The period between the early 1890s and the years 1925 and 1926, which marked the worldwide economic depression, witnessed a flourishing interest in the coal mining industry by the Bengali community. The expansion of the railways into the Jharia field in the early 1890s encouraged the Bengali entrepreneurs in this field. By 1897, sixty-two mines had been opened up by Bengali capitalists. Laik-Banerjee and Company (private) was one of the most remarkable Bengali firms. A.C. Laik, a petty zamindar of the Dishergarh *mouza,* entered into partnership with Jadav Lal Banerjee of Birbhum in the late 1870s.[10] Both Laik and Banerjee worked as clerks in the Bengal Coal Company. Jadav Lal Banerjee was a time-keeper in the company. They realized early, the growing potential of the coal industry. From the mid-1880s, they began to acquire the lease hold of virgin areas on the western bank of the Burrakar River. It was at a time, when the railways stopped short of the western bank of the river. Laik and Banerjee were among the first entrepreneurs to see the commercial possibilities of the then unexploited Jharia field. By the end of the nineteenth century, the firm acquired the rich deposits at Lodna, Jealgora and Jharia Khas. By 1896, the firm possessed ten working collieries and established its headquarters at Begunia, near the new Burrakar bridge. They became one of the original members of the IMA.[11] However, this firm was declared insolvent in 1911. It is altogether not clear how this came about. The popular explanation goes that the European entrepreneurs finally realizing the value of Jharia field began to exert pressure on the firm to give up their leases.

Nibaran Chandra Sircar was one of the most successful of the Bengali entrepreneurs. Born in 1855, at Sitarampur near Asansol, he was the son of a revenue collector. He joined the Bengal Coal Company in the clerical grade in 1879.[12] He gained first-hand knowledge about the coal bearing belt. He soon acted as a selling contractor on behalf of the company for the sale of coal to Calcutta. By the 1890s, he accumulated sufficient capital and took short-term lease of a landed property at Andal. He persuaded Mr R. Bernard, an experienced mining engineer and the English manager of Bengal Coal Company's Gargotia (Gangutia) colliery, to enter into partnership with him in 1899. This partnership prospered. Sircar organized the marketing side, while Bernard looked after mining. The successful strike of the rich Dishergarh seam encouraged the partners to extend their lease and strike new shafts. By 1908, they floated four public joint-stock companies: Baraboni (1905), Imperial, Phularit and (both in 1907) and Bilberia (1908). Though the firm was flourishing,[13] in the same year, Bernard sold off his share to the highest bidder, H.V. Low, and retired to England.[14] At the end of the First World War, the agency's eight public coal companies were annually producing over 600,000 tons of coal. It employed fifteen European managers. The business had diversified into engineering, a brick factory, a boating company and cement works. All were consumers of coal.[15] Nibaran Chandra Sircar was the moving spirit behind the creation of the IMF. He remained its chairman for the next decade.[16] He was called 'coal prince' by the Calcutta press.[17] and elected to the First Legislative Assembly in 1921.[18]

However, the slump of 1924-6, spelt the doom of N.C. Sircar. Shortage of liquid capital made him broach two London Finance Houses in 1924. But the scarcity of the collieries was not enough to elicit the required loan. Sircar was forced to take loan from a Marwari banker, S.K. Karnani. According to a term of the loan, Karnani became member of the Board of Directors of the largest company Baraboni. From the beginning, basic disagreements prevailed between the two men. In 1927, Sircar amalgamated all the collieries into an enlarged Baraboni Coal Company. It was a desperate attempt to materially strengthen the trading position. Sircar was forced to transfer the entire assets of the Company to H.V. Low. Karnani had a controlling interest there. Sircar lived his last days in Benares.

The first two and a half decades of the twentieth century saw a number of Bengali entrepreneurs in the coal industry. Maharaja Nandi of Kasimbazar was the biggest Bengali entrepreneur. But he farmed out the actual management of his collieries to H.V. Low. Maharaja Nandi established a small school of mines at Ethora for training his colliers in the basic techniques of mining.[19]

Indian Colliery Owners *vs.* European Managing Agencies

At the beginning of the twentieth century, there was a striking development of Indian entrepreneurs in the coal industry that led to sharp conflict between the European managing agencies and the Indian colliery owners and coal traders. The confrontation existed mainly between the Indian Mining Association, affiliated to the Bengal Chamber of Commerce, which had long represented the collective interests of the bigger European coal companies and the IMF, newly organized in 1913 to promote unity among the Indian colliery owners. It was affiliated to the Bengal National Chamber of Commerce. In the previous century, the collieries of Raniganj and Jharia were largely controlled by the European managing agencies. But the control of the smaller collieries was never a complete European monopoly. Dwarkanath Tagore was a pioneering Indian colliery owner in Raniganj. However, after the collapse of his business ventures in the financial crisis of 1848, his coal mines passed under the European-dominated Bengal Coal Company. This company was the biggest among all the coal companies in India. The Bengal Coal Company ruined many Indian colliery owners and land owners in Raniganj area. But they could not totally crush the Indian colliery owners. There was no organized lobby of the Indians to counter the European attack but resistance was put up by some of them. In this regard, mention must be made of the Malia brothers of Searsole, Rameshwar Malia and Dakshineswar Malia.

The Malias, a Punjabi Saraswat Brahmin family, owned the coal mines of Searsole and landed estates. Their collieries were leased out so that they had no direct stake in the coal mining and coal marketing business. Yet, the family and the Bengal Coal Company, which were expanding around the same region around Raniganj, were frequently involved in armed clashes and judicial disputes about the proprietary rights in new lands and coal mines. Coal was sent to Calcutta from the Jamuria-Raniganj road to Damodar. While on its way via Searsole, the Malias systematically held up the supplies of the Bengal Coal Company. In one of the armed clashes, two *chaprasis* of the Malias were killed. Rameshwar Malia changed his tactics hereafter. He became a member of the IMA and tried to buy out Bengal Coal Company's shares. Before the formation of any organization of the Indian colliery owners, both Rameshwar and his brother Dakshineswar Malia, owner of the coal mine of Searsole and five landed estates, acted as informal representatives of the Indian colliery owners for more than two decades.[20]

Many of the Bengali entrepreneurs were members of the IMA. They felt their particular interests were not being properly looked after by the IMA which was entirely dominated by the European agency houses. However, it was not until after the death of Rameshwar Malia in 1912 that Indian colliery owners learned to stand up collectively to the pressure of the European coal companies. As long as Rameshwar Malia was alive, the European coal companies could not dominate in the Raniganj coal belt. The Malias always gave a serious challenge to the larger coal companies like the Bengal Coal Company, in the field of production and transportation. In fact, Rameshwar Malia had so much influence that he was appointed to the Labour Enquiry Commission of 1896, as the lone Indian representative.

On the initiative of Nibaran Chandra Sircar, Abinash Chandra Banerjee and Srish Chandra Nandy, the Maharaja of Kasimbazar, a purely indigenous trade federation was established in Calcutta on 14 March 1913. All the key executive positions were held by the Bengalis. The federation proved to be an effective mouthpiece for the indigenous lobby. The immediate occasion for the organization of the IMF in 1913 was a coal boom of 1912 and acute shortage of wagons. At this juncture railway authorities displayed extreme partiality in the supply of wagons. The wagon scramble assumed the shape of a bitter conflict between the big European coal companies and small collieries. The former got liberal supply of wagons at the expense of the leading Indian colliery owners and small Indian coal merchants. These people found that all individual efforts were futile against the powerful European concerns backed by the railway authorities. A meeting was therefore, convened in March 1913. It was attended by Bengali, Marwari and Gujarati colliery owners from distant collieries who came together to form the IMF. The IMF was born as a result. It was immediately affiliated to the Bengal National Chamber of Commerce. It paralleled the European dominated IMA's relationship with the Bengal Chamber of Commerce. It gained sufficient authority to consult those government departments which dealt with the industry. Some indigenous proprietors, however, remained outside the federation along with a small army of coal merchants and wholesalers. Within a few years, almost all Indian collieries joined the Federation. It was an important and representative association, having on its roll two hundred fifty members owning three hundred thirty-one collieries in Bengal and Bihar.[21]

One of the very first acts of the IMF in 1914 was the preparation of a scheme for the establishment of a marketing organization to promote the use of soft coke instead of dung and wood among the public. The war and the subsequent boom in the coal industry weakened the programme. But with the onset of Depression in 1928, the idea was rekindled. Initially the IMF had the support of the IMA. However, their joint negotiations broke down over the question of financing the suggested selling syndicate. The IMF wanted to levy cess on the dispatch of all coals. But, the IMA wanted to shoulder a tax on soft coke alone. The Federation, therefore, proceeded alone. In 1929, under their initiative the Soft Coke Cess Act became law, and a committee consisting of seven IMF and one IMA representative was set up. They were given the power to levy a cess on all soft coke despatches. An up-country office was opened at Cawnpore for publicity. Ten years after the Act had been passed, the annual consumption of soft coke had risen by little more than a lakh ton (889,000 tons in 1939 compared to 754,000 in 1929).[22]

In the second place, the Federation lobbied with the government and the railways for using second class coal where it was economic. In public tenders for coal, rates offered by the Indian colliery owners were lower. But, for the same quality of coal the European companies offered higher rates and the railway authorities accepted the rate. The IMF intervened in this matter and as a result, Indians got some share in the orders placed by the railways. Third, the IMF agitated against the special wagon supply system. The system was that the railways would supply wagons to the coal companies according to their production and demand, irrespective of whether they were European or Indian companies. In this vital matter, it did not make much headway. The First World War broke out within a year of its birth and the general supply of wagons to the larger collieries representing the IMF decreased, causing serious losses. This happened because the railways decided to set aside a major portion of the available wagons for special supply. Some parties benefited at the expense of the rest. As the Secretary of the IMF wrote to the EIR agent:

> A colliery which may secure a contract from a Railway, will get by preferential treatment, the full numbers of wagons it may require to meet the contract; secondly, it may get wagons again for special purposes; thirdly, the same colliery may further get rakes; and, lastly, it will again get supplies with the general body of collieries in the *pro rata* distribution of wagons according to raising and stock; whereas some collieries can get wagons only on the last ground.[23]

As a result, a large number of collieries were unable to despatch enough coal to meet the actual expenses of working the mines. From the middle of 1920s, the Bengali proprietors began to lose their balance of influence. The slump in the period between 1925 and 1928 and the Great Depression of 1929 spelt bankruptcy for many indigenous collieries. Only a few dominant Bengali elements managed to survive. Among the survivors were the Maharajah of Kasimbazar, B.K. Roy, Roy-Dutt and Company, S.B. Banerjee, R.N. Bagchi and Brothers Limited, W.C. Banerjee and K. Pal Chowdhury.[24] However, nothing much is known about most of these entrepreneurs.

The partial eclipse of the Bengalis in the mid 1920s allowed the new immigrant trading communities from Marwar, Kutch, Sindh and the Punjab to set foothold in the coal industry. A few Marwari families had set up trading and shop-keeping business in the coalfields prior to the First World War period.[25] Prior to the slump of 1925 to 1928 and the Great Depression, their stake in the coal trade was marginal. They took the contracting Bengali interest as a great opportunity to extend their colliery holdings. In 1921, the chairman of the IMA accused the Marwaris of being partially responsible for causing general unrest amongst the miners. It led to a series of strikes. In a circular sent to all members of the association the secretary noted that:

In the different coalfields there are a number of shops from which labour draw their supplies of rice, cloth and other essential commodities of life. These shops are for the most managed by Marwaris who are incidentally assisting the present agitators. It is of little consequence to these shopkeepers whether or not the labour is adequately paid and the only interference is that they hope to get more money out of the miner, their sole object being to line their own pockets at the expense first of the local trade and then of the miner.[26]

The secretary then recommended the members of the IMA to establish company owned fair-trade shops to break the Marwari monopoly.

As early as in 1902, two Marwari coal entrepreneurs figure in the returns for the Jharia coal fields. The *Census of India* 1911 listed nine Agarwallas who were Marwaris as colliery proprietors in Jharia and one Agarwalla in Raniganj.[27] By 1923, at least thirty Marwari coal owners appeared in the two coal fields. Their combined output amounted to 400,000 tons approximately.[28]

By 1911, the Marwaris had made fortunes by speculating in jute and company shares. In coal too, the business of trading throughout the subcontinent was increasingly in Marwari hands. Between 1920 and 1925, the market proved bullish. Eleven new jute mills and forty-six new collieries were floated.[29] As the cost of capital escalated, the companies borrowed fair amount of short-term funds from the Marwari families at lower rates of interests, against the security of blocks of ordinary shares. The Marwari lenders were the old *banias* of the companies, viz., Jatias with Andrew Yule; Goenka, Doodhwalla, Bangur and Bajoria with Bird and Heilgers; Kanorias with McLeod and Rameshwar Nathany with Jardine Skinner.[30] Eventually, some Marwari families obtained enough shares to get elected onto the boards of several jute mill companies. These Marwaris had made enough profits while working with the large British firms, be it supplying raw jute from the remotest corner of Bengal or carrying coal from the pit heads.

Till the Great Depression, the jute industry enjoyed the benefits of growing globally. At a time when the jute industry was booming, the coal sector was going through a very bad phase. Many smaller collieries were closed in Bengal and Bihar. The bigger collieries on the other hand, took resort to slaughter mining to increase their production. The years between 1919 and 1924, saw relative prosperity in the coal industry. But the years 1925 and 1930 saw a reverse trend. Railway demand fell sharply as the collieries run by the railways had started production. Therefore, the railways started consuming coal from their own captive mines. It led to fall in prices. In an effort to reduce average costs, many collieries started mining larger output, hoping that demand would rise. But price plummeted to an average of Rs. 6.25 per ton (1925-9) or 52 per cent less than what it was in 1920 and 1924.[31] By 1928, three hundred small proprietary mine collieries, given in lease to small businessmen in the marginal mining areas around Jharia and Raniganj, closed down 'never to open again'.[32] The *India International Year Book* (*IIYB*) of 1928-9 painted a grim picture: 'It is impossible to bring working costs down to keep pace with the drop in prices and the only end appears to be the survival of the fittest (and) collieries expansive to work and companies with no reverses will go to the wall'.[33]

Under the grim circumstances, most Marwaris stayed away from coal sector.[34] However, some well-known Marwari business houses took special interest in coal industry during the second half of the 1920s. The Marwaris were traditionally involved in trade and moneylending. They had no shortage of funds for setting up industries or for working capital requirements. In the period between 1901 and 1914 and during the First World War, Marwari families like Birla, Bangur, Goenka, and the Jatias made fortunes in raw jute trade, share trading and *fatka*. They found it easy to enter into jute and coal. The Goenka and Poddar families directly entered the coal industry as producers in the early 1920s.[35]

Trends were different for the coal sector. During the 1920s, very few shares of the European controlled companies changed hands, because most of the collieries that collapsed were proprietary firms with no tradeable shares. Moreover, European managing agencies always owned a much larger proportion of colliery stock compared to the jute mills. It made takeover bids difficult. In collieries, managing agencies generally owned 35 per cent or more of the equity. For instance, Andrew Yule owned more than 35 per cent of the share capital in 75 per cent of its concerns, whereas the Bird and Heilgers group owned more than 30 per cent of equity in all its collieries.[36] However, the *IIYB* of 1930-1 listed thirteen Marwari directors in the eighty-two collieries which were under European managing agencies.[37] The Jatia family acquired an important stake in the coal companies of Andrew Yule and Kilburns. S.K. Karnani took over the European agency house of H.V. Low.

In 1934, the Indian Colliery Owners Association (ICOA) was formed. It was a second indigenous trade association. It highlighted the decline of Bengali influence on the one hand, and the rising importance of the immigrant groups on the other. During the early 1930, a number of disputes arose within the IMF along community lines.[38] These disagreements were about issues of policy. But the underlying cause was no doubt the Bengali resentment of the immigrant success. A group of non-Bengalis, instead of capturing the executive posts of the Federation, decided to form a rival body. In March 1934, forty colliery proprietors including N.H. Ojha, J.K. Agarwalla, K.C. Thapar, Waliram Taneja and the representatives of the Chanchani and Goenka families formed the ICOA.[39] Over the next few years, the IMF and the ICOA often clashed publicly on a number of important subjects. The most damaging effect of these internecine quarrels was on the output restriction scheme which the IMF and the IMA were jointly preparing since 1933. The IMA was ready to recognize the new break-away group and offer them representation in the new output restriction scheme.[40] But the IMF refused to recognize the new group. Ultimately, the government rejected the entire package. One reason they gave for this decision was this disunity within the trade.[41]

Position of the Indigenous Coal Owners within the Coal Industry

The period immediately after the First World War, was a boom time for the indigenous collieries. In the early 1920s, they mined first over one-third of the total output.[42] From the middle of 1920s, the demand for second class coal began to fall due to substantial fall in the price of first class products. The onset of the Great Depression led to a catastrophic fall in the price of all grades of coal.

Between 1923 and 1924, at the first sign of Depression, many small mines (that produced less than 10,000 tons) went out of work. The indigenous collieries encountered a number of problems. In the very first place, they were denied access to working capital. Their European counterparts enjoyed working capital, as a result of their greater standing in the European-dominated Calcutta money market. It was argued before both the Indian Industrial Commission (1916-18)[43] and the Indian Fiscal Commission (1921-2)[44] that the indigenous collieries faced acute loan crunch.

Actually, the conservative bankers lacked confidence in the small concerns because of their highly illiquid nature of colliery block which applied to all colliery undertakings irrespective of size. In comparison, most of the large European enterprises had a more diversified market, an excellent dividend record and had the backing of a well-known agency house. The small colliery concerns carried a much greater element of risk. One scholar argued:

> Many of the difficulties of which Indian business complained throughout the first half of the century—the inaccessibility of banks and of credit, the high cost of loans, the privileges granted to foreign borrowers and much else—were a perfectly normal response by British banks to business condition of the time ... if they dealt, by preference, with British clients and on easier terms, it was because they had a surer knowledge of their credit worthiness, and because they had close links with them at home.[45]

However, he could not totally deny the charge of racial discrimination. Virtually all branches of indigenous industry in this period experienced great difficulties in obtaining loan finance simply because they were Indian.[46]

In 1921, Amrit Lal Ojha, an outstanding Kutchi colliery owner and founder member of the IMF, complained: 'The small colliery owners have not got sufficient influence to make the banks advance money... I am a colliery proprietor, but they wouldn't recognize me, that is the difficulty.'[47]

Only S.K. Karnani's Industrial Bank seemed ready to extend credit to indigenous collieries, at very high rate of interest.[48] Most of the areas in the Raniganj field having high quality coal were leased out to European companies in the late nineteenth century. In Jharia, however, the all Bengali concern of Laik and Banerjee, originally held the lease of some of the most valuable sites. But by the second decade of the twentieth century, the Europeans managed to gain a virtual monopoly of the better coal lands by purchasing some of the original leases. K.N. Dutta, Chairman of the IMF in the early 1930s, lamented: 'A very large number of the finest coal properties in the Jharia Field were at one time initially exploited by pioneer Indian coal owners ... lack of finance and of marketing facilities led these early owners to make over their fine properties to European houses.'[49]

The Indian entrepreneurs faced a very serious problem from the rail sector also. It was mainly over the matter of distribution of wagon capacity.[50] The Indian owners argued that whenever, there was shortage in supply of wagon, the railway authorities tended to favour the larger enterprises by sending them disproportionate share of the daily allotment of wagons. From 1907 to the mid-1920s, demand for wagons exceeded the supply. At that time, three types of wagon distribution schemes were in vogue: the Rake system (1907-17), under which the railways supplied wagons to the collieries when they needed the wagons, the Special Indent System (1917-22), which arranged for the provision of railway siding and the Preferential system (1922-5) giving preferences to the European collieries enabled the collieries to obtain rakes and the railway sidings.

These systems angered the indigenous entrepreneurs as all of them guaranteed the larger collieries the first call on wagon supplies.[51] In the annual meeting of the IMF in 1920-1, N.K. Choudhury, an important member of the IMF, narrated the experience of J.N. Ghosh of Dharmaband Colliery. N.K. Choudhury saw more than an element of racial prejudice at work:

> Our Mr. J.N. Ghosh stated that after years of trying he couldn't get sidings for his Dharmaband Colliery. He felt it might be due, his English dress notwithstanding, to his dark colour. A Mr. Pringle offered to get him the siding if he would part with half his property. Ghosh followed the adage that 'when the loss of the whole is threatened the wise will part with half to preserve the remainder', and made a gift of half his property to Pringle. Within six months he got his sidings. I mention this to you that you might follow the noble example of Ghosh when you are in difficulty of getting a siding.[52]

Altercation started between the railways and the IMF continued on the nature of railway services in the subject of freight charges, handling facilities, weightment disputes as far as carrying coals and supply of wagons were concerned.

The coal purchasing policy of the railways caused a lot of concern for the Indian entrepreneurs. A large number of the independent indigenous collieries were dependent upon the custom of the railways. Many such organizations had no formal selling platforms of their own as they had disposed of their entire output directly to the monopolistic Railway Board. Their position, henceforth, was slightly better than a raising contractor. The latter used to recruit workers and supervise their work. They also used to get the coal cut and loaded into wagons at an agreed rate. The chief mining engineer to the Board was responsible for all aspects of coal purchase and influenced the terms of the yearly contracts. The railways were constantly trying to reduce their fuel bill by effecting price cuts when the time became opportune. In 1936, the year of economic depression as a last resort, the Federation 'quoted pact prices' when tenders were submitted for the annual contracts. But the attempt ended in a chaos. First, the railway authorities, 'by allotting only small quantities of the total purchases to those owners quoting the pact prices' started cutting prices and second, they threatened to reduce their open market consumption and make up their coal needs by increasing the coal output from their own mines.[53]

Attitude towards Mass Unrest

The IMA and the IMF were equally worried about the industrial strikes which took place during the mass upsurge of the Non-Cooperation movement. In 1921 the IMF noted with alarm that there were no less than one hundred thirty seven strikes in Bengal. Two *swamis*, Swami Biswananda and Swami Darshanand were organizing the coalmine labourers. The two bodies representing the Indian and European collieries agreed that no increase in wages would be considered without a guarantee of increased output. They were determined if needed, to meet demands for increased wages by a complete lockout. The IMF even adopted a hostile attitude towards the newly-formed All India Trade Union Congress and the EIR strike of 1922. Instead N.C. Sircar declared at the annual meeting of the Federation on 21 April 1921, that the *swaraj* for which the Indians have been striving for was far too real and difficult to achieve. However, the trade union leaders and the Non-Cooperation movement, agitators did not aim their movement at the Indian capitalists, though their activities scared the Indian and European colliery owners alike. On the initiative of Darshanand in 1920 strikes occurred at six collieries of Andrew Yule, four collieries of Equitable Coal Company and one colliery of Birds, involving 5,300 miners. In a gathering of five thousand labourers it was said that the real object of trade unionism was 'to stop the work of European owned collieries and to strengthen and enrich the collieries belonging to the Indians'.[54]

Conclusion

The development of the coal industry in Bengal was largely in the hands of the European managing agencies. One cannot deny the contribution of the bigger houses like Andrew Yule and Company and Bird and Heilger's group towards the development of the coal sector in the Raniganj and the Jharia field. Almost all the big coal companies like the Bengal Coal Company were controlled by the managing agencies. They had the finest coal bearing tracts under their wings. They formed the trade association of IMA and virtually guided the Government of India in framing the mineral policies.

However, contribution of the indigenous entrepreneurs in this sector cannot be denied. Ever since the pioneering Dwarkanath Tagore, Bengalis were very active in this sector. They virtually shattered the notion that Bengalis were traditionally shy of entrepreneurial activities. After the pioneering Carr, Tagore and Company, a number of notable Bengali concerns, viz., Laik-Banerjee and Company, N.C. Sircar and Sons entered the field. Laik-Banerjee and Company had important stakes in the Jharia belt. Here, they produced the finest quality of coal. N.C. Sircar and Sons went on to become a major managing agency and rivalled almost all the top ranking British managing agencies in the coal sector. Mention must be made of R.N.

Bagchi and Brothers as the only Bengali joint-stock company in the late colonial era. The Bengali entrepreneurs, along with some non-Bengalis went on to set up the IMF. The aim was to look into the interest of the Indian coal entrepreneurs. But unfortunately, it had some inherent weaknesses as far as structure of the organization was concerned. It lacked a well-knit constitution of its own. Though, both the Bengalis and the non-Bengalis were its members, yet all the top office bearers were Bengalis. Therefore, the non-Bengalis soon began to feel that their interests were overlooked. Thus, the seeds of rupture were planted at the very beginning of the organization.

The onset of economic depression in the 1920s spelt doom for the Bengali concerns. They naturally began to stay away from entrepreneurial activities in the coal sector. It created a vacuum. This vacuum was steadily filled in by the Marwaris and later Kutchis and Sindhis, who had set foot in this sector just before the First World War. Mention must be made of the Marwaris who had amassed enough capital in other trades and later as *banias* to the European managing agencies. They first set foot as directors in the Boards of these houses, taking opportunity of the Depression that threatened the coal sector badly. Later, they went on to become major entrepreneurs in coal mining.

Before 1939, the typical Indian firm consisted of an individual or family proprietorship in mines that produced less than 50,000 tons a year and more frequently less than 10,000 tons. They mined second class coal from very shallow depths. Their investment was, however, minimum. These enterprises quickly responded to any change in demand.

The indigenous coal sector also faced certain problems. In the first place, they faced difficulty in raising loans from the organized and unorganized money market of Calcutta. Second, they did not possess sufficient economic muscle to counter the railway authorities as far as the supplies of wagons were concerned. Finally, despite the endeavours of both indigenous trade associations it proved impossible to reconcile the conflicting interests. There were occasions when the Indians joined hands with the European colliery owners to curb the menace of labour unrest. But these instances were rare.

The indigenous colliery entrepreneurs held a subordinate position to the European corporate concerns. The Europeans always enjoyed the capital, greater resources in personnel and finest colliery property. They also enjoyed the support of a strong political lobby. These factors ensured almost total European hegemony. It continued some years even after India attained Independence.

Notes

1. Kuntala Lahiri-Dutt, 'Kamins Building the Empire: Class, Caste and Gender Interface in Indian collieries', in Jaclyn Gier and Laurie Mercier, (eds), *Mining Women: Gender in the Development of a Global Industry, 1670-2005*, New York: Palgrave Mcmillan, 2006, pp. 71-87.
2. S.B. Singh, *European Agency Houses in Bengal* (*1783-1833*), Calcutta: Firma KLM, 1966, p. 62.
   These were large mercantile houses in Bengal that existed in small numbers before the opening of the Charter Act of 1813.
3. Priyabrata Dasgupta, 'Barddhaman Jelaye Koyla Shilper Bikaser Dhara' (Adiparva), in *Paschimbanga, Burdwan Jela Shankhya*, Kolkata (BS 1403), p. 103.
4. Singh, op. cit., p. 300.
5. L.J. Barraclough, 'A Further Contribution to the History of Development of the Coal Mining Industry in India', Trans. MGMII, 47, no. 1, April 1951, pp. 4ff., in P.C. Simmons,'Indigenous Enterprise in the Indian Coal Mining Industry, 1835-1939', *Indian Economic and Social History Review*, 1976, p. 189.
6. 'Andrew Yule and Company 1863-1963', Calcutta, 1963.
   The main strongholds of Andrew Yule lay in the jute industry, inland steam shipping, cotton mills, flour and oil mills, tea gardens, etc. But in the field of coal mining, Andrew Yule and Company came to occupy a leading position and surpassed all other large agency houses.
7. Letter from A.G. Mackenzie to Macpherson (both employees of the Bengal Coal Company), 12 March 1845.
8. T. Oldham, 'A Report on the Raneegunge Coalfield with Special Reference to Proposed Extension of the Line of Railway', Calcutta, 1859, pp. 18-22.
9. Ibid.
10. Indian Mining Federation, *Golden Jubilee Souvenir, 1913-1963*, Calcutta, 1963.

11. First Annual Report, Indian Mining Association (1892-93).
12. 'Worthy Son of Bengal', *Liberty*, Calcutta, 16 July 1933.
13. *Indian International Year Book, 1909*, Calcutta, 1909.
    Nibaran Chandra began as a Rs. 7 a month porter boy in the Bengal Coal Company.
14. An undeterred Sircar formed a managing agency of his own, N.C. Sircar and Sons, and proceeded to expand further.
15. *IIYB*, 1923.
16. Annual Report, Indian Mining Federation (1913-1923).
17. *Hindustan Standard*, 19 March 1963.
18. For the next three years he acted as the chief spokesman of the indigenous colliery.
19. Maharaja's address to the Mining and Geological Institute of India in 1921, *MGMII*, XVI, 1921, p. 20.
20. Dakshineswar Malia was co-opted as the representative of the Indian colliery owners in a committee for mining legislation appointed by the government in 1895.
21. It represented interests which controlled one-third of the whole coal output of the country.
22. *Report of the Indian Coal-fields Committee*, Delhi, 1946 (also called Mahindra Report), Appendix IX, p. 345.
23. *Bengal National Chamber of Commerce Report,* 1916.
24. Reproduction, Production and Consumption of Coal, 1937, Table 2, pp. 21-53.
25. Annual Report of IMA, 1921, pp.13f.
26. Circular No.14-R., 20 January 1921, ibid., p. 150.
27. *Census of India*, 1911 (hereinafter *COI*), vol. V, Bengal, Bihar and Orissa and Sikkim: Part I Report; L.S.S. O'Malley, Calcutta 1913, pt. II, Table XVE, p. 350 and part III, Table XVE, p. 230.
28. Reproduction, Production and Consumption of Coal, 1923, Table 2, pp. 21-33.
29. *IIYB*, 1925-6, section on jute and coal; Omkar Goswami, 'Then Came the Marwaris: Some Aspects of the Changes in the Pattern of Industrial Control in Eastern India', *Indian Economic and Social History Review,* 1985, p. 232.
30. Ibid.
31. *IIYB*, 1938-9, section on coal.
32. *IIYB*, 1928-9, p. 71.
33. Ibid.

34. Omkar Goswami, 'Sahibs, Babus and Banias: Changes in Industrial Control in Eastern India, 1918-50', in Rajat Kanta Ray (ed.), *Entrepreneurship and Industry in India 1800-1947*, Delhi: Oxford University Press, 1994, p. 238.
35. Reproduction, Production and Consumption of Coal, 1923, Table 2, pp. 21-53.
36. P.S. Lokanathan, *Industrial Organization in India*, London: Allen & Unwin, 1935, p. 187.
37 *IIYB*, 1930-1, section on coal.
38. Annual Report of IMF, 1929-33.
    C.P. Simmons came to the conclusion after speaking to M. Das, N. Mukherjee and N.K. Sanyal, all former secretaries of the Federation.
39. First Annual Report of the Indian Colliery Owners Association, Calcutta, 1934.
40. Letter No. 534-R from the IMA to the Deptt. of Labour and Industries, Government of India, 20 March 1934, Annual Report of IMA, 1934.
41. Letter No. M-76 from A.G. Clow, Joint Secretary to Department of Industry to all provincial government, 28 January 1935.
42. IMF, *Golden Jubilee Souvenir, 1913-1963*, Calcutta, 1964, p. 42.
43. Report of the Indian Industrial Commission, Calcutta, 1919, II, pp. 286-90.
44. Report of the Indian Fiscal Commission, Calcutta, 1923, II, paras 7300 and 7334-9.
45. Michael Kidron, *Foreign Investments in India*, London: Oxford University Press, 1965, p. 9.
46. A.K. Bagchi, 'European and Indian Entrepreneurship in India, 1900-30', in R.K. Ray, op. cit., pp. 178-9.
47. Report of the Indian Fiscal Commission, op. cit., para 7338.
48. Report of the Indian Industrial Commission, op. cit., para 7839, p. 289.
49. Annual Report of IMF, 1931, p. 46.
50. First Annual Report of IMF, 1913, p. 6.
51. IMF, *Golden Jubilee Souvenir, 1913-1963*, Calcutta, 1964, pp. 44-7.
52. Annual Report of IMF, 1920, p. 20.
53. Ibid., 1936, p. 53.
54. Rajat Kanta Ray, 'Masses in Politics: The Non-Cooperation Movement in Bengal, 1920-28', *Indian Economic and Social History Review*, vol. XI, no. 4, December 1974.

CHAPTER 4

Potter's Craft

A Traditional Sector in Colonial Bengal

SUPTI RAHA

Potters constitute one of the major components of the artisan population of Bengal. Pottery is one of the oldest crafts practised everywhere in the world since the Neolithic times. Hand-made pottery was prevalent in lower Neolithic societies until the Egyptian invention of the potter's wheel in about 3000 BC. The surplus production in higher Neolithic societies and the wheel-turned pottery enabled the emergence of pottery as a specialized craft and potters as specialized craftsmen.[1] In Bengal as well as in other parts of India, earthen pottery of various kinds had been in existence from antiquity.

With the establishment of foreign rule in India, the domination of capital, enterprise and skill of industrially-advanced countries of Europe was increasingly felt over trade and manufactures of India. The long colonial rule in India and the social and economic changes that followed it invariably impacted her traditional industries. This study seeks to find that unlike in the case of some other traditional industries, colonial rule did not prove fatal to the craft of potters in Bengal. This traditional industry faced less direct competition from imported wares than others. On the other hand, due to the influence of factors like patronage of the landed aristocracy in Bengal, contact with the Europeans, beginning and spread of community worship, we notice changes in the pattern of goods produced by the potters. Along with the production of traditional items, some branches of the craft, for example, manufacture of clay models, making of clay images for worship of popular gods and goddesses and towards the close of the colonial rule, sculpting by some of the clay-modellers began to flourish. The period also witnessed Western method of manufacturing pottery. We notice both elements of continuity and change in artisan production.

Producers and Production till Mid-nineteenth Century and Technique of Production

Potters are commonly designated as *kumbhakars*. The etymology of the word *kumbhakar* shows that it has originated from making pots. So far as the origin of the *kumbhakars* was concerned, the accounts given in the old treatises vary from each other. According to *Brahmabaibarta Purana*, the union of Vishwakarma and a Shudra woman resulted in the birth of nine craftsmen castes among which *kumbhakars* were considered to be an important one.[2] Quoting the *Brahmabaibarta Purana*, Risley mentioned that the *kumbhakar*, or maker of water jars (*kumbha*), was born of a vaishya woman and a brahman father. The *Parasar Samhita* says the father was a *malakar* (gardener) and the mother a chamar. Risley also mentions that:

> The kumhar says that at the marriage of Shiva, a *ghot* (water jar) was wanted, but no one knew how to make one. The god, therefore, took a bead from his necklace and with it created a potter, while with a second; he made a woman who became the potter's wife. This man was the father of all those who work in pottery, and in the memory of their creator, all potters bear the title Rudra Pal.[3]

It is said that divine association and origin of caste indicated introduction of a new craft by primitive talent in a remote period when primitive society had recourse to magic which could produce strange things for the benefit of their household operations.[4] In Bengal, the common appellation for the potter caste was *kumar* or *kumhar*. They were considered a part of the *nabasakha* and so regarded as *jalchal*. The Bengali *kumbhakars* put a clay image of Lord Shiva or Mahadeva on their wheel and worshipped Mahadeva on the first day of Baisakh. The wheel was not used for a whole month.

On the day of Poush Sankranti, they placed all their tools of trade in front of Vishwakarma and worshipped him.[5]

The potter's craft was mainly a cottage industry in Bengal. There were generally two types of potters—artisans who produced unglazed earthen pottery and the artistic potters who made artistic wares often glazed.[6] The former confined themselves to the ordinary articles of household and articles used in worship, thereby, meeting the primary necessities of the people, while the latter satisfied the craving for decoration. Among the non-glazed earthen wares produced were water vessels, viz., *jala, kalsi, kunja* or *surahi*; cooking pots, viz., *hanri, malsa, sara*; eating and drinking utensils, viz., *thala, khuri* and articles used in worship, viz., *ghat, dhunachi, pradeep,* etc. They supplied those goods which not only served the utilitarian needs of the common people but were also associated with rituals and occasions. The fact that there prevailed in Bengal, the practice of throwing away the pots in use and obtaining fresh ones during every festival provided an impetus to the trade of making earthen vessels. On the occasion of an eclipse or a death occurring in the house, the practice was to throw away all the cooking pots in use. Again, plates and dishes for eating food or cups for drinking water could not be used more than once.[7] It is to be noted that though colonial rule brought about many changes in our social life, many traditional ceremonies and rituals persisted almost unchanged. Hence, there was always an internal demand for their products.

Terracotta tiles have been used in Bengal from the earliest times. Walls of most temples in Birbhum, Bankura, Hooghly, Burdwan and Midnapore, were covered with terracotta tiles. The artistry and the significance of the symbols on these tiles have received much attention of the scholars. A section of the potters under the patronage of the landed aristocracy produced terracotta tiles. It appeared that these terracotta tiles were made with moulds but finishing was given by hand.[8]

The equipment of pottery, not only in Bengal but all over the world, was very simple. The tools and implements of the potters consisted of the wheel which enabled specialized pottery craft, the wooden beater, the scraper and a few others. Other than these tools, there were kilns or ovens which made possible firing with a higher temperature and efficient painting on pots. Unlike most other industries, the manufacture of ordinary pottery required little capital. Clay, temper and colour were the three essential raw materials required for the potter's craft. These materials usually did not require heavy capital investment and were locally available. The durability and finishing of the vessels depended upon the quality of the clay which was classified according to texture, colour and composition. The clay was procured either from river or tank bed or from a fallow land. Two broad categories of clay used in Bengal were loam and porous. The former is somewhat sandy while the latter is sticky. Glossy or sticky clay was considered suitable for use on the wheel. In order to improve the quality of clay, certain tempering materials, such as ash, husks, cattle dung, saw-dust and sand were used.[9]

For preparation of clay, cleaning, mixing and kneading were certain processes adopted by potters. Usually, cleaning was done at home. The clay was first dried in the sun and then sprayed out in an open courtyard. A wooden mallet was used for breaking and pulverizing clay clods. The clay was then sifted through a bamboo or iron sieve for removing pebbles, fine gravel and other materials. The pulverized clay was moistened with water and the entire mass was ready for the subsequent process of mixing and kneading. The latter was a laborious task and done by menfolk.[10] In Bengal, women and children also participated in this process.[11] The processed clay was covered with a piece of wet cloth to keep it damp until it was taken out for throwing on the wheel.

The potter's wheel was of the simplest and crudest kind. It was a horizontal fly-wheel put in motion by the hand. The clay to be moulded was heaped on the centre of the wheel and the potter squatted down on the ground before it.[12] The beating tools were required in a subsequent process of pottery manufacture. A pot after being thrown from the wheel passed through the stages of beating, enlarging and smoothening in order to get the required shape. The unfinished pots were beaten, enlarged and smoothened with a wooden beater on a clay or stone anvil. These were the most important tools of a potter because these were used for both wheel-thrown as well as hand-made pottery. Size and weight of the beater varied even within a group of potters, but the shape remained more or less same. Functionally, there were three types of beaters—one was used for enlarging the vessel, another for smoothening the outer surface of the vessel, the third for making decorative impressions on the pot.[13] Beating was a man's job.

Slip treatment was used to give bright or dark red colour to the pot after firing. All the pots were coated with a slip, i.e. a yellow or red ochre (a type of earth varying from light yellow to brown or red, used as a pigment) which gave lustre to the pot. When the slipped pots were fired, they got highly lustrous red or black according to the condition of firing. After oxidation, the pot came out red and under reduced temperature firing the same slip, may give a shining black colour to the pot. In Bengal, the work of slipping was usually done by women. To brighten the surface of the pot polishing was done. The pots could be varnished with a piece of cloth, a stone pebble, coconut shell, or any other tool, especially made for the purpose. This job too was done by women. The pots were painted either before firing or after firing. For the pre-firing painting, various types of ochre and metallic colours are used. For the post-firing painting, vegetable or chemical colour were used.[14] It is to be noted that the tools and materials needed for potter's craft and technique of production remained almost unchanged for centuries.

Principal Variants of Pottery in Late Colonial Bengal: Product, Market and Industrial Performance

The construction of railroad with foreign capital and active support of the colonial administration unleashed new forces. The railways, especially the East India Railway Company which operated over a larger area, played a significant role in the growth of urban centres in the late nineteenth and early twentieth centuries. The trade of large villages near railway stations increased. Calcutta became one of the foremost commercial centres of India. The period witnessed the beginning of money circulation on a large scale and the growth of capitalist enterprise in the form of mills and factories. Population of Bengal had been growing steadily and there was evolution of the upper middle class of professionals. In the colonial period the range of goods used in middle-class Indian household expanded. Again, the structural change in the composition of the old landed aristocracy in Bengal, as a consequence of the Permanent Settlement, provided new patrons, with new taste for arts. All these factors changed the character of the market for some of the artisan products. It is to be noted that as India remained predominantly agricultural even in late colonial period, the domestic system of industry was still at work. Ordinary household pottery was made almost in every large village and town in the country. But side by side, opportunities were created for some of the artisans to cater to new demands of the market. A section of them adapted to the changing needs of the people.

A late nineteenth-century official report states that common pottery remained one of the principal indigenous industries in Bengal.[15] A large number of potters was widely spread out geographically at the close of the nineteenth century:

The Census of 1891 returned 4,62,483 persons as makers of earthen pottery in Bengal.[16] According to the Census of 1901, potters constituted 0.3 per cent of the total population.[17] The same Census report mentioned pottery as one of the leading handicrafts of Bengal. The Census of 1921 mentions that the kumars were distributed over the whole province and were generally, employed in their traditional occupation.[18] In fact, throughout colonial rule, potter's craft was extensively practiced in different parts of Bengal.

Table 4.1: Potters of Different Divisions of the Province of Bengal (1890s)

Division	*No. of Potters*	*No. actually engaged in making earthenware*
Burdwan	71,918	52,918
Presidency	75,985	53,259
Rajshahi	45,216	31,125
Dacca	66,793	52,459
Chittagong	21,171	25,006

Source: T.N. Mukharji, *A Monograph on the Pottery and Glassware of Bengal*, Calcutta: Superintendent Government Printing, 1895, p. 4.

Though the industry was spread throughout Bengal, it was chiefly located in Dacca, Khulna, Howrah, Hooghly, Midnapur, 24-Parganas, Nadia, Burdwan, Birbhum, and Bankura. Various kinds of pottery were produced in different districts. In the 1870s, there were 3,788 potters in the Dacca division.[19] The best pottery in the Dacca division came from Dacca town and its neighbourhood.[20] Large black earthen jars buried under the floor of living rooms were common in districts like Barishal and Dacca. Different varieties were used in different areas to store paddy and rice. On the banks of the Dol Samudra in Faridpur district in Dacca division, immense earthen jars, some of 20 maunds or more than 13 cws (hundredth weight, origin from the Latin *centum*, i.e. a hundred) capacity were made for storing grain. Earthen pitchers were widely used as containers by the manufacturers of molasses.[21] By 1938, about 8,000 people remained engaged in this industry in the Dacca district. Earthenware constituted one of the important items of export from the district.[22]

It has been reported that the potters in both the districts of Pabna and Bogra, were comparatively well-to-do men in the 1920s.[23] In the Bakharganj district, unlike weavers and carpenters who adopted agriculture as a subsidiary occupation, potters and workers in metals appeared to be entirely independent of agriculture.[24] Pottery of the coarsest description was made in Dinajpur in Rajshahi district. It may be mentioned that even by the 1920s, potters of this predominantly agricultural district were occasionally remunerated by service lands.[25] Potters in the district of Jessore turned out earthenware of all sorts for which, there was a great demand. However, there was no organization among them and nothing was done to improve their craft or export their products to other places.[26]

Manufacture of black pottery at Khanja village in the district of Khulna and at Sewan in the district of Saran deserves notice. Apart from exporting big *jalas* (a kind of earthen pot), ordinarily used for storing food grains, to Calcutta by the river route, Khulna had a high reputation for black pottery without any kind of ornamentation.[27] The articles usually made in these were betel leaf holders, oil pots, smoking bowls, etc. These articles were praised for high polish and elegant shapes. It may be mentioned that at the Calcutta Exhibition of Indian Art Manufactures in 1882, among ninety-one specimens which represented the industry in Bengal, Bihar and Orissa, thirty were from Khanja. A few specimens from Khanja were also sent to the Colonial and Indian Exhibition at London in 1886.[28]

The Sewan pottery produced in the district of Saran (now in Bihar) was the only pottery in Bengal which had artistic merit. The ware was white, red or black. The black ware was most admired. The articles usually made were *surahis* (water goblets), *farsi* (smoking bowls), *chilam* (tobacco pipes) and *abkhora* (drinking vessels). Sewan pottery was remarkable both for its shape and decoration. The vessels were baked in earthen jars so that it could not come in contact with the flames, and when so baked the vessels became black. They were glazed with a mixture of clay and Fuller's earth. The mixture was combined with mango bark and when dried, was powdered up, mixed with water and applied as a glaze. The patterns for decoration were copied from designs supplied by the Europeans. The art had been adopted mainly to meet the requirements of the European customers. The Sewan pottery had some reputation outside the place of manufacture. However, demand for their products among the ordinary people was so small that at the close of the nineteenth century, it did not give employment to more than four families of potters. [29]

Vijaypur in Tippera district was also famous for its pottery. The appliances used by the potters were extremely primitive. A section of the potter's caste, known as the Rajmahalia *kumars,* thatched their houses with green grass and when their grass dried, they used it as a fuel for the kiln. This section of the caste made cooking pots for vegetables, milk pans and salvers on which sweets and other delicacies were handed round at weeding feasts. They were prohibited to make idols or platters used at religious ceremonies.[30] Haripur, Budhanti and Brahmanbaria were the other centres of the potter's craft in Tipperah district. There is an instance of a person in Haripur who started producing bottle-filter.[31]

Pottery was an important industry in Howrah district. The Census of 1901 returned 1,650 persons as actual workers. The village potters made earthenware vessels in the primitive manner during the dry months of the years and sold them in local *hats*. The clay in parts of the Sadar subdivision provided the best material and the vessels made there were preferred because they could stand the fire better and lasted longer. They were exported to Calcutta, Howrah and other towns. Among such vessels, the cooking vessels of Patihal in Jagatballabhpur P.S. and the large jars of Sankrail had local reputation. Some artisans produced painted earthen articles. Among the painted earthen articles, the toys of Chandipur, the masks, brackets, imitations of fruit and pots made in Domjur P.S. and Uluberia were noticeable.[32]

Common pottery was made in many villages of Hoogly district. As reported by the Census of 1872, there were 4,185 potters in the district.[33] Although the manufactures of Hoogly were of ordinary descriptions, they were produced in large quantities because they not only met local demands but also supplied the demand of the Calcutta market. By the 1870s, the East India Railways ran through the district for a distance of about 45 miles. Since the opening of the railway, the trade of large villages near the Chandernagar railway station, like Baidyabati and Bhadreshwar had been increasing.[34] Uttarpara supplied the Calcutta market *gamla* (a flat open mouthed vessel used to keep water, steep rice and for other purposes), *bhanr* (oil pot), *delko* (lamp stand), *chakmaki* (tobacco holder), *khuri* (a small shallow cup used to hold offerings for gods and also in feasts for providing the guests with beverages), etc. Chandernagar supplied to Calcutta *ghats* (water vessels) used as a symbol for any god when no image was made. Baidyabati supplied lamps to Calcutta. Smoking pipes were produced at Serampore, Bali and other places in the district. Milk-pot was brought to Calcutta from Tarakeshwar.[35]

Apart from supplying the ordinary household articles to the Calcutta market, the pottery of Hoogly also presented the only examples of Bengal faience in the Economic and Art section of the Indian Museum Collection. The specimens consisted of two flower tubs and two water goblets. The body of the ware was the usual red clay, coated over with a semi-vitrified green glaze. This seems to be an attempt to introduce the manufacture of glazed pottery in the country. Glazed pottery was definitely an improvement upon non-glazed one and had the ability to revolutionize the household industry of a country. However, the industry did not appear to have made much of an advance.[36]

The making of earthen tiles for country houses, known as *khola,* was one of the non-specialized utilitarian industries pursued by both men and women. Kotrung in the district of Hoogly, was an important centre for making of earthen tiles.[37] Maurigram and Jhapardah in Domjur P.S. in the district of Howrah were also famous for the good quality of tiles.[38] The *kumbhakaras* near Akhauda in Tipperah district produced tiles which not only supplied the needs of the local people but also to more distant areas.[39]

The pottery industry was indigenous to the district of Murshidabad. By the mid-1880s, the number of potters in the district was about 11,278. Kanthalia was the chief centre in the district. There was no organization whatever of the nature of a trade guild. The price of each kind of pot was settled by the potter himself. Advances were rarely made to potters. They kept a regular stock for trade and also made articles to order. The cost of finished articles varied according to the size and quality of the pots. The price of a first rate pot was 8 *annas*, and that of an inferior one was 1 *paise* and sometimes less than that.[40] The industry expanded in different villages of Kandi subdivision of Murshidabad from earlier times, because of easy availability of clay from the local land and sand from the river Mayurakshi. Panchthupi in Kandi was the centre for making shells of percussion instruments of music like *tabla* and *khol*, etc. This non-specialized utilitarian industry was pursued by both men and women.[41]

Apart from making pots for eating and drinking purposes, some potters in Kandi produced vessels for marriage painted with different scenes of the ceremony. This unique piece of pottery was made mainly for the local landed aristocracy who were their patrons. Under the patronage of Maharaja Manindra Chandra Nandi of Cassimbazar, the image-making industry also expanded in Murshidabad. In his royal palace, he used to organize competition of artisans by bringing artists from Krishnanagar, Calcutta and Nabadwip.[42]

Among some interesting items of pottery, mention may be made of the terracotta tub-like *tulsimancha* (a pedestal, on which *tulsi*, the sacred plant of the Hindus, is planted and worshipped) with decorative motifs mainly of gods and goddesses. *Tulsimancha* is a noteworthy example of the cultural heritage of the folk art of Bengal that is centred around popular rituals. Considerable numbers of these ritual objects were turned out by some potters at Ghatal, Midnapur proper,

Raghunathbari under Panskura P.S. and at Gopalpur. They were sold in local *hats* and fairs. Another interesting piece of pottery, known as *bara-murti* was found in the south of the 24-Parganas district. It was basically a *ghat* (vase), shaped in the figure of a local village deity, *bara-murti*, the worship of which was widely prevalent in the region. *Bara* was one of the most popular gods in south 24-Parganas, associated with an environment of forests, which is likely to be the Sunderbans. Thousands of painted terracotta vase-heads of *bara* were produced by the potters of this area during the celebration time of the worship of *bara-murti* in winter. The rituals were observed on mass scale on the last day of the Bengali month of Pous and the first day of Magh, corresponding to 14-15 January.[43] The potters in different districts also produced *mangalghat* (auspicious vases) of various sizes and shapes. They were essential requisites in all kinds of rituals.

A study of the Bankura pottery, Krishnanagar pottery and the image-making industry in celestial colony at Kumartuli offers an interesting picture.

Bankura Pottery

Potters were numerous in Bankura district by the first decade of the twentieth century. There were potters for furnishing a temple with earthen vessels. The *kumhars* (potters) in many places were rewarded with a small plot of rent-free land, but earthen vessels for domestic use were paid for in money.[44] It was the production of popular ritual objects—terracotta horses, elephants, *manasa-ghats* (the vases of the serpent goddess) with spouts of serpent's hoods arranged in a semi-circular order and life-sized terracotta snakes with raised and flushed hoods—that marked the specialities of the potters of Bankura. The principal centres of production of terracotta horses and elephants in the Bankura district were Panchmura (P.S. Taldangra), Rajagram (P.S. Bankura), Sonamukhi (town) and Hamirpur (P.S. Patrasayar). The Panchmura-style of pottery was by far the best and finest of all the four types.

The terracotta horses and elephants were turned out in separate parts on the wheel, and then joined by hand. The figures were then scraped and made even by a semi-circular piece of bamboo, used for surface finishing, locally known as *ucha* and *chiari*, used for decorating clay figures. The figures were then heated in the sun. The potters of Bankura followed pre-firing colouring, i.e. the work of colouring was done before firing in the kiln locally known as *poan*. They used not chemical paints but natural colours prepared from clay. This was quite unlike the Krishnanagar-potters who did painting after firing and used chemical products for colouring. The whole work of colouring, including the preparation of natural colours from clay collected from riversides and other places, was done by the women in a potter's family. The normal terracotta red colour was obtained by letting out the smoke through the vents of the kiln after firing and the black colour was obtained by sealing the vents and not letting out the smoke. Eucalyptus leaves were used as fuel for the kiln.[45] This technique of manufacturing continues even today.

Panchmura retained the tradition of pelleted and incised terracotta toys. Baked and hand modelled incised clay dolls decorated with pellets, made at Panchmura by *kumbhakaras* were never painted or coloured because they did not require to be so treated. They were resplended in consummate, primitive, modeling skill which alone imparted all the finish that they required. They provide supremely important document of a stage when *kumbhakaras* did not need to use colour on toys or images to heighten their excellence.[46]

The Bankura pottery had ritualistic functional basis, the origin of which is to be found in the religious urge of the local people. It had a link with rural life. The terracotta horses, elephants, serpent-hoods (spout-like snake-hood jars called *manasha bari*) were popular ritual objects. They were made by the potters of Bankura almost exclusively as votive offerings to local deities, not worshipped generally by upper caste Hindus. It seems to have originated in a pre-Hindu totemic system of beliefs and rituals which survived among some castes of Bankura. The origin of these religious cults and rituals is shrouded in the misty social milieu of the pre-historic age. How and why these terracotta horses and elephants became the objects of votive offerings is not very easy to explain. It might have been, as argued by one scholar, that the forest of this region was infested with elephants. As to the reason for the spread of horse-motif in this region as an object of ritual oriented folk art, it has been suggested that it was introduced in the Muslim period, probably in the thirteenth century. It may be pointed out that in all the shrines of the Muslim *pirs* in Bengal, including those in Bankura, Midnapur and other parts of western Bengal, the terracotta horse was the most important votive offering.[47]

The Bankura pottery is important for its unique cultural significance and is an example of achievement in the history of clay modelling in India. The terracotta figures of horses and elephants have been accepted by All India Handicrafts Board as an artistic symbol of Indian handicrafts.

Krishnanagar Pottery

The Krishnanagar clay-modelling industry of realistic objects has been mentioned in the nineteenth-century official and administrative reports and also by different admirers and critics. The clay modellers of Krishnanagar probably did not originally belong to any village around Krishnanagar or even to the district of Nadia. It is said that the introduction of clay-image worship of the popular deities during Maharaja Krishnachandra's rule in Nadia created the need for making idols for worship. In the beginning of the eighteenth century, the potters were probably brought to Krishnanagar either from Dacca or from Natore by Maharaja Krishnachandra or his father Raghuram for image-making. Thus, a clay modellers' colony was established at Ghurni, a place in the north-eastern suburb of the town of Krishnanagar,[48] The location of Ghurni near the river Jalangi (locally known as Khoray) provided the potters with good quality clay for modelling.

The potter's craft of image making got an impetus from the introduction of *barowari puja* (community worship) in Bengal from about 1790. Till then, the *puja* was a private affair in the elegant *thakurdalan* (hall of the deity). The first recorded Durga Puja seems to have been celebrated by Bhabananda, ancestor of Maharaja Krishnachandra, in or about 1606. The oldest Durga Puja in Calcutta was the family *puja* of Sabarna Chowdhury of Barisha, which dates back to 1610. Durga Puja broke free from the confines of the *thakurdalan* at Guptipara in Hooghly district in about 1790, when twelve young men were stopped from taking part in a household *puja*. They formed a twelve man committee, which held the first public or community Durga Puja financed by subscription. Hence, such *pujas* came to be called *barowari*.

An interesting account of its beginning and spread in Bengal, especially in Hoogly, Nadia and the adjacent districts, can be found from the *Friend of India* of Serampore Baptist Mission which observed:

> . . . a new species of Pooja which has been introduced into Bengal within the last thirty years, called Barowaree. About thirty years ago, at Goopti-para, a number of Brahmans formed an association for the celebration of a pooja independently of the rules of the Shastras. They elected twelve men as a committee, from which circumstance, it takes its name, and solicitates subscription in all the surrounding villages. A way having been thus opened for the gratification of the senses, in addition to those regular festivals which their books enjoin, the example was imitated in other parts of Bengal. Within a few miles of the metropolis, more than ten of these subscription assemblies are annually formed. The most renowned are those are at Bulubh-poora, Konnugura, Ooloo, Gupti-para, Chugda and Shree-poora.[49]

Thus, community worship in Bengal began to spread rapidly from the second quarter of the nineteenth century. It gave a boost to the craft of image making.

The clay-modelling industry in Krishnanagar received the patronage of the local landed aristocracy. An important feature of the district of Nadia in the first half of the nineteenth century was the transformation of British indigo planters into local zamindars on a large scale. Being zamindars, the planters became great patrons of local arts and crafts of which clay models were most important. European patronage gave further fillip to the clay-modelling of Krishnanagar. The British gave a new orientation to its style towards realism. T.N. Mukharji, Assistant Supervisor of Indian Museum, wrote:

> Krishnanagar modelling industry originated from this making of idols for worship. Gradually, the gods and goddesses came to be furnished with attendants and in public worships got up by subscriptions, more for

amusement than for a religious obligation, life-size mythological scenes, scenes from daily life, portrait figures of athletes and other celebrities, caricatures, comical subjects and figures representing any scandal current at the time were gradually introduced. The manufacture of toys and miniature figures was a natural growth from this stage of the industry. The modellers owed to Dr. Charles Archer, Assistant Civil Surgeon of Krishnanagar in the 1850s, the notice which the Europeans now take of their work.[50]

The traditional idol-makers of Krishnanagar, thus turned into modellers of realistic objects largely under the influence of European ceramic arts of the time, and mainly with European patronage. The golden days of the clay modellers of Krishnanagar may be traced to this time when the famous modeller Jadunath Pal (1821-1920), and his contemporary modellers, viz., Paranchandra Pal (1828-1924), Bakkeswar Pal (1875-1924), Gopeswar Pal (1896-1952) and others flourished.[51] The new tradition for modelling realistic subjects, in naturalistic style, reached its peak during the time of Jadunath Pal who had no equal in clay-modelling in India. He worked for some time as government modeller also. In *Atmakatha,* Pramatha Choudhury, an eminent literary personality of the contemporary period, wrote admiringly of the Krishnanagar pottery. He remembered that he had seen in his childhood days excellent 'Ahladi' dolls made at Krishnanagar. In his opinion, Jadunath Pal, who could make the model of Venus from its pictures in the English book, could undoubtedly be designated as an 'artist'.[52]

In most of the international exhibitions held since 1851, Krishnanagar clay-modellers had won medals and certificates. The excellent life-sized models of some of the indigenous tribes of India, which they had made for the International Exhibition, were marvellous for their honesty and were of considerable educational value. There was considerable delicacy and fineness in their work.[53] In this connection it may be mentioned that technical education was necessary to improve skill or to increase knowledge in a particular industry. The Calcutta Art School was established to secure artisans conversant with the new techniques. However, with the exception of Jadunath Pal who had his education at the Calcutta Art School, the artists who made excellent clay human figures at Krishnanagar had received no art instruction. They attained perfection in the art of reproducing the human figures in clay, though they did not pass through a course of teaching in anatomical drawings.[54] All these modellers charged very high prices for the models.

The subjects and the prices of these models highlighted in Table 4.2 indicated that they were not within the reach of the common people. Indeed, the customers of these models were mainly Europeans. Indigenous social scenes, the people, the different castes and racial types, reproduced realistically in clay-models, not only served the purpose of the British administrators, but also satisfied the curiosity of the European people in general. The British period witnessed the glorious days of Ghurni. [55]

In the last quarter of the nineteenth century, the clay-modellers of Krishnanagore grew into a fairly well-to-do middle class. The Census of 1872 reported that the *kumars,* potters and makers of earthen idols numbered 20,420. They were generally of moderate means, more or less respectable and held high in local public esteem.[56] Unlike in the case of indigo manufactures of the district of Nadia, the potters worked for themselves and in their own homes and there was no distinct separation between the capitalist and the labourer. [57]

In this connection, mention may be made of some other well-known doll and toy-making centres of Bengal. Indeed, potters of Bengal made large varieties of dolls and toys for which there was an

TABLE 4.2: PRICES OF THE CLAY MODELS IN 1888

Clay Models	*Prices*
Tea-garden scene	Rs. 1,200
Durga Puja	Rs. 175
Marriage and marriage processions	Rs. 375
Landlord's court	Rs. 150
Car festival	Rs. 360
Collector's court	Rs. 275
Charak festival	Rs. 180
Collection of fishes	Rs. 300
Collection of fruits and vegetables	Rs. 100

Source: Benoy Ghose, *Traditional Arts and Crafts of West Bengal*, Calcutta: Papyrus, 1981, p. 51.

internal market. For instance, the *allahadi*, *benebau* and *narugopal* toys of Kalighat were well known all over the province and outside. In Birbhum interesting dolls such as *jantraghurni* or *grinding women*, *chulbadhuni* or a woman combing her hair and so on were made. Unique pieces of mother dolls were made at Panchmura, Rajagram and Sonamukhi in Bankura. Unfortunately, however, from the close of the colonial rule, toy-making was fast becoming a lost art owing to the competition of foreign mass produced toys.[58]

Potters made large varieties of dolls and figures with the help of 'moulds'. Different types of moulds were used for shaping different types of vessels, toys, images and terracotta figures. The moulds for vessels were made of clay. The moulds for terracotta figures were made of clay as well as plaster of Paris and cement. A couple of bowl-shaped baked clay pots were used as a mould for moulding vessels. Earthen vessels of different sizes, made solid by filling them with plastic clay, were also used as moulds. Moulds for shaping clay toys and terracotta figures were also prepared by the potters themselves. These moulds were prepared by the potters out of models. The latter were prepared by the skilled potters.[59]

Although small clay toys, dolls, animals and birds of various kinds and pots were generally made by the women of the Kumbhakar caste it was not their monopoly. They were also made by women of the Patidar-Chitrakar (painter) castes. In fact, in Bankura, Birbhum and some areas of Howrah, Hoogly and Murshidabad districts, women of Kumbhakar and Patidar-Chitrakar castes remained engaged in making hand-modelled pottery as part-time occupation, even after Independence. The women of the Sankhari (conch-shell carvers) families in Bishnupur made painted clay figurines of mother dolls for ritual purposes.[60] These hand-made figures, small toys and dolls were produced both by the pressing and moulding methods. In the pressing method a lump of clay was pressed in hand between thumb and fingers. Sometimes, the cooking pots and water jars were made by this method. In Bishnupur (Bankura), Chaurigacha-Katalia (Kandi, Murshidabad) and some other places in Midnapore and Bankura, perhaps the most primitive method of hand-modelled pottery was pursued and that too almost exclusively by women. Big jars were usually prepared by men, and comparatively small pots by women.[61]

Over the years the popularity of the clay toys of Krishnanagar in and outside India was affected by certain factors. Freight charges were a standing hindrance to this industry. These dolls and toys being made of clay were easily breakable and not as easily portable as those made of wood, metal or lac. Hence, they required special packing. Again, the common people preferred wooden dolls to breakable and expensive clay-models. Gradually, most of the reputed modellers like Kartick Chandra Pal, Biswanath Pal, Ganesh Chandra Pal, Narendranath Pal and Biren Pal moved away from clay modelling to sculpting in stone.[62]

It is important to note that realistic figures were made at Ghurni only, and from the beginning the number of artists remained confined only to a few families. This indicated that behind the fame of Krishnanagar pottery remained the high proficiency of a number of clay modellers. It was not the manifestation of excellence of an entire artisan society, i.e. the potters' society, because the tradition did not originate from any demand for folk culture. Unlike the Bankura-pottery, which served mainly ritualistic purposes because the terracotta horses or elephants were offered as their humble token of devotion and faith to the village god, the Krishnanagar pottery was mainly used for decorative purposes. From the very beginning, it was patronized by the English art-lovers and landed aristocracy. It was their active and direct inspiration and the individual competitive mentality and reward and recognition that some of the artists got, which provided impetus to some clay-modellers.[63]

Certainly, there were problems and difficulties which the Krishnanagar modellers faced. But quite unlike the average potter of Bankura, even the humblest modellers of Krishnanagar did not face similar problems of subsistence and survival, because the social roots of pottery of the two regions in Bengal were different. It is true that the descendants of Jadunath Pal earned fame and social recognition for modelling clay figures of rural characters and scenes, and for producing dolls of various kinds throughout the colonial period and even after Independence. However, there was practically no impact of status elevation of some clay-modellers as winners of medals and certificates or their better economic position due to European patronage on their fellow artisans.

Potters of Kumartuli

Kumartuli was a traditional potters' quarter in northern Calcutta. With the colonization of Bengal, which started from the second half of the eighteenth century, separate districts were allotted to Company's workmen by Holwell under orders from the Directors of the East India Company. Some neighbourhoods acquired work-related names like the Chuttarparah (the place of carpenters) and Kumartuli (Potters' quarters). Kumartuli was famous for clay images of gods and goddesses, which it retains till today and was in the periphery of the area in which the aristocracy of Bengal once prospered. Some of the most famous Bengalis of the eighteenth century, viz., Nandaram Sen and Gobindaram Mitra, who were the deputies to the English collectors, and Banamali Sarkar, who had a grand house, lived there. Before 1911, Kumartuli was the police station area with Calcutta's highest concentration (95 per cent) of Hindus.[64]

Unlike most of the artisans living in the north Calcutta neighbourhood, who dwindled in number when they were pushed out of their area in the late nineteenth century by the invasion from Barabazar, the potters of Kumartuli managed to survive in the area. It may be mentioned that John Anderson, Esq, Superintendent, Indian Museum, Calcutta, walking through Chitpur where the potters resided, visited the hut of a man who lived by making terracotta figures, brackets and toys, all the work being conducted by himself and his wife. It appeared to him that the potentials of Bengal in that department were great.[65]

The potters of Kumartuli fashioned the clay from the river beside their homes into pots to be sold at Sutanuti market. Gradually, they took to making images of gods and goddesses, worshipped in increasing numbers in the mansions all around and later at community *pujas* in the city.[66] The image-making industry in celestial colony at Kumartuli got an impetus from the community worship or *sarbojanin pujas*. The word *sarbojanin* (for all men) came to be substituted for *barowari* at the time of the Indian National Congress (INC) held in Calcutta in 1910. The fun and excitement of the old *barowari puja* took a serious turn in the early *sarbojanin pujas*. The celebration of the first community *puja* in Calcutta at Balaram Basu

Ghat Road in 1910 was used as a nationalist forum in religious guise. A pledge of solidarity was taken and the country was identified with the goddess. Fencing with sticks (*lathi khela*), *yoga* and drill displays provided moving demonstrations of a people preparing to fight for freedom. *Swadeshi* goods were sold in the stalls around the *pandals* (temporary structures where the *pujas* are held). In 1926, the 'Simla Byayam Samity', a nationalist group at Simla Street, organized an important *puja*. In this *sarbojanin puja* in 1939, Subhas Chandra Bose unveiled a 21 feet high image of Goddess Durga created by one Netai Pal.[67] This community *puja* still survives.

In Bengal, when a large image was made, the potters prepared a framework using paddy straw. The making of the bamboo frame or the straw *kathamo* for the idol was purely a man's job. The skeleton of the image was finally plastered with clay, and the head, usually moulded, was joined with the body. Other limbs too were fitted into the body. The use of the straw framework was intended to prevent sagging, and obviously it appeared to have originated from pressing the soft clay with fingers. The use of mould for preparing the head of the image, however, combined the techniques of pressing and moulding.[68] Before festivals, potters would come to Kumartuli from Nabadwip and Krishnanagar to execute commissions. The authorities of community *pujas* commissioned the *kumbhakars* to make their images according to their own satisfaction. This practice continues even today.

The Sarbojanin Durga Puja at Kumartuli dates back to 1933. Gopeswar Pal, popularly known as G. Pal was the image maker. Pal (1894-1944) started to work as a clay-modeller at Ghurni, Krishnanagar. He got his training from his grandfather, Paran Chandra Pal, his maternal uncles Satish Chandra Pal and Kshitish Chandra Pal and also from Jadunath Pal. He was the first among the clay modellers of Krishnanagar to go abroad. He participated in the British Empire Exhibition held at Wembley in England in 1924 where he gave a demonstration. *Daily Telegraph*, London, reported on 7 July 1924:

> Remarkable talent in clay modelling is being shown in the India Pavillon at Wembley by Srijut Gopeswar Pal, who hails from Krishnanagar in Bengal.

Taking a handful of clay, he changes it into a horse's head within forty-five seconds, with a deft touch here and there the staid features of the horses are transformed into snarling biting, distorted mask with ears lying wickedly flat, hair flying of a wild horse under the first restraint of a Vein. With a sweep of the hand, Mr. Pal wipes out the image. A poke here and a twist there, and within thirty seconds the head of a dog appears placidly contemplating the spectators. Someone wonders if the sculptor is capable of moulding a bust.[69]

He also went to Italy to learn sculpting. After coming back to India he established his studio at Kasimitra Ghat Road in Kumartuli. It is said that as he went abroad, he was an outcaste at Ghurni. The land where the studio was established was taken as lease from one Sunil Ghosh. Gopeswar Pal used pressing method in making models and did not use moulds. He initiated a new line by accepting stone as a medium of art. Sculpting as a medium of art was difficult and expensive. It also required extra imaginative power, labour and the exact striking of chisel and hammer. The new line of sculpting initiated by Gopeswar Pal was subsequently followed by some other clay-modellers in Ghurni and Kumartuli because of its profitable side. Although he switched over to stone he did not renounce clay as medium of art altogether. He also accepted cement as medium. The coloured cement models of a man and woman in his studio at Kashimitra Ghat was a reflection of Krishnanagar style. The small clay figures in the studio were a mixture of Krishnanagar and European style. Initially, the Goddess Durga and her four children were modelled in a single frame (*ekchala* image). The idea to make the separate images of Durga, Lakshmi, Saraswati, Kartick, and Ganesh, which was subsequently followed by the image-makers of Kumartuli, was initiated by him.[70] Gopeswar Pal's innovative power and talent is still remembered with respect by the potters of Kumartuli.

By virtue of their artistic production, the potters of Kumartuli became prominent. During the colonial period, goddesses Durga and Kali were mainly worshipped in clay images. The image makers of Kumartuli were patronized by the aristocratic families. With an ever increasing number of community *puja* celebration the demand for clay idols was on the rise. The economic condition of those associated with making images started improving.[71]

Problems and Prospects in the Craft of the Potters

Clay was one of the important raw materials on which the quality of pottery depended. Previously at many places, the potters used to collect suitable clay from fallow land free of cost. With the growing value of land, the lands hitherto used by the potters, had been brought under cultivation. The source of clay was, thus gradually restricted. Non-availability of good clay was a problem which many potters had to face. The process of manufacturing was laborious and time-consuming. The technological backwardness of their tools and techniques of manufacture, the problem of marketing and the changing values in the profession were some of the problems which confronted the potters in the age of machinery. Again, the method of firing was very defective, the furnace being exposed to external conditions of wind and temperature. A large number of potters adopted open firing and even those who fired their pots in the kiln failed to construct a permanent roof of the furnace. Therefore, with onset of rains, the potters had to stop work. It was for this reason that pottery work was not possible all the year around. The modern brick kilns could help the artisans to eliminate the breakage, ensure uniform burning and reduce the cost of fuel. However, the modern brick kilns were too costly to be arranged for by the artisans.[72] Cooperative method was the way out of this difficulty. But, there was lack of cooperative societies among the potters prior to the independence of the country.

From the close of the nineteenth century, porcelain dishes and cups were gradually coming into fashion. Enamelled iron ware had also appeared in the market. In the pre-First World War period, the imports of earthenware and porcelain came to India mostly from the UK, though an appreciable quantity was imported from Germany and Austria, as well as from China, Belgium and Holland. During 1902-7, import rose from Rs. 9.5 lakh to 14.5 lakh of which the UK contributed over one-third and the rest was shared by Germany, Austria-Hungary and Belgium. The greatest demand in the Calcutta market was for De Grelle Houdret and Co's earthenware which was made in Holland. Earthenware, bowls and rice dishes were sold in large quantities to Muhammadans locally and to other customers in various districts of Bengal. No local earthenware competed directly with De Grelle Houdret's ceramic brands of earthenware as they could not be imitated exactly by other makers. There was a good demand for soup plates, rice dishes and curry cups and saucers. Imports of earthenware from Germany to Calcutta consisted principally of cups and saucers of various prices and designs, for which there was a very large demand.[73]

The beginning of the twentieth century saw the efforts made by the *swadeshi* entrepreneurs to organize the traditional pottery industry on modern lines. One of the earliest successful ventures of *swadeshi* entrepreneurs into the ceramic industry was the Calcutta Pottery Works. Satya Sunder Deb, one of the pioneers of Indian Ceramics, was in charge of business in the Calcutta Pottery Works. Before 1914, the Calcutta Pottery Works was equipped with most up to date German and English machinery and furnaces with best quality fire clay brick. Tea cups, saucers, tea-pots, jars, ink-pots, tumblers, insulators and dolls manufactured at the Calcutta Pottery Works had a local as well as an export market.[74] In 1919, the Calcutta Pottery Works was converted into a public company under the name of 'Bengal Potteries Ltd.'. There was a factory at Uttarpara in Hoogly district where high class terracotta wares, including tea cups, saucers, pots, bowls, flower vessels and many other articles were manufactured by local hands. The factory was owned and managed by a rich zaminder of Uttarpara.[75]

From the late nineteenth century, attempts were made in Bengal to organize pottery industry using modern methods. Mention may be made of the pottery works of Raniganj, which was conducted on a large scale on Western methods. The work was commenced in 1860 by one Mr Macdonald. In 1869, Messers Burn & Co. took it over. Glazed drain-pipes, bricks, tiles and every variety of pottery was manufactured.[76]

With the introduction of porcelain dishes and cups and enamelled iron wares, the future of village pottery was shaken to some extent. The upper- and middle-class people started using steel and bell metal. Towards the close of the colonial rule, earthen pitchers were being replaced by canisters as containers of molasses. But as earthen vessels were cheaper than other kinds of metal vessels, they were used in the villages by the poor people even after the emergence of the modern industry. There was a market for goods produced by the potters throughout the year because earthen pots were considered more sacred and auspicious than glass-pots or metal-pots. The demand for their commodities was unlimited, the earthen pots being an indispensable domestic necessity with the cultivators and also the middle class people. It was the continuity of tradition and the link between the craft and the social and religious life of the people that led to its survival in Bengal as well as in India to a large extent.

Table 4.3 indicates that the potters, other than their traditional occupation, had drifted either towards agricultural labour or skilled labour in industry. The percentage of literacy among them tended to remain low. It has been argued that the potters who could improve their condition through wealth and education looked down upon this craft. They left the traditional occupation.

Nevertheless, that the major section of potters was employed in their hereditary craft at the end of the colonial rule is evident from Table 4.4.

Table 4.4 indicates there were numerous potters in Dacca, Mymensingh, Khulna, Nadia, 24-Parganas, Midnapore, Bankura, and Burdwan. At the end of the colonial rule, potters in Bengal still retained their profession to a large extent.

TABLE 4.3: A STUDY OF OCCUPATIONAL CHANGES IN REGARD TO THE POTTERS

	1901	*1911*	*1921*	*1931*
Population	1,95,533	2,78,206	2,84,514	2,89,654
Earning members	–	92,659	75,326	53,506
Percentage of literates	6.56	8.04	10.18	9.66
Percentage in traditional occupation	75.16	73.80	61.69	58.87
Agriculture	16.60	13.40	19.76	19.89
Industries	–	78.14	64.50	65.66
Higher professions	–	0.86	1.29	4.26

Source: N.K. Bose, 'Some Aspects of Caste in Bengal', *Man in India*, vol. 38, April-June 1958, no. 2, p. 126.

TABLE 4.4: DISTRIBUTION OF POTTERS IN BENGAL TOWARDS THE CLOSE OF 1930S

Districts	*Males*	*Females*
Bengal (British Territory)	1,22,104	1,14,272
Burdwan	6,019	5,218
Birbhum	3,030	3,073
Bankura	6,503	6,285
Midnapore	10,968	10,877
Hooghly	4,368	3,893
Howrah	4,883	4,285
24-Parganas	6,547	5,761
Calcutta	776	459
Nadia	6,998	7,111
Murshidabad	3,992	3,662
Jessore	5,616	6,005
Khulna	6,693	6,487
Rajsahi	3,217	2,991
Dinajpur	5,042	3,865
Jalpaiguri	1,610	1,432
Darjeeling	157	167
Rangpur	2,970	2,418
Bogra	2,006	1,808
Pabna	4,969	4,665
Malda	1,318	1,296
Dacca	10,332	9,922
Mymensingh	7,4652	7,203
Faridpur	3,057	2,866
Bakarganj	3,728	2,954
Tippera	5,965	6,005
Noakhali	2,590	2,398
Chittagong	1,292	1,226
Chittagong Hill Tracts	6	–

Source: R.A. Dutch, Superintendent of Census Operations of Bengal, *Census of India,* 1941, vol. IV, Appendix Caste Tables, Delhi: Manager of Publications, 1942.

Conclusion

The potters in Bengal fulfilled the needs of the people by performing a variety of functions in which they manifested their skills. There were three categories of potters according to the nature of their work. They were *kuchols,* i.e. those who produced small items, *hammors,* i.e. those who produced large vessels for storing fodder and *deoras,* i.e. those who were specialized in making clay images.[77]

The pottery industry of Bengal was carried out by the *kumbhakaras.* Although the Patidar-Chitrakar (painter) castes also took to the industry, the monopoly of the *kumbhakaras* did not break down. In Bengal, pottery was essentially a family craft, where men, women and children of the family worked together. It is to be noted that a particular group or family of *kumbhakaras* sometimes specialized in one or two items, while others living in the same area remained quite unaware of that particular technique. This is particularly true in the case of Ghurni at Krishnanagar. Ghurni was the only centre in Bengal where specialized crafts were practised by men and women. Life-like miniature dolls in dramatic poses made of baked or sun-baked clay dressed in cloth or materials other than clay were its specialities. However, neither from the point of technique nor subject, did it influence the traits of the *kuchols* living around.[78]

A conspicuous social phenomenon of the colonial period was the steadily rising wave of idolatry in Bengal. The upsurge of idolatry had proved economically beneficial to the clay-modellers. The economic condition of those associated with making images started improving. Again, tendency towards immortalization in stone by people gave a new incentive to sculpting, i.e. stone-modelling. Considering its profitable side, a section of the clay-modellers started switching over from clay to stone as medium of art. The modellers and the image-makers received the patronage of the enlightened landlords of the period.

The working process of the potters and their crafts indicated that they mostly remained attached to traditional methods. The course of historical evidence suggests that the changes that had taken place throughout the colonial rule were not able to extinguish the pottery industry. Similarly, the emergence of modern industry did not offset the decline in this traditional industry. The craft of pottery maintained its existence due to inherent strength which it accrued from religion and culture. There was no general deterioration of this trade unlike some other traditional industries. The artisans have preserved and continued to preserve the distinctive heritage of art, culture and craftsmanship on which India prides itself. Some of the very ancient techniques in pottery manufacture survive to the present day. The potter's craft has future possibilities as the province of Bengal possessed certain advantages in its geographical and socio-cultural situation.

Notes

1. Benoy Ghose, *Traditional Arts and Crafts of West Bengal: A Sociological Survey*, Calcutta: Papyrus, 1981, pp. 16-17.
2. *Census of India 1951*, vol. VI, Part I-C, Delhi, 1951, p. 436.
3. H.H. Risley, *The Tribes and Castes of Bengal*, Calcutta: Bengal Secretariat Press, 1891, pp. 517-18.
4. A. Mitra, *The Tribes and Castes of West Bengal*, West Bengal: West Bengal Govt. Press, 1953, p. 318.
5. *Census of India, 1951*, vol. VI, Part I-C, pp. 436-7.
6. G. Watt, *The Indian Art at Delhi*, Calcutta Superintendent of Govt. Printing, 1903, pp. 83-4.
7. T.N. Mukharji, *Monograph on the Pottery and Glassware of Bengal*, Calcutta: Superintendent of Govt. Printing, 1895, p. 2.
8. *Census of India, 1951*, vol. VI, Part I-C, p. 439.
9. Ghose, op. cit., pp. 29-30; *Census of India, 1951*, vol. VI, Part I-C, 1951, pp. 436-7.
10. B. Saraswati and N.K. Behura, *Pottery Techniques in Peasant India*, Calcutta: Anthropological Survey of India, 1966, pp. 42-7.
11. J.K. Majumdar, *Cottage Industries of Bengal*, Calcutta: Chuckervarty, Chatterjee & Co., 1927, p. 48.
12. George C.M. Birdwood, *The Industrial Arts of India*, London: South Kensington Museum Arts Handbooks, 1880; rpt. London, 1971, pp. 310-11.
13. Saraswati and Behura, op. cit., pp. 129-30.
14. Ibid., pp. 66-8.
15. E.W. Collin, *Report on the Existing Arts and Industry in Bengal*, Calcutta Bengal Secretariat, 1890, p. 3.

16. *Census of India, 1891*, vol. III, p. 284.
17. *Census of India, 1901*, p. 11.
18. *Census of India, 1921*, vol. V, Part 1, p. 357.
19. W.W. Hunter, *A Statistical Account of Bengal,* vol. V, London, 1877; rpt., New Delhi: D.K. Publishing House, p. 37.
20. *Report on Administration of Bengal* (henceforth *R.A.B*), *1879-80*, p. 185.
21. *R.A.B.*, 1875-76, p. 207; *R.A.B.*, 1876-7, p. 154.
22. Dhakar Shilpo Banijya', *Arthik Unnati*, Asar, 12th year, no. 2, 1341BS, pp. 99-100.
23. *Final Report on the Survey and Settlement Operations in the Districts of Pabna and Bogra for the years 1920-29*, Calcutta, 1930, p. 32.
24. *Final Report on the Survey and Settlement Operations in the Bakharganj District, 1900-1908*; Calcutta, 1915, pp. 13-14.
25. *Final Report on the Survey and Settlement Operations in the District of Rajshahi, 1912-22,* Calcutta, 1923, p. 38.
26. *Final Report on the Survey and Settlement Operations in the District of Jessore 1920-24*, Calcutta, 1925, p. 81.
27. *R.A.B., 1879-80*, p. 183.
28. Mukharji, op. cit., pp. 3-4.
29. Collin, op. cit., p. 7.
30. Mukharji, op. cit., p. 3.
31. Ibid., pp. 9-10.
32. L.S.S. O'Malley, *Bengal District Gazetteers*, Howrah, 1909; rpt. New Delhi: Logos Press, 1985, p. 99.
33. W.W. Hunter, *A Statistical Account of Bengal*, vol. III, London, 1877, rpt. New Delhi: D.K. Publishing House, 1973, p. 374.
34. Ibid., pp. 370.
35. Mukharji, op. cit., pp. 5-6.
36. Ibid., p. 4.
37. A. Mitra, ed., *The Tribes and Castes of West Bengal*, West Bengal: West Bengal Govt. Press, 1953, p. 315.
38. *Arthik Unnati*, Kartick 1341 BS 9th year, no. 7, p. 386.
39. Mukharji, op. cit, pp. 9-10.
40. Letter from H. Farrer, ESQ. Covenanted Deputy Collector in charge of Murshidabad to the Commissioner of the Presidency Division, General Department, Misc. Branch, Prog. B, July 1886.
41. Mitra, ed., op. cit., p. 315.
42. Surajit Chakraborty, 'Mritshilpe Murshidabad', *Ganakatha,* Special issue, Murshidabad, 1985, pp. 401-2.

43. Ghose, op. cit., pp. 21-2.
44. L.S.S. O'Malley, *Bengal District Gazetteers*, Bankura, Calcutta, 1908; rpt. 1995, p. 118.
45. Interview with Jhankar Kumbhakar and Bhairab Kumbhakar, Panchmura, Bankura on 24 December 2012.
46. Mitra, ed., *The Tribes and Castes of West Bengal* , West Bengal, 1953, p. 316.
47. Ghose, op. cit., pp. 32-4.
48. Sudhir Chakraborty, *Krishnanagarer Mritshilpa O Mritshilpi Samaj*, Calcutta: K.P. Bagchi, 1985, p. 2.
49. Jaya Chaliha and Bunny Gupta, 'Durga Puja in Calcutta' in S. Chaudhuri, ed., *Calcutta The Living City*, vol. II, New Delhi, 1990; rpt. 2011, pp. 331-2; *Friend of India,* May 1820.
50. T. N. Mukharji, *Art Manufactures of India*, Calcutta, 1888; rpt. New Delhi Navrang, 1974, p. 62.
51. Ghose, op. cit., pp. 44-5.
52. Pramatha Choudhury, *Atmakatha*, Calcutta: The Book Emporium, 1353 BS, pp. 24- 5.
53. Mukharji, op. cit., p. 59.
54. Letter no. 6T dated 12th January 1884, from John Anderson, Esq, Superintendent, Indian Museum, Calcutta, To the Hony. Secretary to the Trustees, Indian Museum, Govt. of India, Department of Finance and Commerce, August,1886, Calcutta; Govt. Printing 1886, pp. 453-60.
55. Interview with Kartick Chandra Pal, one of modellers at Ghurni, Krishnangar on 14.11.09.
56. W.W. Hunter, *A Statistical Account of Bengal,* vol. II, op. cit., pp. 48-9.
57. Ibid., pp. 101-2.
58. *Census of India,* 1951, vol. VI, Part I-C, p. 439.
59. N.K. Behura, *Peasant Potters of Orissa: Sociological Study,* New Delhi: Sterling, 1978, p. 137.
60. *Census of India, 1951*, vol. VI , Part I-C, p. 439.
61. Saraswati and Behura, op. cit., p. 91.
62. Interview with Sailen Pal, Krishnangar on 14.11.09.
63. Chakravarty, op. cit., pp. 5-6.
64. P. Thankappan Nair, 'The Growth and Development of Old Calcutta' in Sukanta Chaudhuri, ed., *Calcutta: The Living City*, vol. I, Calcutta, 1990, p.16.
65. Letter no. 6T dated 12 January 1884, from John Anderson, Esq, Superintendent, Indian Museum, Calcutta, To the Hony. Secretary to

the Trustees, Indian Museum, Govt. of India, Department of Finance and Commerce, August,1886, Calcutta; Govt. Printing 1886, pp. 453-60.

66. Bunny Gupta and Jaya Chaliha, 'Chitpur', in *Calcutta: The Living City*, vol. I, Calcutta, Oxford University Press, 1990, p. 27.
67. Bunny Gupta and Jaya Chaliha, 'Durga Puja in Calcutta', in S. Chadhuri, ed., *Calcutta: The Living City*, vol. II, New Delhi, 1990; rpt. 2011, pp. 332-5.
68. Interview with Nemai Pal, an image maker at Kumartuli on 5 December 2012.
69. Interview with Sailen Pal, an image maker at Krishnanagar on 14 November 2009; *Daily Telegraph*, London, 7 July, 1924, cited in Sudhir Chakraborty, op. cit., pp. 38-9.
70. Interview with Byomkesh Pal of Kashi Mitra Ghat Lane, Kumartuli, on 12 April 2012.
71. Interview with Babu Pal and Ranjit Sarkar of Kumartuli on 5 Decmber 2012.
72. Saraswati and Behura, op. cit., p. 191.
73. Finance Dept. Commerce Branch, File no. 2R, February and March 1915.
74. Amit Bhattacharya, *Swadeshi Enterprise in Bengal, 1900-1920*, published by Mita Bhattacharya, Calcutta, 1986, pp. 189-92.
75. J.K. Majumdar, *Cottage Industries of Bengal*, Calcutta: Chuckerberty, Chatterjee & Co., 1927, p. 51.
76. *R.A.B.*, 1875-76, p. 20.
77. Mitra, op. cit., p. 319.
78. Ibid., pp. 315-16.

CHAPTER 5

Genealogies of Sports Associations in Bengal

Historicizing the Institutionalization of European Clubs with Native *Akharas*[*]

Amitava Chatterjee

Introduction

Sports began to acquire relevance in the middle class cultural world of Bengal at the close of the nineteenth century as a leisure and health option, moulded by ideas imported from Europe. With the advent of colonialism, Bengali society witnessed the diffusion of modern sports which had colonial origins. The sporting clubs, an European prerogative in India, had a distinctive identity of 'colonial public sphere'.[1] They allowed for a relatively greater degree of openness. The stereotypical portrayal of the 'weak and inferior' Indian body as compared to the strong and superior body of the European and the subsequent effort to discipline Indian bodies to improve them was at the heart of the politics of colonialism.[2] J.A. Mangan emphasizes that sport was self consciously employed in British educational institutions for Indians as a part of the programme to discipline their bodies in line with the manliness and hardihood of the English public school boy.[3]

Western sports slowly caught the fancy of Bengali society and attracted the rich and middle class sections. The sporting clubs and associations that emerged as an institutional novelty in the sporting arena in the course of the nineteenth century, made the public sphere critically important for a modern sporting culture, in which public patronage and public viewing of sport replaced the older connection with patrician patronage. The growth of physical culture in an institutionalized form became integrally linked with this club culture. The patronage of indigenous sporting associations came mostly from relatively affluent men, whose ambition to achieve fame in the public sphere accounted for their interest in promotion of traditional games. In the process a distinct locus of sporting activity was created, in which the involvement of the public mattered. The most significant issue concerning the sporting culture in Bengal in late colonial times relates to the transformation of traditional sporting activities from leisurely practice to the larger process of institutionalization and as aspects of a public culture. The purpose of this paper is to explore the history of institutionalization of traditional sporting *akharas* of colonial Bengal from its marginality as a counterpart to European sporting clubs.

Conceptualization of Club Culture in Bengal: Formation of European Clubs

The club was a European implantation in India. In the late eighteenth and nineteenth centuries, a variety of associational forms emerged across South Asia. Of these, clubs were just one type and when taken as a whole, they formed a supra-network of associational life. A club may be broadly defined as an association of individuals sharing some common interests and goals.[4] In South Asia, the majority of clubs have been social or sporting in nature. They opened in different settings: large urban clubs in colonial centers; hill station clubs; clubs in princely states; and clubs in dusty countryside towns.[5] Mrinalini Sinha argues that the role of the clubs in reproducing a rigidly exclusive 'Britishness' in the colonies has been considered so self-evident as to preclude any systematic exploration of its actual imbrications in the ideologies and practices of imperial rule.[6] George Orwell, a bitter critique of colonialism, wrote in *Burmese Days,* that in every other town in India, the European club was 'the spiritual citadel, the real seat of British Power'.[7]

English education and ideology inevitably brought in their wake English sports like cricket, hockey, rugby, football, tennis, and golf, mainly from around the early part of the nineteenth century. The

Calcutta Cricket Club which traces its origin to around 1792[8] is generally regarded as the oldest cricket club outside of the British Isles. The first organized match, watched by the bemused natives, was played on the *Maidan* in January 1804 between the Old Etonians (who were in Calcutta as East India Company writers) and the non-Etonians, designated as 'Calcutta'. As in England at the time, there was heavy betting on the result. Odds of two to one were offered against the Old Etonians,[9] but they won the match by an innings and 152 runs, with Robert Vansittart scoring a century.[10]

Ballygunge Cricket Club was established in 1864. The formation of this club is linked with the early genesis of cricket in the region. A speaker at a function reported in *The Englishman* of 2 March 1894, that

> The idea of starting a Cricket Club at Ballygunge, so I am told, arose very much in this manner. Our worthy President (C.E. Brock) many years ago was in the habit of renting the Bodyguard Bungalow at Ballygunge during the absence of the Bodyguard in the hills. The love of cricket learnt in the Canterbury fields' years before broke out again, and Mr. Brock used to ask a few of his more intimate friends to come and have a game of cricket on Saturdays at Ballygunge. Mr. Brock's cricket got to be so attractive that the idea of a cricket club took root and grew up in Mr. Brock's mind and in 1864 the idea was mooted among the then European inhabitants living in and around Ballygunge.[11]

The Calcutta Rowing Club was established in 1858. John Courie was the first honorary secretary. This is considered as one of the oldest athletic clubs in eastern India. The Club took off with a six-oared boat which was purchased locally in 1859. Just after the cyclone of 1864, the club was left homeless, boatless and destitute. The club got somewhat restructured in 1865 with purchase of some Chinese boats. One of the original promoters and chief patrons of the club through its early struggles for existence was F.A. Goodenough of Messrs. Mackillop Stewart and Co., then one of the leading mercantile houses in Calcutta. Thus corporate patronage which was essential for substantial financial support was very much present. At this stage in the club's history, the Regatta course was 1 mile from Fort point to Shalimar or from Shalimar to Botanical Gardens. Records reveal that the first institutionalized competition took place with Howrah Boat Club in 1866. C.G. Norman's account of a Regatta reveals that on 19 January 1869 the Governor-General along with the Lt. Governor of Bengal witnessed this event.[12] By the turn of the century, the club was affiliated to the Amateur Rowing Association. A sculling match between Hoare and Charles was held and was won by the former after a very close and fast race. These events were supported by plenty of indigenous spectators and they enjoyed this institutionalized colonial sport. Gradually the number of competitions increased. The Hooghly Cup became a prestigious competition for all oarsmen. Foreigners from Madras and Rangoon paid visit and competed with the members of Calcutta Rowing Club. Apart from Ganges the institution also recognized Regatta in the Dhakuria Lake and the canal of Behala.[13]

The Calcutta Football Club was established in 1872 exclusively for the British expatriates and military personnel stationed in Calcutta. It was the oldest rugby club outside the UK.[14] Though named as a football club, the members actually played rugby until 1876 when the club was disbanded. The Calcutta Cup trophy was made accumulating the club fund and it was presented for the annual Rugby championship between England and Scotland. The club was reformed in 1884 and took part in the Trades Cup and eventually concentrated on football from about 1894.[15]

The membership of this club was restricted to expatriates who had the good fortune of going to a university or, at least, one of the better-known British public schools or were members of the services, either civil or military or were professional men such as lawyers, doctors, bankers and so on but who all bore the stamp of belonging to the upper echelons of British middle class society. However, there was no entry for the tradesmen of Calcutta, though amongst them there were many brilliant exponents of Association Football.[16] The history of the Dalhousie Athletic Club is linked with this episode of Indian football. It was set up in 1880 by some football enthusiasts among the tradesmen of the city led by Towfett who was an assistant in the well-known department store, Whiteaway, Laidlaw and Love, working with the noted jewellers, Hamilton and Co., whose entry was barred to the exclusive Calcutta Football Club. It was known as the Trades Club and the name was later changed to the Dalhousie Athletic Club. This body was brought into being in the year 1893 and to get things going, Dalhousie donated a handsome trophy called the Trades Cup. In all justice, the donors became the first winners from a field of thirteen which included four Indian teams of which the Sovabazar Club was the best known.[17]

It was largely through the initiative of the Dalhousie Athletic Club that the meeting at which the Indian Football Association was founded was convened. The Association immediately set about inaugurating a tournament under its own auspices and for a trophy to be arranged by itself and so, the IFA Shield was brought into existence but it was largely through the generosity of certain Dalhousie members such as J. Sutherland, A.R. Brown, the first Hon. Secretary of the IFA, M.D. Lindsay and others, who made handsome voluntary contributions, that the cost of the splendid trophy was defrayed. The Calcutta League, or the First Division thereof, was started in 1898 and Dalhousie was one of the Clubs to participate from the year of inception. It was not, however, until 1910 that they were to become champions and their further successes came in 1921, 1928 and 1929.

Dalhousie, at one time, used to field a very strong cricket team. This was in the years when they were led and inspired by the famous Australian Frank Tarrant, who had been brought out to these parts by the Maharaja of Cooch Behar. The Cooch Behar XI used to play a number of matches in Calcutta, mainly against representative sides, during the winters and Tarrant used to be made available for Dalhousie when the State team was not playing. This was in the years from 1907 to 1917. In November of 1917, a special 2-day match had been arranged to be played at Eden Gardens between the Governor of Bengal's XI and Cooch Behar. Murray Webb, K.B. Harper and H. Hannay, all of Dalhousie were invited to assist the Governor's XI.[18]

Early Initiatives of Institutionalization of Indigenous Physical Culture: Hindu Mela

The public culture of sports is inconceivable without the institutions and ideologies that came to sustain it. The ethos of a public celebration of sports, articulated through clubs and associations, succeeded in transforming the character of physical culture in Bengal in the later half of the nineteenth century. The patronage of landed aristocracy and other magnets of the society manoeuvred the process of institutionalization of traditional sporting practices.

The importance of physical culture was well realized by the patrons of Hindu Mela and it was included in its regular proceedings. The first assembly of Hindu Mela was held on 12 April 1867. It was decided to invite and felicitate the renowned wrestlers of the town in the *Mela* and to spread the consciousness about physical exercise among fellow Indians. In the following year (1868) the performers showed their prowess in indigenous style. Then there was demonstration of *lathi*-play and wrestling which was thoroughly enjoyed by both native and European spectators. In the eighth session of 1874 tickets were sold at the rate of 50 paise for muscle posing shows. Competitions of physical feats were arranged for young enthusiasts in the Mela and the champions were presented with medals.[19]

The movement started by the Hindu Mela and National Society for the widespread consciousness about the value of physical prowess among the youth compelled the government to introduce physical education in the schools and it was also included in the syllabus of Civil Service Examination. There were instances where students from government as well as local schools demonstrated their physical feats in the Mela.[20] *Amrita Bazar Patrika* reported that National Society was the pioneer in fostering physical education among the school students. Moreover most of the trainers of physical exercise department set up by the government in schools and colleges were the students of National School founded by Nabagopal Mitra, chief patron of Hindu Mela.[21] Nabagopal Mitra founded the National School on 1 April 1872 for the cultivation of arts, music and for physical training. In the following years horse riding was also introduced as a part of the physical exercise course. Some of the eminent students of this school were Jitendranath Bandopadhyay, Bipin Chandra Pal and Dr. Sundari Mohan Das. Shyama Charan Ghosh after successfully graduating from this institute joined Civil Service Institution as a physical trainer.[22] Prior to the establishment of National School, Nabagopal imparted horse riding training in his private stables and Satyendra Nath Tagore and few of his peers were trained there.[23]

Institutionalization of amateur wrestling *Akharas*[24]

Wrestling created a distinct meaning as a part of the physical culture that flourished during the height of the *swadeshi* movement. This was another indigenous martial sport that gradually found useful support of the *akharas* (physical culture clubs). The first three and a half decades of the twentieth century covered the phase of revolutionary movement in Bengal. The revolutionaries urged for a programme of all round development, which was channellized through a set of organizations known as Samities, *sanghas*, *akharas* (gymnastic clubs), study circles or libraries. In Calcutta Simla Byayam Samiti, Baghbazar Gymnasium, Manik Babu's Camp, Ballygunge Bhatri Sangha, Gobor Babus Gymnasium, to name a few, were the famous ones. These *akharas* organized several competitions apart from regular physical training for the Bengali youth, the prospective recruits in the revolutionary movement.

With time, the *akharas* acquired the features of a club, crossing the limits of the courtyard of a rich household. Some of these were located in the house of a trainer, but there were others which were public associations devoted to physical culture and wrestling. The *akhara* in the house of Khetu Guha of Durzeepara attracted wrestlers from different provinces of India. Eminent wrestler Gobor Guha was also trained for some time in this *akhara*. Another distinguished disciple of Khetu Babu was Bhabendranath Saha, popularly known as Bhim Bhabani though his initial training started under the guidance of Khudiram Babu, the founder of Simla Byayam Samiti.[25] Such *akharas* were not always nationalist in nature. Phanindra Krishna Gupta, a doctor by profession, was an earnest disciple of Ambu Babu.[26]After the death of Ambu Babu, he set up an *akhara* near his house. Along with native Indians, Europeans also trained in this *akhara*. In 1914 during the World War he assisted in the formation of Bengal Ambulance Core under the patronage of Maharaja of Burdwan and Dr. Sarbadhikari. He himself trained the volunteers how to combat and went to Mesopotamia as their Adjutant.[27]

Somewhat different was the character of the Simla Byayam Samiti. The latter one of the premier *akharas* in Bengal organized regular wrestling competitions of which 'Bengal Wrestling Competition' was an important event. On one occasion, the final bout was witnessed by J.C. Mukherjee, Chief Executive Officer of the Calcutta Corporation and J.C. Guha (Gobor Guha). The clubs which contested the final rounds were Simla Byayam Samiti, Manik Babu's Camp and Ballygunge Bhatri Sangha. One striking feature which is evident here is the importance of a particular Manik Babu who happened to be a Guru and he himself maintained an *akhara* successfully and challenged some of the best gymnasiums of that time.[28]

The overwhelming enthusiasm on the part of Calcutta crowd clearly contradicted the construct of 'effeminacy' imposed on the Bengalis by our colonial masters[29] and occasional newspaper reports about wrestling and athletic events points to the existence of several *akharas* and clubs in Calcutta and its neighbourhood. In an athletic competition which included a wrestling bout, organized by the Kiddirpore Byayam Samiti, participants from Rishra Byayam Samiti, Ghosh's College of Physical Culture and Vajrang Vyayamagar joined the fray. In that competition, Rishra Byayam Samiti, which was located in the small town of Rishra in Hooghly district at some distance from Calcutta, achieved distinction.[30]

The Proliferation of New Associations for Physical Culture

This was the historical backdrop against which it is important to trace the proliferation of a new crop of physical culture associations. With a view to providing healthy recreation for the youngmen of their locality the Aheeritolla Club was founded in 1898. In those days the members played football, cricket, tennis and games like swimming and rowing in the Ganges. Towards the beginning of the year 1922, Krista Lall Bysack, proprietor of Hippodrome Circus, after his extensive world tour came back and helped the members of the Executive Committee in organizing the gymnastic section which was started in March 1922. The gymnasium followed an elaborate training manual. The first year was spent in simple physical culture, while in the second year the members gave displays of their skills.[31]

There were other public spirited men in different localities who took similar initiatives. Prof. B. Ghosh's school, popularly known as Bishtu Ghosh's Akhara, at Bosepara Lane in Calcutta was a unique institution. Bishnu Charan Ghosh, the founder of this institution was himself a well-known physical culturist who devoted his life for the cause of physical education among Bengali youths. Within a very short time after its establishment it proved its worth, participating in an acrobatic performance.[32]

Teachers Physical Training Camp was another institution that provided such training. Operating from the grounds of the School of Physical Culture in Wellington Square, the institution was meant to train physical instructors for the schools in the province. This had initially been started in Rajsahi a few years earlier. The centre at Calcutta was set up to train some of the interested teaching and non-teaching staff.[33] The National YMCA School of Physical Training which began its pioneering work in Madras in 1920 achieved grand success in this matter. The Bengal government while trying to imitate the above-mentioned physical training programme announced its intention of employing physical instructors in schools from amongst the trainees of these institutions.[34]

At times physical training sessions were organized by leaders of revolutionary societies. Pulinbehari Das, the noted revolutionary of the Dacca Anushilan Samiti, was the first to train the educated Bengali youth in *lathi*-play using modern techniques. In 1905, Advocate P. Mitra, Bipin Pal and other nationalist leaders set up various physical culture institutes. Pulin Das was selected as one of the trainers who was sent to Dacca. His mock fight training tried to inculcate the warrior spirit among his followers. But his most notable contribution, as far as this martial sport was concerned, was perhaps the book *Lathi-khela o Asi-khela* (Stick and Sword Fighting). With an illustrated description of the martial sport, the book was a path-breaking example in sports literature.[35] The example set by Pulin Das early in the twentieth century continued even in later decades. A promoter of physical culture in the 1940s Prof. Basanto Kumar Banerjee successfully organized a group of pupils who used to perform as a physical culture team, popularly known as *Basanto-scheme*. On the inauguration of Hindusthan Athelete's Union on the day of Kali Puja in 1941, a group of 400 boys and girls demonstrated *Basanto-scheme*. On the same day the disciples of Sinthee Rash Behary Adarsha Byayam Mandir held a three hour show of Basanto-keep-fit culture.[36]All these demonstrations included unique aerial and ground feats like loop exercises and chair vaults on aerial trapeze, brick-juggling, hand athletics on high chairs, etc., invented by Master Basanto which became a favourite among the masses.[37]

Several well-known residents of Calcutta interested in boxing and physical culture formed an association which was called The Calcutta Sporting Club. After months of labour they succeeded in acquiring a really first class gymnasium in Indian Mirror Street which had been fitted up at a cost of Rs. 7,500. The gymnasium was placed at the disposal of the soldiers taking part in the boxing tournament of 1918. A military officer who was in Calcutta for the tournament, and had considerable experience and knowledge about boxing in England remarked that it was one of the best fitted Gymnasia he had seen. The Club was expected to organize Boxing on sound lines following the National Sporting Club Rules.[38]

Gradual Shift of Interest from Physical Culture Movement to Western Sports

Western sports actually penetrated the psyche of the Bengalis who had a profound interest in the activities of indigenous physical culture. In an article written in 1890 Mr. Ananda Charan Sen wrote about a revival of interest in physical exercise due to the introduction of Western style of education. Earlier, as Sen tells us, men who played *kabaddi* or *gollachuth* were considered foolish, but gradually things changed and in schools, just as pupils received prizes for academic excellence, students also began to receive good amount of recognition and awards for achievements in sports. According to him the fact that people were becoming conscious of the merits of exercise was because of their affinity with the English lifestyle. The English kept themselves fit through exercise. Due to the progress in education, students carried out physical and mental exercises. He profusely thanked the English for introducing games like cricket, football, lawn tennis, badminton, etc., which provided scope for physical culture movement.[39]

The second half of the nineteenth century saw Western sports catching fancy of the urban middle classes, just as folk theatres were replaced by a modern theatre, inspired by Shakespeare, in the cultural sphere. The emergence of what came to be known as a refined taste by marginalizing a more eclectic culture of early colonial Calcutta has been the main theme of Sumanta Banerjee's work. The urban middle class, as Banerjee suggests, while representing the elite culture reconstituted the lines of the deference, patronage and moral authority in Calcutta society by distancing itself from the popular cultures of the lower orders.[40]

Sports began to acquire relevance in the middle class cultural world of late nineteenth century as a leisure and health option, moulded by ideas imported from Europe. By the end of the nineteenth century, members of the aristocracy and bourgeoisie from the cultural centre of Calcutta started to play English sports. Western sporting games which began to be introduced in the educational institutes with an aim of promotion of disciplinary regime resulted in a general movement known as athleticism.[41] Its early development, however, was intertwined with the spread of other kinds of physical activities which were traditional pastimes and practiced in the *akharas.* Prior to the adoption of Western team sports, leisure activities consisted of the so-called field sports, such as hunting, shooting and fishing, all of which related to the lifestyle of landed aristocracy of the eighteenth and nineteenth centuries.

Western sports, particularly football were considered a source of improvement necessary for the bodies of the Bengali 'race'. The game, however, was considered important by the Army for ensuring the enduring capacity of 'martial' Indian bodies for war. Other colonial sports also got a solid footing in the Bengal presidency which altered the sporting culture of the colony to a greater extent. By the close of the nineteenth century, Bengal witnessed proliferation of Western sports into mass culture by the way of formation of Indian clubs for Western sports.[42] The patronage of indigenous clubs came mostly from relatively affluent men, whose ambition to achieve fame in the public sphere accounted for their interest in the promotion of physical culture and sporting clubs. Clubs flowered into different branches of sports—like football, cricket, hockey, etc., which were always a male dominated game. It was through such institutions like clubs and tournaments, alongside public patronage of the games that sporting activity which had an element of strangeness in local society began to strike their roots in the Indian milieu. This made the public sphere critically important for a modern sporting culture, in which public patronage and public viewing of sport replaced the older connection with patrician patronage. The circulation of information about sporting activities and achievements through the print media created heroes out of the sportsmen. People who had earlier depended almost entirely on upper class patronage began to establish their distinctive identity in the public arena.

There cannot be a better description of how a Western sport became an integral part of Bengal's sporting culture by the close of the nineteenth century than what was reported by the anonymous correspondent of *The Hindoo Patriot*: 'Bengal has taken kindly to cricket and unquestionably very kindly to football. There is hardly a village where it is not played, a large batabi (melon) fruit often doing duty for football, where the means of the players would not allow them to purchase it'. [43]

Conclusion

It seems, therefore, that since the early part of the twentieth century sporting culture in Bengal began to feature as an aspect of mass culture. This implies that all the different branches of sporting activities did not achieve the same degree of popularity. Certain types, particularly team sports which blended finally with mass participation started attracting the notice of contemporary press to an extent that newspaper coverage of such sport became more extensive from early part of twentieth century. From this period the popularity of indigenous physical culture in Bengal actually showed a downward swing. Popularity of Western team sports gradually superseded the interest in physical culture and with passage of time mass interest was shifted to the Indian clubs for Western sports.

Thus the institutionalization of traditional physical culture lost its momentum and became very much limited within a particular time frame.

Notes

* I am indebted to Dr. Anindya Sekhar Purakayastha, Associate Professor of English, Kazi Nazrul University for suggesting the title.

1. Mrinalini Sinha, 'Britishness, Clubbability, and the Colonial Public Sphere: The Genealogy of an Imperial Institution in Colonial India', *Journal of British Studies*, vol. 40, no. 4, 'At Home in the Empire' (October 2001), pp. 489-521.
2. James Mills and Paul Dimeo, 'When Gold is Fired it Shines: Sport, the Imagination and the Body in Colonial and Postcolonial India', *Sport and Postcolonialism*, ed. John Bale and Mike Cronin, Oxford and New York: Berg Publishers, 2003, pp. 107-22.
3. J.A. Mangan, *The Games Ethic and Imperialism: Aspects of the Diffusion of an Ideal*, London: Frank Cass, 1998 as cited in James Mills and Paul Dimeo, 'When Gold is Fired it Shines: Sport, the Imagination and the Body in Colonial and Postcolonial India', 2003.
4. Benjamin B. Cohen, *In the Club: Associational Life in Colonial South Asia*, Hyderabad: Orient BlackSwan, 2015.
5. Ibid.
6. Sinha, 'Britishness, Clubbability, and the Colonial Public Sphere: The Genealogy of an Imperial Institution in Colonial India', op. cit.
7. Charles Allen, *Plain Tales from the Raj*, London: Andre Deutsch, 1975 as cited in Ronojoy Sen, *Nation at Play: A History of Sport in India*, Penguin, 2015.
8. *Madras Courier*, 23 February 1792 first mentions about Calcutta Cricket Club in an article about a match between The Gentlemen of Calcutta and The Gentlemen of Barrackpore (Rowland Bowen, 'Some Dates in Indian Cricket History', *Wisden Cricketers' Almanack*, 1967).
9. N.S. Ramaswami, *From Porbandar to Wadekar*, New Delhi: Abhinav Publications, 1975.
10. Krishna Dutta, *Calcutta: A Cultural and Literary Companion*, Oxford: Signal Books, 2003.
11. Ramaswami, op. cit., 1975.
12. L.H. Macklin (compiled), *A Summary of the Records of the Calcutta Rowing Club, 1858 to 1932*, Calcutta: L.H. Macklin, 1932.

13. *The Englishman*, 16 October 1931.
14. R.B. (Rakhal Bhattacharya), *Kolkatar Football*, Calcutta: Calcutta East Light Book House, 1955
15. Tony Mason, 'Football on the Maidan: Cultural Imperialism in Calcutta', *International Journal of the History of Sport*, vol. 12, no. 1, 1990.
16. P.H.R.S., 'Dalhousie Athletic Club: A Brief History', *Dalhousie Athletic Club Centenary Souvenir*, 1980.
17. Ibid.
18. Ibid.
19. Jogesh Chandra Bagol, *Hindu Melar Itibrittwa*, Calcutta: Maitraee, 1945.
20. Ibid.
21. *Amrita Bazar Patrika*, 14 February 1875.
22. Jogesh Chandra Bagol, *Hindu Melar Itibrittwa*, Calcutta: Maitraee, 1945.
23. Ibid.
24. For detailed discussion, see A. Chatterjee, 'From Courtyard Sport to Competitive Sport: Evolution of Wrestling in Colonial Bengal', *Sport in Society*, vol. 18 (1), 2015.
25. Birendranath Ghosh, *Bangalir Bahubol*, Calcutta: Saratchandra Chakrabarti & Sons, 1341 BS (1934).
26. Ambika Guha, the grandfather of renowned wrestler Gobar Guha, was the founder of the gymnasium in 1857.
27. Anil Chandra Ghosh, *Byame Bangali*, Calcutta: Presidency Library, 1928.
28. *Amrita Bazar Patrika*, 6 March 1940.
29. Mrinalini Sinha, *Colonial Masculinity: The Manly Englishman and the Effeminate Bengali in the Late Nineteenth Century*, Manchester: Manchester University Press, 1995.
30. *Amrita Bazar Patrika*, 13 March 1940.
31. Ibid., 7 April 1925
32. *Amrita Bazar Patrika* reported how the Club performed in Sovabazar Rajbati in the presence of a large and respectable assembly. The performance began at 9:30 p.m. and lasted till midnight. It opened with an excellent display on the triple horizontal bar. Wire dancing of Monmatha, balancing of trapeze by Bidhu, boneless play by Sanathan, wonderful performance of Ramen, a boy of eight, on trapeze, Prof. Bose's canon ball play exhibited Herculean strength. He also showed barrel play and jugglery which was applauded by all. The Maharaja of

Sovabazar was highly pleased with the performance and awarded a gold medal along with a purse of Rs.100. The reporter mentioned that this kind of institution needs patronage and support from the elites as well as ordinary people of the society (*Amrita Bazar Patrika,* 21 October 1907). The same institution under the able guidance of Prof. Ghosh displayed their performance at the Calcutta orphanage. All the items were so skillfully displayed that the gentlemen of the locality highly appreciated them (*Amrita Bazar Patrika*, 6 November 1907).

33. *Amrita Bazar Patrika*, 19 May 1933.
34. Ibid., 23 May 1933.
35. Ibid., 7 April 1925.
36. Ibid., 21 October 1941.
37. Ibid., 29 October 1941.
38. *Indian Planters Gazette*, 1918 (British Library Holding).
39. *Sakha*, February 1890.
40. Sumanta Banerjee, *The Parlour and the Streets*, Calcutta: Seagull Books, 1998.
41. J.A. Mangan, *Athleticism in the Victorian and Edwardian Public School,* London: Frank Cass, 2000.
42. For detailed understanding of the topic see, Kausik Bandopadhyay, *Scoring off the Field: Football Culture in Bengal, 1911-1980,* London: Routledge, 2011.
43. *The Hindoo Patriot*, 11 June 1919.

CHAPTER 6

The Missionary among the Khasis

Arpita Sen

The British Empire did not rule by military and physical force alone. It endured by getting both colonizing and the colonized people to see their world and themselves in a particular way, internalizing the language of the Empire as representing the natural, true order of life.[1] This may be particularly applicable in the case of the Khasis, a matrilineal tribe of Meghalaya, renowned for their prowess in archery, where such a thing was made possible through the process of conversion. Even though British colonialism and Christian missionary activities cannot be put together within one register to emplot the Khasi story of conversion, in the long run it eased the work of the British by helping to subdue the Khasis and, thereby, making it easier to reconcile the war-like Khasis to colonial rule. The Khasi conversion to Christianity in the second half of the nineteenth century was a Welsh missionary project. The first Welsh missionary, Thomas Jones who arrived in 1841 in Cherrapunjee to share the loving grace of the Gospel of Christ to those who did not know, was not invited by any British official. In fact, he was encouraged by the glowing report given by another missionary, a Baptist, Reverend Jacob Tomlin en route to China via the Khasi Hills, who highlighted the superstitious and simple character of the Khasis, described them as cheerful, active and enterprising and felt that blessed with the knowledge of the Gospel, they would become faithful and noble allies of the British government.[2] The conversion of the Khasis to Christianity in the second half of the nineteenth century was never at any stage entangled with British colonial rule, but it had the latter's tacit support and protection, otherwise there would have been many a martyr in the Khasi Hills! Ultimately it was the missionary, with his supremacist instincts who became part and parcel of the West's spiritual, physical and intellectual conquest of the Khasis.

This article basically probes and investigates the conversion of the Khasis to Christianity in nineteenth-century colonial India. By focussing on the process of religious conversion, this article illustrates how Edward Said's Orientalism can be adopted to approach and explore the mechanics of conversion among the Khasis by according them an inferior status, thus ascribing them with the identities of 'pagans', 'heathens' and 'animists'. The Khasi way of life was compared with European ideas of God, man, nature, society, science and history and consistently found inferior and backward. This article argues that conversion was made possible by the denigration of Khasi religion, culture and tradition through factors such as education, medicine and a natural calamity like the Earthquake of 1897 that shook the Khasi Hills causing widespread havoc and destruction. Apart from all these factors were also British political paramountcy and perhaps an interpretation of Khasi cosmology in more refined Christian terms.

As a race the Khasis are divided into sub-tribes such as the upland Khasis occupying the central high plateau; the Khasis bordering the plateau in the south, presently north of Bangladesh known as the Wars; the Bhois bordering the plateau in the north, south of Assam; and the Lyngams in the west of the plateau. Though speaking different dialects, often dissimilar, they derive their origin from Khasi roots. What bind the Khasis together are their clans. The origin of the word Khasi can be traced to the words *kha* which means born of and *si* which means ancient mother. Khasi, therefore, means born of a mother. Khasi clans are strictly exogamous. An early colonial account describes them as a handsome, muscular race of an active disposition, fond of martial exercises, who always went about armed, in general, with bows and arrows, and a long naked sword and shield.[3]

The Khasis were perceived, like any other people of the Orient, as inferior. The European trader, the missionary and the official 'thought about, the Orient because he could be there, or could think about it, with very little resistance on the Orient's part'.[4] This was especially true of the Khasis who could not boast of a written script in their first encounter with the British in late eighteenth century. As the story goes, it got lost as a result of a great flood that brought their once flourishing civilization to an end. The Khasi escaped by swimming a great river and held the book of knowledge in his mouth that he unfortunately swallowed. On reaching God's house in a state of repentence, he was graciously consoled by the latter who said that it was the same thing to have a book in his belly as in his hand. So, for a Khasi, it was not necessary to study books for knowledge. He had the infallible guide within him!

The need to enter the Khasi Hills was urgently felt at the end of the Anglo-Burmese war followed by the Treaty of Yandaboo in 1826, when, for the convenience of the British, a road had to be constructed through the Khasi Hills connecting Sylhet with Gauhati, Assam. To realize this plan, negotiations were entered with the *Syiem* (chief) of Nongklaw, U Tirot Singh, by David Scott, agent to the Governor-General on the north-east frontier of Bengal. Since no Khasi chief had any right to give such pledge without consulting his *durbar*, Tirot Singh informed Scott that he would convene a meeting of his assembly and place his proposal before it. He invited Scott to be present at Nongklaw during the *durbar*, which the latter accepted. Major White, who accompanied Scott, was astonished to see five or six hundred warriors come 'bounding along the hills armed with two handed swords, bows and quivers and arrayed in the picturesque garb of the *Cossyas* (Khasis), resembling the Roman Toga'.[5] He was also impressed by the order and decorum that characterized the debates as no shouts of exultation and indecent attempts were made to put down the orator of the opposite party.[6] On the contrary, every speaker was heard out. He further opined that even though he often witnessed the debates in St. Stephen's chapel, but those of the *Cossya* parliament appeared to him to be conducted with more dignity of manner.[7] The Khasis refused to drink spirits till they arrived at a consensus.[8] Finally, a decision was reached in Scott's favour. But things took to a different turn when an attack was made on the British party by the people of Nongkhlaw in 1829, said to be among other things, provoked by the false and foolish speech of a Bengalee *chupprasee*, who, in a dispute with the *Cassyas*, had threatened them with his master's (Scott's) vengeance, and had told them that it entered in his master's plans to subject them to taxation, in the same way as the inhabitants of the plains.[9] Considering that Assam and Sylhet were already a part of the Company's dominion there must have been some truth that the British intended to integrate these hills into their expanding Indian possessions.[10] This led to the commencement of the Anglo-Khasi war which culminated in the defeat of many Khasi chiefs who had entered the war and the surrender of Tirot Singh in 1833. The strength of the Khasi warriors was 'measured' during the Khasi insurgency, by their sheer prowess to chase the British soldiers on horse-back.[11] Following the end of the war, twenty-five Khasi chiefs made their feudal submission to the East India Company by means of treaties and engagements, with only three villages close to the British settlement at Cherrapunjee annexed to British India. The chiefs were bound to the British government by treaties and agreements to run the administration of their respective states on behalf of the paramount power.

The Missionary Perception of the Khasis

European colonization and culture gained in strength with the coming of the missionaries to the Khasi Hills. It did so by setting itself against the Orient as represented in this case by the Khasis as a surrogate and underground self. The missionary view that persisted throughout the colonial period was the notion of religion as something expressed objectively in written creeds, doctrine or stated belief. The usual assumptions of commentaries in the seventeenth and eighteenth centuries was that there were four religions, namely Judaism, Christianity, Islam and Paganism or Heathenism. The same idea of a fourfold religious system is reflected in William Carey's well-known *Enquiry*, published in 1792. 'Paganism' or 'heathenism' were broad and loosely defined terms which were meant to include all non-Christian religions apart from Judaism and Islam.[12] The Missionary regarded Christianity to be superior to all other religions. Though he was aware that there was a difference between Hinduism and tribal religions, which was encouraged at least as much by official reports as by his own experience of work among tribals, the missionary portrayed both the religions as irrational, immoral and inhuman. The feeling that the Khasi was inferior and had nothing to offer religiously was reinforced by the Khasis' lack of material and scientific progress. David Scot, an evangelist himself argued that the introduction of Christianity in the region would benefit the indigenous tribes who were not under the influence of the traditional Hindu and Islam religions. He maintained that the Khasis were in a rude state of civilization, whose ideas of further state, and the Supreme Being, were vague and indistinct and were much more likely to be converted than races further advanced.[13]

It was William Carey of Serampore Baptist Mission who sent the first Bengali convert, Krishna Chandra Pal, to work among the Khasis in Sylhet who were apparently refugees from inter-tribal wars in 1813. But he met with little success. So did the efforts of Alexander B. Lish, also of the Serampore Mission. As Lish was to opine about the Khasis, he found the people, 'so steeped in ignorance as to make it almost impossible to convey any religious idea to their minds', and the only religion they understood consisted in endeavouring, 'to appease the demons with sacrifices of goats, fowls, sheep and pigs'.[14] It was not that he was not able to make an impact on their minds as they would listen to his message with incredulity, and when told of salvation through the merit of another, end up saying—'How can God be pleased with us unless we ourselves will do something good to merit His favour?' The most important contribution of the Baptist missionaries was the creation of a Khasi script in Bengali in the Shella dialect. The records of the Serampore Mission indicates that even though much had to be done in the way of schools in the Khasi Hills, as early as 1816-17, a few of the Khasis, widespread in the southern plains nearest to Bengal, could read and write since they had acquired the knowledge of the Bengali character.[15] The letter of the Sylhet Collector, dated 20 May 1816, pointed out that five or six boys, sons of rich persons and people of consequence in their tribe, can be obtained through the different Rajahs to help in the translation of the scriptures. This proved that education was more confined to the chiefly families and even state nobles in a foreign medium. In 1819 two Khasis—U Bi Tham and Ram Singh Rani pursued their studies in Serampore College. No records exists that the two Khasis ever embraced Christianity.

The Baptist missionaries had to surrender their field to the Welsh Calvinist Methodist Mission in 1841, proponents of missionary activity who argued in favour of a general 'civilizing mission's project for the enhancement of the moral standards of the Khasis'. When the Welsh missionaries, Reverend Thomas Jones and his wife, landed in Sohra, a tract of hilly country nearly as big as Wales, on 22 June 1841, they found its inhabitants 'living under the darkness of fear, superstition, ignorance and disease.... And when anyone is ill, all that he and his family have saved through depriving themselves of the bare necessities of life is spent on baskets of eggs, and on fowls, pigs, goats, cows for sacrificing.... The whole history of their race throughout the ages has been a repetition of these practices.'[16] It is interesting to note what Jones had to write in his first letter from the Hills, where he described the Khasis as, 'multitudes upon multitudes of untutored heathen, naturally lazy and sluggish, living in filth and rags, afraid to wash a rag lest it should wear out the sooner; depriving themselves of proper clothing; niggardly hoarding up every pice they can get; and if asked the reason why, they answer that 'they may have something to sacrifice when they or their friends are ill'.[17] The picture painted by Jones was in sharp contrast to what some British traders and colonial officials had to say about the Khasis in the previous century, where they were all praise for the enterprising and hardy nature of the Khasis. The Khasi people were regarded as simple and upright; an open-hearted, cheerful, loyal and honest people, possessing qualities which raised them considerably above their Bengali neighbours in the scale of moral worth.[18] It can also be assumed here that the Khasis that Jones initially encountered were the poor people who came from the lower echelons of the social ladder. In fact, politically and socially the Khasis were divided into the ruling class which included *syiems, wahadadars, sirdars* and *lyngdohs;* the aristocrats, such as the *mantris, basins, dolois* and *lynqskors*; and the subjects or *raid.*[19] The subjects included the *plebian* class, soldiers, agriculturists, common villagers, bondsmen (sold in slavery), criminals attached to *syiems* and people who were made outcastes. But, all Khasis were definitely not poor. Sometimes photographs of the most primitive and sad looking Khasi people were sent to Wales by a Welsh missionary for the purpose of raising money from the members of the Welsh Presbyterian Church in order to elicit their sympathy and raise cash for the mission.[20] If the Khasis were not portrayed as people in distressful condition and in need, then donations would not pour in and the work of the mission would stop. It also deserves mention here that cleanliness of person was not unknown to the Khasis before the advent of the missionaries. Natural substances such as nub and *sohphirah* were used by the Khasis to clean their person, and ground charcoal and the skin of areca nut (*saep kwai*) were used for the cleaning of teeth.[21]

It was a common practice among the missionaries to identify a tribe with drunkenness, and the Khasis were no exception. When the Welsh missionaries first came to the Khasi Hills, they found that drunkenness was 'a common vice which prevailed to a large degree throughout the country … and every family in the possession of a moderate degree of prosperity, distills spirituous liquors at home, from rice and other grain.'[22] The Khasis did brew liquor at home and rice beer (*yat um*) was consumed in large quantities but it did the work of Vitamin B12 and contained some therapeutic and restorative qualities. Liquor was also needed for wine libation, which was an important part of Khasi religious ceremonies that consisted of scattering of wine on the ground from a gourd, by the priest with the expectation that the soil would become fertile. In marriage ceremonies, too, libations were poured from two gourds, all the time invoking the gods and the ancestors to witness and bless the couple. But it seemed that though the Khasis consumed large quantities of rice beer, the habit of drinking wine and spirituous liquors was formerly unknown. Liquor with a high alcoholic content was introduced into the Hills, according to Lish, by the European soldiers temporarily stationed at Cherra. The advice of Lish to his fellow European was: 'A nation (the Khasis) just emerging from barbarism may be naturally expected to follow the example, be they good or bad, set them in the character and conduct of their superiors.'[23] The Khasi newspaper *U Khasi Mynta*, reported in 1904 that consumption of liquor, which was brewed in the English way, was unknown to the Khasi and consumption of alcohol by women was not prevalent at all. But it was the British who introduced this intoxicating drink through one Padre at Sohra. The fact that Jones taught the Khasis the distillation of liquor corroborates the report of the newspaper.[24]

The Welsh missionaries challenged the traditional belief system amongst the Khasis that provided the Khasis with the guarantee of security and the totality of the 'cause' of their existence. Their traditional rituals and ceremonies were shown as having no direct link with God and even their sacred places such as the consecrated forests or Law Kyntang, sometimes near the sources of drinking water, were shown as not necessarily sacred and so disrespect to these elements were allowed. Like many other tribes, the Khasis maintained sacred groves—meant to be forest patches where multiple plant species were maintained for a diversity of uses, economic, medical and cultural, and where the community's collective interest and identity were vested. In order to prevent people from exploiting its resources, the forests were given religious sanctity and it was said that they were inhabited by spirits or demons (*Ki Ksuid ki Khrei*). This was wrongly interpreted by the Welsh missionaries as strong prejudices of the Khasis, and with total disregard to their feelings John Roberts, a Welsh missionary, secured a land in a high hill covered with jungle, supposedly inhabited by village demons.[25] By building a bungalow there, the sanctity of the forest was questioned and its resources made vulnerable to exploitation by men. The point to be emphasized here is that the social backgrounds of the missionaries were different. Even though most of the Welsh missionaries came from very poor coalminers and farmers' backgrounds, the knowledge of science made many of them look down on tribal beliefs with scepticism. It did not strike them that the sacred forests of the Khasis instead of being objects of ridicule were an important and healthy means of environmental protection and preservation of the eco system.

The missionaries, however, could not make any headway when they goaded the converts to reject their matrilineal system—the *khein kur khein kha*—as it did not comply with Christian doctrine, belief and teaching. The Khasi converts immediately retorted—'If you interfere with our social system—the *khein kur khein kha*—we would rather leave the Church.'[26] Clan exogamy, an injunction from God according to Khasi belief, was also strictly maintained as any attempt on the part of the missionaries to encourage intra-clan marriages, which is considered as a sang or taboo by the Khasis, affected the process of conversion adversely.

Salvation through the Ultimate Saviour

The first task that lay before Jones was to open schools in the Khasi villages, the purpose of which was, 'to teach the Khasis—children and adults—to read their own languages; and to instruct them in the principles of the Christian religion; … to train native teachers; and to make use of the natives to teach their fellow-countrymen to read …'[27] that would mark important steps towards evangelization.

1842 was an important landmark in the Mission's history as not only was the 'First Khasi reader' prepared by Jones and the 'Mother's Gift', both of which were printed, but three schools were opened, the first in Mawsmai, the second in neighbouring Mawmluh and a third at Cherra. Mr. Jones resolved to adopt Roman characters amidst much opposition from home and abroad. The dialect adopted was the Cherrapunjee dialect, learned by the missionaries resident there. The argument put forward by the missionaries was that the Khasis found it difficult to read Khasi in the Bengali script, which was preposterous as the Khasis were at that time more familiar with the plains of Bengal and had considerable interaction with the Bengalis through trade relations. A few of the chiefs, founding clans and businessmen in Cherrapunjee and the 'war' areas were able to use and even write the language to some extent.[28] Obviously, the main reason as to why the Welsh missionaries adopted the Roman characters was because that was the easiest course for them to take, in so far as it was in which their own languages were written.[29]

The first decade of missionary work gave little evidence of progress. The missionaries found it difficult to convince the people of Sohra (*Cherra*), who were economically sound, very cultured, strong-minded and much exposed to the outside world through their contacts with the progressive peoples of the plains of Bengal, that the imported religion of the West was far superior to the Khasi religion. Minimal early response to Christianity was also due to the strict rules laid down by the missionaries, which were to disclaim all traditional religious practices and rituals, to observe *Sabbath* on Sundays, to have knowledge of the fundamental principles of Christianity and to lead a life in a manner befitting the Gospel. Some Khasi children were sent to missionary schools by their parents to learn how to read and write, which was important to them as traders. But the parents vehemently protested and stopped their wards from attending schools because of one lesson in the Khasi Primer which says '*u kpa uba pop* (father is a sinner), *ka kmie kaba pop* (mother is a sinner) and *baroh ngi pop* (all are sinners)'.[30] They felt it was not relevant as they were taught to know God the Creator, to pray and offer thanks to Him every morning and every night for His protection and guidance in their everyday life and respect others and all creations.[31]

According to the missionaries it was not an easy task to teach the Khasis, as they were 'wild and uncultivated as the Hills on which they lived'. They would sit quietly for some hours each day to read write and count but often would madly rush out of the schoolroom only to return a few days later and promise never to run away. What the missionaries failed to note was that the content of the syllabus must have appeared rather unfamiliar, difficult and unexciting for the Khasis as there were only two secular books, two catechisms, 32 Christian Hymns, translation of the Gospel, the Acts of the Apostles and Hall's *Come to Jesus*. It was alleged that though most of the boys made excellent progress in reading and writing, the mysteries of arithmetic completely baffled them and was attributed to the influence of demons and the evil spirits who were unwilling them to learn arithmetic. The problem was in regard to the girls. The counsel of the village 'divine' or 'egg breaker' in the matter of female education was that any female who touched a book would become childless and, thus the clan would become extinct. However, due to the persistent efforts of the missionaries some Khasi girls were taught sewing, knitting; and also reading without being conscious of actually picking up these skills!

The missionaries made the economically weak their targets for conversion. Inducements to the students like a reward of 6 pence was given to every Khasi child who mastered the first two pages of the Khasi Reader and a bright coloured garment if they mastered the whole book that contained eight pages.[32] This encouraged an increasing number of children of various degrees of cleanliness and clothing to gather around the missionaries. Jones assisted them with proper clothing and scholarships. The people of Wales donated many of these gifts and articles of clothing. The Welsh missionaries Mr and Mrs Lewis undertook to support some of the poor promising pupils, boys and girls, by allowing them to live with them in the Mission compound. Upon learning of their intention, Lieutenant Lewin, an officer at Cherrapunjee, generously offered to support twelve of the boys and contributed for many years until his removal from the Hills. Thus, the early converts were those who served the missionaries and lived in and around their compound.

The hard work of the missionaries bore fruit when in 1846 two Khasis—U Amos and U Rujon—converted to Christianity; in 1848 there were thirteen converts, six of them females; in 1850 the first Khasi marriage was solemnized; in 1852 the first Khasi child was baptized; and in 1854 the Khasis were given to use Mr Lewis's expression, 'couple of living advertisements of the temporal advantages of education', in the appointment of two pupils from Nongswalia (near Cherra) as clerks in the East India Company—the first among Khasis to receive such appointments; and also further in the appointment of U Jarkha as postmaster at Cherra.[33] In the subsequent years a large number of men reared in mission schools and churches began to occupy important government posts such as Babu Mohon Roy who was appointed Stipendiary Magistrate—a post which was occupied after his death by another Khasi Christian, Babu Dohory.

In 1854, Lord Dalhousie, the Governor-General's Council, recommended a monthly grant to the Welsh Mission of Rs. 50 and it is of note that this was the first grant made by the Government of India towards education through the agency of religious organizations. By the close of 1857 the mission schools numbered sixteen with 240 pupils. B.C. Allen gave a favourable report of the mission's work in educating and 'civilizing' the Khasis. He attributed the phenomenal increase in conversions (which trebled in 1881) as a result of schools which were in the hands of missionaries, where children came early under the influence of Christian thought and principles.[34] Allen also laid stress on the effect of the introduction of the Medical Mission. In 1861 the grant was increased to Rs. 150 and by the end of 1866 to Rs. 500 monthly. Around 1865, it is estimated that with the exception of Nongkrem Syiemship, all other Syiemships in Khasi Hills had at least one school in their territory.[35] Besides assuming the financial burden of education, the government gave 'incentive' to vernacular language by introducing the practice of admitting petitions and documents in the courts and public offices of the district in Khasi.[36] It was around this time that a school was opened in Nongsawalia where 150 boys were drawn from twenty-five villages, the greatest numbers of whom were to be trained as teachers. The first six months of the year were spent in school, for the remaining six months the pupils were sent to teach in their villages. In this way the work spread in all directions. The opening of a number of schools in the Khasi Hills by the Welsh missionaries earned the praise of A.J.M. Mills, officiating judge at the Sudder Court (Calcutta), on a visit to the Khasi Hills which he felt was dispelling the 'darkness and superstition of the people', and also referred to the Khasis as being without invidious distinction of caste and without religion.[37] It deserves mention here that at this stage the Khasi indigenous religion was without organization; also there was no established church and no hierarchical central structure as in European religious movements. Defined differently as 'a rather vague cult of the spirits supposed to live in trees, mountain peaks etc.' (*Meerworth*); 'demon worship or a jumble of enchantments muttered by priests who are sorcerers' (*Bivar*); 'animism or spirit worship, or rather, the propitiation of spirits both good and bad, on certain occasions, principally in times of trouble' (Gurdon);[38] the Khasi religion and its meaning eluded Western scholars.

The 1860s and 1870s witnessed the further spread of schools and churches penetrating the Nongkrem Syiemship considered to be the most difficult of all Khasi kingdoms to accept Christianity and other places in the Bhoi area. The period is particularly significant in that Christianity touched the royal families or clans.[39] A political explanation appears readily at hand. After the Queen's Proclamation in 1858, W.J. Allen made a report in 1859 where it was decided that each of the Khasi chiefs had to execute a general agreement on their succession with the district deputy commissioner who was also to function as government's political officer in relation to the Khasi states. Periodic changes in the terms of the agreements taken from the chiefs were made between 1864 and 1875 when it was decided that appointments of chiefs should rest with the Governor-General in the case of the larger Khasi states and the Chief Commissioner in the case of the smaller states. In November 1875, the system of agreements was replaced by the granting of *sanads* to the newly recognized chiefs. The operation of paramountcy meant that the Khasi chiefs had to be loyal to the British crown and the recognition of any person as the chief of the state was within the exclusive discretion of the paramount power. There were many Khasi villages brought under direct British rule. Often the paramount power took advantage of the dissensions and inter-village disputes within a Khasi state to allow villages to secede from states and become British villages.[40] Probably with many of their subjects becoming Christians, the *syiems* felt that the only way they could still retain their authority over them was to become Christians. Moreover with the advent of British administration, a political vacuum was created as Khasi political structures started to crumble. The importance of the village *durbars*, Raid councils and the state *durbars* were undermined and ceased to be as powerful as before. This void was filled with the establishment of the ecclesiastical structure of the Presbyterian Church. The first Presbytery was formed in 1862. With the setting up of the executive committee, similar to the village *durbar*, the pastorate or district level committee comparable to the Khasi Raid council and the Presbytery synonymous with the state *durbar*, the Khasis belonging to different clans, hailing from different places and possessing different dialects were brought together. Thus, the church administration was organized among the Khasis taking into consideration the democratic principles inherent. Many of the *syiems* who converted were made deacons of the Church. There were more rewards. Morris mentions that when the *durbar* was held in Delhi, on the occasion of the Proclamation of His Majesty King Edward VII, as Emperor of India, the King of Khadsawphra, the faithful deacon U Kinesing, was invited and honoured with the title of Rajah.[41] However, there were exceptional cases. One *syiem* just would not convert much to the disgust of the missionaries and in another instance Bor Sing was ready to give up his kingdom for a place in the kingdom of God.

1867 was an eventful year as the Welsh missionaries in Cherra set up two printing presses (much to the incredulity of the Khasis) and an important step was taken with regard to the appointment of Khasi teachers to spread the message of the Gospel. The first Evangelists Examination was held in 1869, and finally six were approved and became the first 'licensed preachers' of the Khasi Hills. As Morris writes in his book it was only after competent teachers from among the Khasis were obtained that the beginning of the great progress of the Mission can be dated.[42] This was in 1870. It is interesting to note that in spite of their condemnation of Khasi rituals and culture, the missionaries were extraordinarily accommodating towards Khasi doctrine and cosmology in which they and their Khasi converts systematically sought points of entry for Christian terms and ideas. Being well acquainted with Khasi customs and cosmology, the native preachers employed their Christian knowledge with wonderful skill. The Khasi preachers and evangelists went about their work by first speaking of the Khasi religion, then drew a comparison with Christianity, and later came to conclusions in favour of Christianity.[43] The God of the Christians, whose name could be expressed, assumed greater significance than the God of the Khasis, whose name was not known.

The Khasi evangelists worked hard to assimilate Christian ideas, names and terms into the Khasi's religious universe such as Khasi beliefs in monotheism, concept of devil, heaven and hell, covenant between God and man, concept of sin and the mediator. Originally the Khasi religion was monotheistic—one God and that is, Blei Nongbuh, Blei Nongthaw (God the Creator and God the Maker), but later became polytheistic. With the advent of the Welsh church and the evangelization carried out by the native preachers the Khasis were given to understand that they should identify with one God. As a result, the animistic rites that they had earlier followed, such as the worship of mountain and river spirits, divination and glorification of ancestors were discarded as they involved elaborate rituals and huge expenses.[44]

The Khasis strongly believe that they are the chosen people of God. At the beginning, they were the children of God as members of the sixteen families—Khadhynriew Trep, Khadhynriew Skum—the sixteen huts and the sixteen roots. In accordance with the decision of the divine council (*dorbar blei*) in heaven called by God, U Blei, seven families were sent down to earth to rule over it. The nine families that stayed behind were known as 'Ki Kyndai Ha Jrong' or the nine above. It was arranged that the seven families would have access to heaven through a golden ladder (in some versions it is referred to as a giant tree, *Diengiei*). God made a covenant with the seven families called '*Ka Jutang*' promising to communicate with them so long as they lived a good life.

But it so happened that at the behest of the demon, the two brothers, Sormoh and Sorphin, tore down the ladder or cut down the tree. *Ka Mei-Ram-Ew* (mother earth) died of sorrow due to man's sin. Her children, the sun and the moon, ceased to shine and, thereby, the whole world was plunged into complete darkness. Man was in great trouble so he prayed to God to forgive his sins. The all-merciful and forgiving God summoned a divine council to find someone who was pure, had not committed any sin and who could act as a mediator for Man. The choice fell on the poor and ugly cock.

To the Khasi the sacrifice of the cock was made only because of the covenant between man and God. As sacrifices became superfluous with the discovery of modern medicines, the Khasis turned to Christianity as an alternative means to re-establish their relationship with God. The acceptance of Christianity would, thus redeem the Khasis from their sins and rescue them from the fate of Hell. A small incident illustrates this point. In 1845, three Khasis approached Mr Lewis for baptism. When asked if the Saviour would receive such as they, the three men answered, 'O, yes, He will; why shouldn't He? Did He not come into the world to die for sinners such as we?' In 1896 in Wales, John Roberts, the Welsh missionary gave a lecture followed by thunderous applause when he mentioned that by asking Khasi children to repeat the line, 'I am a sinner, you are a sinner and we are sinners,' he was able to convince the Khasi children to embrace Christianity in order to be freed of sins.[45]

The main purpose of the mission schools was to preach and in this way each school had become a Sunday school. A reference may be made here to the Calvinist doctrine that became an essential part of the Presbyterian Church. An important facet of Calvinist doctrine is predestination, which implies that everything a person does is predetermined and there is nothing the individual can do about it. Such an idea was naturally the cause of great anxiety among the Khasis for whom the tortures of Hell were an accepted reality and the only way out was to be among the pre-ordained few whom God had chosen to save. By embracing the Church, it was hoped by the Khasis that divine grace might descend on them. A few lines may be quoted here to give an idea of how the Khasi evangelist, U Sohonrai went about his work of preaching by giving a sermon:

> 'For this purpose the Son of God was manifested that he might destroy the works of the Devil.'
>
> 'Son of God … Jehovah of the Old Testament, and the angel of the covenant appeared in our nature and bore our trangressions. He conquered sin. He appeared and now appears before the Father for us. . . . He continues to appear to us through His Spirit in our hearts. . . . If the Son of God has appeared in your hearts, the works of the devil will certainly be destroyed.'[46]

In short, one can see here a fusion of literacy and religion. Literate Khasi men who were made teachers and evangelists in schools started by the Welsh missionaries would explain to the Khasi villagers the tenets of Christianity and how U Blei was the high God in both Christianity and the Khasi religion. Thus, U Blei was not an alien God imposed upon the Khasis from outside, but their own generic term made universal by the Bible's message, and made possible by print technology. Jesus Christ was indeed the ultimate Saviour.

Added to the work of education was the commendable work done by the missionaries in the medical field. In the 1870s, reports describing the desperate plight of the Khasi people who suffered frequent plagues of cholera, malaria, tuberculosis, etc., resulted in the conviction of the Welsh Missionary Society in Wales that the setting up of a Medical Mission in the Khasi Hills was justified, not only on humanitarian grounds, but also to attract the Khasi people to convert to Christianity.[47] In 1879 when a terrible cholera epidemic broke out, Jerman Jones remained in Shillong, day and night, visiting the deserted villages, succouring the forsaken sufferers, rescuing babies and little children from the arms of dying mothers, caring for the sick, giving them medicines and food, and burying the dead with his own hands.[48] When again in 1892, cholera broke out, this time in Cherra, Dr Griffiths took care of the sick. By destroying the ailments of the Khasis, the missionaries were able, 'to get at them' and in an effective way, to undermine their belief in their old religion. The use of chloroform by Dr Griffiths (1878-1906) at first alarmed the villagers but having come to realize that it did not harm them, they began to shun the ministrations of the *augerers* (egg breakers) and flocked to be treated by Dr Griffiths.[49] The latter in his report of 1887 mentioned that the Khasi 'heathens' who visited his dispensary not only found bodily relief, but an effort was made to bring to their 'guilty and corrupt souls' the 'unfailing remedy to be found in the blood of Jesus Christ'.[50] Several were, by these means, drawn nearer to Christianity, and some had also been received into various churches in consequences of their visits to the dispensary run by Dr. Griffiths.

The role of the Medical Mission as a valuable adjunct to the evangelistic work was further corroborated by the report of Dr Hughes, another missionary who reported from Mawphlang district, that the patients who came from distant villages to his dispensary heard the name of Jesus for the first time from the lips of the medical missionary, and carried the gospel seed to their heathen homes.[51] A Khasi evangelist, U Ksan-bin, wrote from Cherrapoonjee that for many Khasis, medicine was synonymous with the Christian religion, and when they saw that the Christians were healthier than them, they began to consider Christianity a little.[52] In fact, in Dr Griffiths' opinion, many Khasis would not have heard or rather would not hear the gospel had they not been brought into contact with the Medical Mission. In this respect the Khasi evangelist, U Kypa Ka Loi, played a very important role. He would not only preach to those at the dispensary, but sought the opportunity of speaking to each one personally. Afterwards he would visit the homes of the more promising ones. In this way many were received into the Church with whom Kypa took a lot of trouble. Religious meetings were held at the dispensaries and many who regularly attended them joined the churches later on. Dr Griffiths admitted this part of the missionary's work was blessed as one means of bringing many souls to the Saviour.

According to a Khasi evangelist U Juramon's report, once the Khasis realized that medicine, which they earlier considered as poison and something to enrage the demons, possessed greater healing power than their egg-breaking and other sacrifices, they began to believe and seek the medicines of the missionaries.[53] In this way their faith in the demons rapidly departed. Another interesting fact that induced many Khasis to come for medicine and put their trust in the missionary was the number of deaths among the heathens from various diseases was far greater than those in the Christian villages. They began to see clearly that their gods were not able to save them from sickness and death. These influenced their minds to such a degree that hundreds of them came to hear the gospel preached and to learn and read the word of God.[54] In this way medical care began to play a more important role in conversion than did the message of the gospel. Wherever medical work was carried out, the seed of the gospel was sown in villages where it was not known before. This led Dr Griffiths to comment that the Khasi religion would never be strong again in those villages as many of them were thinking of having teachers and schools and scores of people were already learning to read the Bible even before they had regular teachers. This, Dr Griffiths, saw the beginning of what promised to be a great harvest.

Mr Evans, another missionary, saw malarial fever, which had been raging in his district, Mawphlang for two years, as a dark cloud with a silver lining[55] as it would prevail upon the Khasis the worthlessness of their religion which could not cure malaria and thus, demonstrate the value of Christianity and Christ as the saviour. As Khasi beliefs vis-à-vis health and healing became ineffective in the face of diseases, the traditional healers became discredited in the eyes of the people who naturally turned to the missionaries, abandoning their older beliefs in the malign supernatural causation of illness and embracing the new Western medicine wholeheartedly. It was not surprising that the number of converts increased to 500 in 1871 and to 6,941 in 1891. However, there were exceptional cases where, in spite of medical care rendered, the patient proved to be very stubborn when the question of conversion to Christianity came up. Such was the case of an old sacrificer who was usually called upon to sacrifice for the children of the King of Cherra. He thought he would die though he had only a case of mumps! Though he expressed his gratefulness, he was determined not to have anything to do with Christianity. In fact, many Khasis articulated the view that even if their religion was false and the Christian religion the best, it was difficult for them to cast off at once the practices of their mothers and fathers for generations. It also required great courage on their part to break off from old associations and customs and begin the life of a professing Christian.[56]

Apart from the stated factors, it would seem that the early success of the Welsh mission had been much assisted by the empathy that these former, mainly rural, peasant Welshmen were able to display towards the peasant Khasi.[57] The missionaries understood the trials of those forced by circumstance to scratch a meagre living from the land, weather and circumstance beyond their control, threatening the ever-present menace of disease and famine.[58] Thomas Jones, the first missionary, used his native agricultural knowledge to enhance Khasi well-being by the introduction of the saw, which seemed to the untutored Khasis a miraculous happening and to conclude that the material advantages of the Western world were inseparable from its religious beliefs. He also strongly opposed the naked and cruel exploitation of the Khasi people by Henry Inglis, Assistant of Captain Lister (political agent in the Khasi Hills 1835-54) and also a trader, proprietor of the Inglis and Company who carried out lime trade in the Khasi Hills. Not all Welsh missionaries could be said to be racists or imperialists or ethnocentric. Neither did they act superior and arrogant. Many of them regarded the Khasis with much regard and affection. If that was not the case Dr Griffiths would not have allowed his baby son to be baptized by the native evangelist, Reverend Amirkha Chyne at Sohra in 1897, an event recorded in the Griffith's family Bible.[59] The Welsh missionaries were all praise for the ability, knowledge and degree of faithfulness of the native preachers who they felt could worthily adorn the office of any church in Wales. Talented Khasi preacher U Ramjan was quick to grasp the difference between the Welsh missionaries who came to Khasi Hills, 'with their love of men . . . who do not hate us in our filthiness of body and apparel' and the *sahebs* who had come to serve the government 'who are not missionaries and do not allow us to approach'.[60] From this he concluded that the Spirit of God had entered the missionaries.

In the midst of such tranquillity and steady progress, there struck a massive catastrophe, this time a natural calamity. On 12 June 1897, Shillong and the nearby regions suffered a terrible earthquake. It is to this earthquake I turn now in order to understand how the Orientalist attitude as represented by the Welsh missionaries of regarding the 'other' as inferior beings, heathens and pagans not following the true religion, Christianity, roped in more Khasi converts to the Presbyterian Church. The earthquake provided the Welsh missionaries a golden opportunity to make use of the circumstances, 'in the furtherance of the work of our Lord'. In the words of Morris the earthquake and its impact has been described briefly as follows:

> The first shock occurred shortly after five o'clock on Saturday afternoon, June 12th. In a few seconds every building in Sylhet, Khasia and Jaintia, was levelled to the ground; the Government offices, mission premises, including the mission houses (sixteen in number), the two hospitals (Cherra and Jowai); thirty chapels; the Theological Institution, and a large number of schools, many of which, in the principal villages, were handsome and substantial buildings; the fruit of the sacrifices of the home and the native churches for over half of a century swept away at a single stroke! Whole villages were likewise completely destroyed, large portions being buried, with their inhabitants, under the terrible landslips following the upheaval. All the missionaries were providentially saved, but the number of deaths among the native population was appalling. The disaster occurring at the height of the rainy season, the sufferings of the homeless missionaries and natives were painfully intensified. Added to this, fevers and epidemics following the shock and exposure, made fearful ravages among the terror-stricken people.[61]

Morris has further things to say about the results of the earthquake. In his words:

> The splendid conduct of the native Christians throughout this time of great suffering afforded further indubitable proof of the depth and reality of their convictions, and impressed visibly their heathen neighbours, hundreds of whom soon sought admission into the Churches. The returns for the year show that as many as 2,373 were received on probation, while the number

of adherents showed a clear increase of 2,101. Thus wonderfully did an all-wise Providence over-rule the Mission's great adversity for good![62]

A destructive earthquake of such a massive intensity was something that the Khasis had not experienced for a long time. Epidemics swept away a lot of the people and disrupted trade. Many Khasis were reduced to penury. One of the consequences of this traumatic experience, and the help that was extended to the victims by Christians, was that large numbers of victims became Christians.

It deserves mention here that the Welsh missionary, Reverend Robert Evans saw in it, 'God's purpose through famine, pestilence, storms and earthquake the liberation of the inhabitants of India from the enslavement of paganism and idol worship to the glorious freedom of God's children, as, through the plagues in Egypt.'[63] Evans was of the opinion that there were many people in Khasia who had heard the gospel and accepted its truth, but without obeying its demands and many who had got close in some ways but nothing they had heard had made them forsake their old faith and their sins and claim Christ as their saviour.[64] Therefore, he felt that a big event was needed to force them to realize the presence and sanctity of God. According to him, 'the earthquake was literally a kind of pentecost in that it converted sinners and became a huge pouring forth of the Holy Spirit upon the country's Christians'.[65]As for the non-Christian Khasis whom he describes as pagans, the earthquake forced thousands of them to pray in the name of Jesus Christ to save them, for if He would save them, they would not again sin against Him. For others, the devastating earthquake pushed them forth in the quest for a real God, whom they found in Jesus as a God who loves and suffers for others, who died on the cross, rose from the dead, and ascended into heaven and was to come again.[66] To the Christian Khasis, the earthquake acted as a means of strengthening their faith in God and affirming it in a marvellous way in the truths of the gospel, so much so that it was a disappointment for many of them that the Son of Man did not appear in the firmament, as they had been led to expect.[67]

It is clearly evident that the Welsh missionaries propagated the message that in the earthquake lay God's great purpose, which was the perfection of His people and the salvation of souls. What took place was not only a psychological conversion where many Khasis started to deeply appreciate the doctrines or teachings of Christianity, but also a spiritual conversion where many of the Khasis underwent a mental anguish, due to the earthquake, resulting from conviction of sin and then came to accept Jesus Christ as their saviour and master. This became more pronounced as nothing happened to the missionaries indicating that God would not abandon His own in times of crisis, but give them strength and even greater faith.

It is interesting to note that many fallen Christians or backsliders came from the class known as earthquake victims—people who sought refuge amongst the Christians. The calamity, according to Reverend Jones, had succeeded in drawing many a backslider to Christ, weeping and trembling, to seek a place in God's house and also more readiness among the heathen to hold intercourse with the Christians, and a stronger desire to hear more of the religion that gave great peace in the midst of such fearful circumstances. Not all of them, however, stuck to the Church once the excitement had passed. The earthquake victims were helped by the missionaries, who distributed valuables and useful things as well as different articles of clothing among them that had arrived from kind friends at Cardigan, Aberystwyth, Cardiff and Whit-Church.[68] G.A. Jones pointed out that around 2,373 people became Christians in 1897 itself.[69] But the picture was not the same everywhere. In the case of Cherra, the people continued to be very hard and inflexible, in spite of the fact that the earthquake had destroyed the Khasi religion in a sense, according to the Report of Reverend John Jones, 1898, by destroying the most sacred things they possessed, the *maw-shing* (cromlechs), or stone chests, in which the ashes of different families were kept after being burnt.[70] In this context it may be mentioned that it was normal practice among the Khasis to carry the dead person's bones after the cremation to the receptacle or ossuary (*mawkynroh*) where the calcinated bones of the family were deposited, to the accompaniment of a number of rituals. Some time later when the dead person's relatives could afford to perform other ceremonies, the bones were taken out from the *mawkynroh* and carried to the clan ossuary (*mawniam, mawbah*). Stone monuments were raised to commemorate the dead, the standing stone or menhirs were called *maw-shynrang* meaning male stone, and the flat stones in front of them were known as *maw-kyntiew* or female stone. All these activities involved active participation of the clan members.

Responses and Reactions

The conversion process among the Khasis was not without its share of trials and tribulations. Though the missionaries were left untouched, many of the early Khasi converts had to suffer much persecution. Had it not been for the intervention of the colonial state, the work of evangelization would have been halted. Some instances may be cited. When Ka Nabon, a Khasi girl, converted she was confined in her mother's house at Mawmluh and Mrs Lewis, the Welsh missionary, had to seek the help of Colonel Lister for her release.[71] In another instance in the village of Nonjiri, a Khasi Christian woman suffered much persecution, as she would not join the heathen ceremonies after the death of her mother. When the matter was explained to Major Peet, the Deputy Commissioner, the latter decreed that all her inheritance should be restored to her. Again, a *syiem,* who had bound and beaten a Christian Khasi girl, was ordered by the Deputy Commissioner to refund the fines that he had inflicted upon her.

Often the death of a Khasi Christian led to scenes of wild excitement and violence as the missionaries insisted on burial that was against the Khasi custom of cremation. Burial of the dead happened to be against Khasi religion and belief, as it was commonly believed that by burial the spirits of the deceased would not find a resting place among their ancestors, who freed from earthly bondage were elevated to a supernatural status capable of aiding mortals in times of crisis. The Khasis did not mourn the dead with outward signs and bid goodbye to the departed souls with the words *kublei khie leit bam kwai sha iing u blei ho* (Goodbye, go and chew betel nut in the house of God).[72] On more than one occasion large and excited crowds rushed to the burial ground, armed with sticks and weapons, but although they frequently threatened violence to the missionary, their hands were miraculously restrained,[73] perhaps by the presence of the British forces.

The remarkable progress of the mission work was threatened by frequent backsliding on the part of the Khasi converts, some of whom had been Christians for many years. The reasons given for backsliding were strange. One man gave his reason that while in the Church he did not feel himself free to use his tongue as formerly when he happened to have a quarrel or disagreement with anyone.[74] Many felt the strict principles of the Presbyterian Church put them in a prison and they were hindered from leading a life of sport, fun and freedom like their non-Christian brethren. Others attributed their deviation from the Christian path to the evil influence of Satan.

Since the missionaries had full monopoly in the spread of education, the Khasis attending their schools were subtly influenced to look down upon their own culture and gradually lured to embrace the Christian religion. Promising young students were roped into the Christian fold by means of free scholarship, free studentship, by providing hostels and government jobs, etc. Recommendation from a missionary was a must to get into any government job.[75]

Gradually, the years witnessed how some of the pupils in the missionary schools toed the missionary's repugnance for the religion and beliefs of the Khasis, as by now Evangelical notions that equated Indian culture with depravity had gained widespread currency. The Welsh missionaries looked down on Khasi marriage customs that they described as simple and of primitive character, as well as the naming of their children that they felt was done in consultation with the demons.[76] It was not surprising, therefore, when two Khasis—U Mohsin and U Sor—on being baptized took Christian names, U Solomon and U Stephen, respectively, and set the trend for converts to adopt Biblical names such as Ka Hannah, Ka Rachael, Ka Rebecca, U Moses, and U Josiah. Some of the pupils also refused to take part in the performance of Khasi rites in tribal sacrifices that were a communal affair and in which it was imperative that all the members of the clan should join or the observance would be void. The missionaries interpreted these actions as a desire of the new converts to severe themselves entirely from their former heathen associations.

The native Evangelists in no way lagged behind in their denigration of Khasi religion and culture. Under colonialism, colonized people are made subservient to ways of regarding the world that reflect and support colonialist views. U Juramon, the most popular and powerful of the native preachers in the Khasi Hills, famous for his sermon in the Cherra Presbytery 1880, on the Resurrection of the Dead which lasted for more than one and a half hours, toed the missionary's point of view as far as the sacred groves of the Khasis were concerned. In one of his reports he wrote that Christianity had made much progress and the people were much wiser and more enlightened than before as faith in the demons and fear of them had subsided. He further wrote that several of the groves and the places, which were considered sacred because the demons and the gods were thought to dwell in them, had been turned into arable land.[77] U Juramon did not realize that this act had led to the failure of crops in the following summer. As a consequence the people had to resort to consuming herbs and leaves. In another instance U Ramjan, one of the oldest Christians in Khasia and one of the most talented preachers wrote:

> I thank our Heavenly Father, that He has plucked me out of the miry clay and the mouth of Hell, that He has called me from the darkness and the power of the demons to the hope which is in the Gospel of the Son of God. I thank Him also that by His mercy He has moved your minds in Wales to send out the light of the Gospel to us, the Khasis ... people without God, and who had given themselves entirely to the demons; people without knowledge and understanding, almost like the brutes that perish.[78]

Not far behind was U Larsing, a devoted young evangelist, who stated in a letter to the directors that if he could fly as a bird he would go to Britain and kiss the boots of each of them, as he felt so grateful to them for sending the gospel to the Khasi Hills.[79] His desire was fulfilled. Probably he was the first Khasi to visit Britain where in Wales he moved to tears of joy thousands who heard him sing hymns in Khasi, on Welsh tunes. The climate of Wales did not suit U Larsing and he died prematurely on 24 August 1863. At his burial a paper was read out which narrated how the Welsh missionaries, Mr and Mrs Lewis found him an orphan amongst a people debased to the utmost by heathenism.[80]

Once converted, a taboo was imposed on the Khasis forbidding them to witness and take part in Khasi dances, to touch or play Khasi indigenous musical instruments, to take part in the death ceremony and the naming ceremony and even to touch or play with bows and arrows or to witness the village archery games held once a week. Christians, upon conversion, sold even their dance costumes and jewellery, thus dissociating themselves with the early dances.[81] The game of archery was condemned as the degrading and demoralizing sport of the heathens and the Khasi song and dance that accompanied the winning side in the game as the yelling and howling of dogs.[82] It may be mentioned here that the Khasis renowned for their accurate marksmanship, like many other peoples who came into contact with Hinduism, took pleasure in linking their history with the legends of the *Mahabharata* and claimed that they had acquired their skill in archery from the hero Arjuna himself, who is said not only to have taught the Khasis how to use the bow and arrow, but also taken a wife from among them.[83]

The Welsh Presbyterian Mission also prevented the Khasi converts from staging dramas, something which was close to the hearts of the Khasis, frowning upon it as a insidious medium. From time to time through their journal *U Lurshai* (The Shinning Star), they would instruct their flock to be on their guard against the pernicious influence of pleasurable scenes.[84] Gradually, the Christian taboo that differentiated Christians, known as *skul,* from non-Christian Khasis, classed as *shnong*, radically uprooted the converts from their legitimate cultural heritage.[85] It is seen that the missions set norms to control the behaviour of their members both within and outside the religious sphere. The converts were cut off from any activity that savoured of heathenism or primitivism and forbidden to partake in any ritual and ceremony. In these ways Christian converts were stirred away from their traditional moorings. Their cultural heritage was fast becoming a thing of the past. The erection of megaliths to commemorate the dead had almost disappeared by the end of the nineteenth century.

The report of 1891 that marked fifty years of service of the Welsh Mission in the Khasi Hills summed up the impact of the spread of the gospel as having gradually raised the whole (Khasi) population in morality and civilization from a deplorable state, where in the absence of the gospel, the latter had been 'savages and in a state of degradation and misery'.[86] Thus, it is seen that Christian missions, as they functioned in the colonial context, were destructive of the culture and social cohesion of tribal life and so contributed to a profound demoralization.[87] In the final analysis, the missionary discourse provided a confirmation of what the Orientalist representations had always advocated—the inferiority and backwardness of the Orient.

The Khasi converts began to mimic the culture, behaviour, manners and values of the missionaries. A particular value system was taught to them as the best with the truest world-view. Not surprisingly, the Khasi converts began to regard Christianity and Christian ways as the best. They even voiced their feelings about the superiority of Christianity and its value system by saying that the man who followed Christ became sober and honest and truthful and this religion was the hope of the country (*Syiem* of Mawnai's words),[88] and looked down with total contempt the Khasi religion as being superstitious, ritualistic and centring around the belief in demons. Any opposition to conversion by one's clan members was looked upon as an act of foolishness.[89] Thus, some of these Khasis acted as ideal surrogates, fulfilling the ultimate desires of the missionaries by going the distance that even the missionaries would not go by giving up their customs and traditions. In this case mimicry was indicative of resemblance but a flawed mimesis in which to be a Christian was emphatically not to be a true Christian like the Welsh. The identity of a Khasi Christian was almost the same but not quite the same. Often the missionaries lamented that the converts were unable to free themselves from the influence of heathen preconceptions. Though having renounced entirely their former religion, it was frequently found, nevertheless, that their previous notions largely coloured their Christian beliefs.[90]

But this was just one side of the story. Some of these mimic men, Khasi converts, did not completely succumb to the power of the missionaries. Contrariwise, they went back to the folds of their traditional Khasi religion and challenged the representations that attempted to fix and define them. Some went to the extent of forming separate churches. The menace of mimicry did not lie in its concealment of some real identity behind its mask, but came from its double vision, which in disclosing the ambivalence of missionary discourse also disrupted its authority. In this respect the names of three Khasi men come to prominence—Radhon Singh Berry Kharwanlang, U Rabon Singh Kharsuka and U Hormurai Diengdoh. All three were Presbyterian Christians but reverted back to the Khasi religion. Kharwanlang later on joined the Unitarians.

In order to counteract the missionary propaganda about Khasi religion and also the fact that the missionaries had inculcated moral principles among the Khasis and taught them to be truthful and honest, Kharwanlang collected the oral traditions/moral code of the Khasis in the last hundred years passed by the Khasi Elders in his book *Ka Jingsneng Tymmen* (*The Teaching of Elders*) published in two parts at the Ri Khasi Press in 1902 and 1903. The book contains several rhymes on how the Khasis should live, work and conduct themselves honestly, honourably and decently at home and in society. One important theme was how, why, and when one should respect Man, revere Khasi ancestors and worship the Creator. Ancestor worship among the Khasis is based on the belief that the chief ancestors and progenitors of the house or clan should be appeased in order to get their blessings.[91] The book clearly indicates that the Khasi Elders stressed on the monotheistic aspect of Khasi religion and the importance of the clan and its interrelationship with the Khasi religion.

Kharsuka—wrote three books, *Ka Kitab Jingphawar* (1898), a vivid description of religious ceremonies and sacrifices, *Ka Jingiathuh Khan Puriskam* (1900), a collection of twenty long folk tales which preserves some elements of Khasi mythology and *Ka Kitab Niam Khun Ki Khas* (1911), which throws light on the Khasi religion where a special treatment was laid on Khasi rites and sacrifices, ordeals and divination, funeral ceremonies and other like elements. It is in the last book that Kharsuka makes an attempt to explain the reason behind Khasi divination ceremonies and also the Khasi belief in monotheism. At the beginning of time, Man lived face to face with God who daily descended down to teach *Ki Hynniew Trep* or the Seven Huts, the ancestors of the Khasis about cultivation, iron smelting and mode of living.[92] But God withdrew owing to Man's commitment of sin; yet God, since learning of the latter's persistent prayers, became merciful and promised to meet Man at the altar, where he would let his ways be known by the auguries to be revealed on the shells of the egg and the entrails of the cock after the latter agreed to be sacrificed, hence, *Ka Niam Khasi*, the divination system. Khasi religion was entirely monotheistic at first, but became polluted afterwards with the polytheistic trend-beliefs in other deities, appeasement rituals of both good and evil spirits, propiation of the ancestors and others.[93]

The man who contributed enormously to Khasi journalism was Hormurai Diengdoh who brought out the first monthly in 1895 called *U Khasi Mynta* (*The Khasi Today*) where, through his articles on Khasi traditions and religion, he pointed out the elements of Christianity, which did not suit the Khasi tradition.[94] Probably the reasons could be that Khasi tradition does not believe in Prophets, does not trace the origin of the Khasis to Adam and Eve but to the primeval ancestress, the first grandmother of the clan, *Ka Iawbei*, her husband, U Thawlang, and the first maternal uncle of the clan, U Suidnia, and is matrilineal where the children carry the title of the mother's clan. In fact, to marry within one's clan is a *sang* or taboo. It is believed that a baby is born into a clan through the will of God and the ancestress. Thus, it may be observed that for a freedom-loving race like the Khasis to whom liberty is like the air they breathe, Khasi religion at its best is not to have a place or altar of worship where they would congregate from time to time to worship one of God's prophets, but to lead a life of righteousness and purity through one's words, actions and deeds. Incidentally, when Swami Vivekananda visited Shillong in 1901, Diengdoh met him and expressed his unhappiness about the way the Welsh missionaries were condemning the followers of Khasi indigenous religion as animists and heathens. Swamiji laughingly retorted that the Absolute Soul was manifested in all creations of God and those who believed in this concept and worshipped mountains, trees and rivers were at the same time worshipping the Supreme Being.[95] In that sense the Khasis were animists. If someone believed in God he could not ignore His creations or Nature. As for heathens, Swamiji was quick to point out that those who were prejudiced towards other religions and regarded only themselves as true believers, called the rest heathens. The word heathen, therefore, was indicative of intolerance and narrow–mindedness.[96]

Some Khasi Presbyterians backslided from the Calvinist Methodist Church and formed their own churches. One was Hajom Kissor Singh who questioned the rigid and sectarian teachings of the Welsh Calvinist Mission and started a new liberal movement called *Ka Niam Wei Blei* (The Religion which worships One God).[97] Hajom Kissor Singh went to Calcutta along with a Brahmo friend where he became acquainted with the work of Raja Rammohun Roy and the Unitarian Church. Much against the wishes of the Welsh Presbyterian Church he established the Unitarian Church in 1887. It is interesting to know that Singh observed that the Welsh missionaries had done no more than replace the fear of demons with the fear of Hell.[98] Though entirely locally born, it received the aid and support of foreign Unitarian missionaries. B.C. Allen, the Superintendent of the Census Operations, opined that one Khasi Christian of his acquaintance became a Unitarian because the Christians had so many sins and were prevented from going to market on a Sunday.[99]

A new church by the name of Church of God came up in 1902 as a result of differences of opinion between the Presbyterian missionaries and some Khasi converts on matters of salvation, baptism and the practice of foot washing. U Donrai Diengdoh and his son Wolley Mohan Roy Laitphlang started this church movement and it was with the association of U Jobin Roy Khain that the latter established the church. This church believed that though human beings were sinners they could achieve salvation through God's grace and that baptism is antecedent to faith, therefore, they baptize only after a person asserts his faith in Christ.[100]

As for those sections of the Khasis who stuck to their traditional religion right from the beginning and vehemently opposed missionary propaganda with self-representations of the Khasis and the revivalism and revitalization of the Khasi religion, the name of Babu Jeebon Roy Jaid Mairom stands prominent. He was responsible for starting a cultural awakening among the Khasis through a literary movement and may be rightly regarded, as the apostle of Khasi Renaissance. He was the mentor, inspirer and guide of the Seng Khasi. The Seng

Khasi initially began as the Young Men's Association or Ka Seng Samla Samiti on 23 November 1899, the purpose of which was to develop the fellow Khasis in mind, body and spirit, irrespective of religious affiliations. It was started by sixteen young educated men some of who were partly *dkhars* (outsiders) hailing from Cherra.[101] (If the lists of the Cherra clans are examined, a large number bear the name of *dkhar* or its abbreviation '*khar*', the Khasi word applied to the inhabitants of the plains. The ancestresses of these tribes were plains women carried off, no doubt, in the raids made by the Khasis over the border into Assam and Sylhet.) Incidentally it was housed at the Brahmo Samaj Hall at Mawkhar. It may be mentioned here that the Brahmo Samaj had secured a foothold in Cherra in 1889 through the efforts of Nilmani Chakravarti who had worked tirelessly among the Khasis for their social, moral and economic uplift.[102] In fact, he had succeeded in making a few converts among the Khasis and many prominent Khasis of that time had close relations with him. Nilmani wrote two books in Khasi—one on the Principles of the Brahmo Dharma and the other on Brahmo *Upasana*. It may be suggested here that perhaps this revivalism among the Khasis was influenced by Brahmo tenets and ideas as well as Christianity. However, it is beyond the scope of this article to discuss this issue at length.

Whatever the external influences might have been in 1901, the Seng Samla came simply to be known as Seng Khasi (The Khasis Association) whose chief aims were to cultivate a sense of togetherness among the Khasis who retained the traditional socio-cultural and religious heritage, create consciousness of God as the sovereign Lord, Almighty Creator, the omnipotent and omniscient and in no way lacking from the Christian Godhead,[103] to bring about educational advancement among the Khasis, promote and foster traditional sports, art forms and all traditional socio-cultural or religious festivals and undertake welfare activities, like maintenance of cremation grounds, for the general advancement of the Khasis according to their tradition and religion.

It goes to the credit of this association for holding an archery competition at the Polo Grounds in 1905, a sport that had been condemned by the missionaries as, 'degrading and demoralizing sport of the heathens'.[104] In 1907, it turned its attention to the development of indigenous music and collected Khasi musical instruments, drums and *tangmuri* (a *sehnai* like flute) for the purpose. The Seng Khasi also focused on drama, which they felt was an easy medium to educate the by and large illiterate Khasis. In the early years, the dramas were based on either stories with morals from the Indian Classical Literatures, such as the staging of *Ka Savitri* in 1910, or on legends and historical episodes of the Khasi people. At a time when the name of Tirot Singh was shunned and rejected, and even just mentioning his name was banned, Seng Khasi staged a play on his life and his war against the British. In 1911, the Seng Khasi held *Shad Suk Mynseim* (thanksgiving dance) in spite of Christian opposition.[105] It adopted and published its constitution in 1913 and gave the Khasis of the traditional faith an organized religion for the first time in their history with regular prayer services in church-like assemblies and songbooks, like the Christians.

Thus, it is seen that the Khasi society was able to negotiate with itself, along with the shifts and changes that it went through, the outward manifestations of which were visible in these acts of resistance. Right from the start, the missionaries viewed the emergence of the Seng Khasi with suspicion and concern and a threat to their activities. Any Khasi Christian found to have attended the *Shad Suk Mynsem* dance or any function organized by the Seng Khasi were excommunicated from the Church.

In order to counteract missionary propaganda and defend Khasi religion and culture, Jeebon Roy founded the Ri Khasi Press in 1896 in competition to those presses owned by Europeans. This press was to publish in subsequent years an enormous amount of literature on Khasi religion and culture. Jeebon Roy consistently fought to check the detribalization of the Khasis by taking up the cause of higher education of the Khasis and by trying to wean them away from converting to Christianity. He continually exhorted the Khasis to keep the religion of their forefathers.

Apart from counteracting the teachings of the Welsh missionaries in various ways, efforts were made to provide an alternative system of education. In this, Rash Mohan Jaid Nongrum, the first chairman of the Seng Khasi, played an important role. It goes to his credit for establishing the Seng Khasi Morning School on 20 May 1920, at Mawkhar with the sole objective of providing free education to all the poor children in the area. The latter was concerned about the impact that lessons given in the schools run by the missionaries had on their students, as the lessons acted as agencies for spreading Christianity. Rash Mohan was of the opinion that the proselytizing literature written and compiled by the missionaries should not be included in the curriculum of the Seng Khasi School, while the Deputy Inspector of Schools insisted that its students should read such books as were taught in other schools.[106] The textbooks in the curriculum of other schools were printed by the missionaries and included books of their liking and choice, viz., History of Jesus, Abraham, Isaac, Jacob and so on and so forth. In a letter to Mahatma Gandhi, Rash Mohan sent a circular where he pointed out that the British government gave education grants to the Christian missionaries for spreading education among the Khasi people and also expressed his objections regarding the acceptance of those books written and compiled by the missionaries in the curriculum of the Seng Khasi School. It was because of his refusal to accept the latter that the Deputy Inspector did not recommend his school for a grant from the government on the plea that the curriculum was not followed by this school.[107] Gandhi in response wrote in his *Harijan* (March 1940): '… If what is stated is true it enforces the argument advanced by me that Christian Missionary effort has been favoured by the ruling power….[108]

It deserves mention here that on the recommendation of Gandhi the Bharatiya Adimjati Sevak Sangh extended a monthly grant of Rs. 5 to the school through its secretary, A.V. Thakkar, from Delhi for nearly ten years till 1949.[109]

Thus, it may be observed that the resistance to missionization came from the section of Khasis who hailed mostly from Cherra/Sohra. This proved to be quite contrary to Dr Griffith's wish that with the efforts of the Mission, especially education and medicine, the Cherra people would have been brought to such a state that they would soon lose all attachment to their old religion. In his words:

> I believe that we have only to wait for the disappearance of a very few of the oldest influential people here to see the disappearance also of the Khasi

religion from the village, and once the Khasis learn that Cherra does not cling to the religion of their forefathers there will be no more spirit left in them to uphold it.[110]

Conclusion

The impact of the Welsh Revival in the Khasi Hills in 1904 greatly affected the Khasi people. Though there were no mass movements in the sense that large groups decided to become Christians collectively, large numbers of persons were affected by the continuous prayers, singing, dancing, etc., and church membership increased. It is interesting to note that the missionary records take the number of converts to 17,125 in 1901 and 23,000, in 1905. In 1904-5 alone, about 8,000 people were converted.[111] It was not surprising that by 1920 30 per cent of the Khasi population had become Christians.[112] It pleased the colonial power no end to admit that the Khasis, who might, from their warlike character and tribal organization, given them more trouble than any other hill people 'have been the most peaceful of our subjects'.[113] B.C. Allen pointed out that, 'by the beginning of the century it appeared as the most correct thing to become a convert to Christianity (among the Khasis)'.[114]

In spite of the initial difficulties that the Welsh missionaries encountered in evangelization, by the turn of the century there were considerable number of converts among the Khasis. The Khasis were conquered by an outside power that (indirectly) patronized the Christian religion and all were integrated into a broader economic and political order as a result of colonial rule; all had been preliterate prior to contact with British imperialists and Welsh missionaries. Even though the Welsh missionaries and the administrators of the Raj were socially apart (most of the latter drawn from the English upper classes), it was not long before the latter realized the value of the popularization of a faith that preached non-violence and the acceptance of authority, alien and otherwise. The pacific teachings of obedience to authority implicit in the Calvinist theology as promulgated by the Welsh missionaries undoubtedly came to be welcomed by the British rulers, while its educational and medical activities became advantageous to the ruling imperial authorities.[115]

Hence by the mid-century the government not only tolerated but encouraged the work of the missionaries even to the extent of helping to fund the mission schools.[116] Through education, Christian principles were indoctrinated. Simultaneously, the wish of the Khasis to learn English so that they could earn their living anywhere was at last fulfilled.[117] For fifty years education was in the hands of the Welsh missionaries. Many boys educated in Christian schools began to occupy important government posts.

This article has argued that conversion was made possible by the depiction of the Khasis and their religion as inferior, primitive and backward, a false religion that worshipped demons and not the true God. Counterpoised to the Orient (the Khasis) the superior Occident became synonymous with Christianity and served as a yardstick of measurement of modernity. The powers of the missionaries were intimately connected with the construction of knowledge about the Khasis in their discourse. As the Khasis did not have a written script, such knowledge made their management easy and profitable. Knowledge gave the missionaries power and went on to become a profitable dialectic of information and control. The Welsh missionaries were intent on saving souls and the establishment of Christian communities which would survive and outlast all forces of political domination. Mixed with a sense of difference and a general sense of superiority (there were exceptional cases), which was in anything, encouraged by the growth of the Empire and the missionary's association with it, and exhilarated by the Empire's industrial, scientific and technological achievements interlinked with the blessings of Protestant Christianity, the Welsh missionaries were convinced that their efforts were necessary because of the overall inferior position of pagan people, the Khasis. Religion was perceived by them as systems that could be explored like scientific objects. This, while strengthening their notion that rational religion was superior to those based on dogma or superstition, reinforced their antipathy to Khasi religion perceived as demon worship or irrational. While stressing the importance of inner religion for themselves they tended to objectify the religion of others, spending little time in attempting to discover the Khasis' inner life. Modernity became the yardstick for measurement of the intrinsic inferiority of Khasi medicine.

The curative qualities of Western medicine was seen through as the healing power of the Christian religion through its saviour, Jesus Christ. A natural calamity of wide magnitude like the earthquake of 1897 was explained as retribution from Heaven for not following the true religion and resulted in bringing more converts. A major basis for Christian success was the inference of the subjugated peoples that the White Man's deity must be the source of White Man's power,[118] which the Welsh missionaries did not try to dispel but consciously exploited.

The increasing integration of the Khasi Hills with British India confronted all Khasis with a far larger reality than their local beliefs and customs could be seen as controlling. Accordingly, they began to play great attention to the Supreme God, as sovereign in charge of the entire universe, who was more clearly in charge of things. The native preachers laboured hard to refine and elaborate indigenous notions of Heaven and Hell, concept of sin, the Mediator, etc., that finally bore fruit in the form of what appeared to be conversion to Christianity. The undermining of Khasi religion, that did not have a founder and whose historical existence could not be proven as well as its rituals and ceremonies, including divination and hepastoscopy, that could not be explained scientifically by priests as they had been handed orally, was one of the important reasons why many Khasis turned to Christianity. There were distortions in the original beliefs over a period of years. The Khasis felt a deep void in their religious life, a void they themselves could not fill up. As they were not very happy with their own religion, they had a longing for some saviour from outside and kept on looking forward because religion for them was 'incurably eschatological'. It is exactly at this point that Christianity fulfilled their longings. As their own religion could not give them spiritual solace, the Christian converts found in Christ a true solution to their spiritual problems.[119] O.L. Snaitang opines that the trauma created in the minds of the people due to the loss of their traditional authority to alien rulers attracted them to Christianity. Through the introduction of a standard language, through its schools, its indigenous leadership, ecclesiastical structures and ideology, the new religion created a new inclusive tribal identity whereby the Khasis could accommodate themselves to the changes that the new administration forced upon them, and which in due course they themselves welcomed in their own way.[120] There is no doubt that Christianity was accepted for various reasons—it was the religion of the rulers, and accepting it implied obvious advantages. The rewards were two: on this earth and in the next when God took a person into His arms. Admission to educational institutions, hospitals, jobs, help in cash or kind were offered generously to the Khasis by the missionaries, and Christians were given preference over others. But one cannot ignore the fact that the Welsh missionaries were on their part, very gifted, devoted and selfless people and their constructive humanitarian work, particularly in imparting education and providing medical care, drew the Khasis to Christianity.

Acknowledgements

I gratefully acknowledge the financial assistance received by me from UGC-DRS/SAP PHASE II Programme in the Department of History, Visva-Bharati, Santiniketan, for collection of material for this article. I am deeply indebted to Abhijit Choudhury, Kong Sweetymon Rynjah, Ex-Deputy Registrar, NEHU, Shillong, Kong Sitimon Sawian and Bijoya Sawian of the Jeebon Roy Memorial Institute, Shillong, for giving me much of their time and also providing me with deep insights and information while attempting to write this article. My thanks as always go to Pijush Deb, Sheena Panja and Mita Chakraborty for their support and encouragement.

Notes

1. John McLeod, *Beginning Postcolonialism*, Manchester, 2007, p. 19.
2. Amena Nora Passah, 'Choice of Mission Field of the Welsh Calvinistic Methodist Mission (Later known as Welsh Presbyterian Foreign Mission'), in D.R. Syiemllieh, ed., *Proceedings of the North-East India History Association*, Shillong, 1997, p. 256.

   The Welsh missionaries, despite the historical exploitation of their nation, were firmly supportive of nineteenth-century imperialism as practised in the latter decades of that century. Since the empire was the vehicle that provided security that enabled them to carry out God's command to go forth and preach, they could hardly condemn it.

3. Capt. R.B. Pemberton's Account of the Khasis and Jaintias, 1835, quoted in R.T. Rymbai, 'Babu Jeebon Roy and Khasi Culture', in *Jeebon Roy Memorial Lectures* (henceforth *JRML*), Shillong, 2000, p. 21.
4. Edward Said, *Orientalism: Western Conceptions of the Orient*, New Delhi, 2001, p. 7.
5. Memoirs of Major White quoted in Jerlie E. Tariang, *Tirot Sing Greatest Freedom Fighter of North-eastern India*, Shillong, 1990, p. 8.

   For more details on the Khasis before the advent of the missionaries see my article 'The Colonial Impact on the Khasis: An Overview', in B.J. Basu, ed., *Explorations in Economic and Social History, 1200-1900*, Kolkata, 2008, pp. 59-88.
6. Ibid.
7. Ibid.
8. Hamlet Bareh, *The History and Culture of the Khasi People*, Guwahati, 1997, pp. 115-16.
9. D.R. Syiemlieh, *British Administration in Meghalaya: Policy and Pattern*, New Delhi, 1989, p. 8.
10. Ibid.
11. Tariang, *Tirot Sing,* op. cit., p. 7.
12. Geoffrey A. Oddie, *Imagined Hinduism British Protestant Missionary Constructions of Hinduism 1793-1900,* New Delhi, 2006, p. 13.
13. Syiemlieh, *British Administration,* op. cit., pp. 102-3.
14. J.H. Morris, *The History of the Welsh Calvinistic Methodist Foreign Mission to the End of the year 1904*, New Delhi, 1996, p. 84.
15. Hamlet Ngapkynta Bareh, *William Carey in a New Perspective*, Delhi, 2004, p. 136.
16. Maurice P.G. Lyndoh, *Recapture: A Collection of Articles in the Works of the Presbyterian Mission in Khasi and Jaintia Hills*, Shillong, 1992, p. 8.
17. Morris, *The History,* op. cit., p. 88.
18. Ibid., p. 59.
19. Namita Shadap-Sen, *Origin and Early History of the Khasi-Synteng People*, Calcutta, 1981, p. 175.
20. Basil Griffiths, *Khasis and the Welsh Legacy*, Shillong, 2007, p. 50.

    The author is the grandson of Reverend Dr Hugh Griffiths, the first Medical Missionary to the Khasi Hills.
21. Nalini Natarajan, *The Missionary among the Khasis*, New Delhi, 1977, p. 111.

    Nub and sohpirah were seeds of plants that had a soapy texture.
22. Morris, *The History*, op. cit., p. 59.

23. P.N. Dutta, *Impact of the West on the Khasis and Jaintias: A Survey of Political Economic and Social Change*, New Delhi, 1981, p. 207.
24. Natarajan, *The Missionary*, op. cit., p. 107.
25. See Morris, *The History*, op. cit., pp. 169-70.
26. Sawian Sitimon, 'Is Khasi Society Resilient Enough to withstand the Onslaught of Western Influence and Culture', in *Seng Khasi Silver Jubilee Volume 2004-2005* (henceforth *SKSJV*), Shillong, 2005, p. 85.
27. Morris, *The History,* op. cit., p. 90.
28. O.L. Snaitang, *Christianity and Social Change in North-East India*, Calcutta, 1993, p. 122.
29. Syiemlieh, *British Administration,* op. cit., p. 105.
30. Sitimon Sawian, 'Is Khasi Society', in *SKSJV*, p. 84.
31. Ibid.
32. Morris, *The History*, op. cit., p. 95.
33. Ibid., pp. 118-47.
    The articles U and Ka placed before nouns indicate masculine and feminine genders, respectively.
34. Dutta, *Impact*, op. cit., p. 197.
35. Reverend Fortis J. Jyrwa, *The Wondrous Works of God: A Study of the Growth and Development of the Khasi-Jaintia Presbyterian Church in the 20th Century*, Shillong, 1980, p. 27.
36. Dutta, *Impact*, op. cit., p. 194.
    This was in 1864.
37. Morris, *The History*, op. cit., p. 95.
38. Natarajan, *The Missionary*, op. cit., p. 42.
39. Jyrwa, *The Wondrous Works*, op. cit., p. 29.
40. Syiemlieh, *British Administration*, op. cit., pp. 153-4.
41. Morris, *The History*, op. cit., p. 95.
42. Ibid., p. 169.
43. Reverend I. Kharkongngor, *The Preparation of the Gospel in Traditional Khasi Belief,* Shillong, 1973, p. 43.
44. Ibid., p. 20.
45. Shyamadas Bhattacharya, 'Swami Vivekananda in Shillong', in Shyamadas Bhattacharya, ed., *Shillonger Bangalee*, Calcutta, 2004, p. 40.
    This was narrated to Swami Vivekananda when he visited Shillong in 1901 by U Hormurai Diengdoh, editor of the newspaper, *U Khasi Mynta* (*The Khasi Today*).
46. J.F. Jyrwa, *Reports of the Foreign Mission of the Presbyterian Church of Wales on Khasi-Jaintia Hills, 1864-1899*, Shillong, 1998, pp. 227-9.

47. Basil Griffiths, *Khasis and the Welsh Legacy*, Shillong, 2007.
    This aspect of evangelization has been discussed at length in my article, 'The Healing Hand: Missionaries and their Medicines in the Khasi Hills (1879-1899)', *Vidyasagar University, Journal of History*, vol. 2, 2013-14, pp. 141-60.
48. Amena Nora Passah, 'The Welsh Presbyterian Church and Health Care in the Khasi and Jaintia Hills (1841-1969)', in Manorama Sharma, ed., *Proceedings of the North-East India History Association*, Shillong, 1999, p. 279.
49. Griffiths, *Khasis*, op. cit., p. 123.
50. Dr. Griffiths, Report in 1887, in Jyrwa (compiled by Reverend Fotis), *Reports*, op. cit., pp. 125-6.
51. Ibid.
52. U Ksan–bin's letter in Khasi translated by Mrs Roberts, 19 February 1890 from Cherrapoonjee in ibid., p. 142.
53. Ibid., p. 333.
54. Ibid., p. 466; Reverend Robert Jones Report; Unfortunately many of these reports have not been dated.
55. Ibid., p. 513.
56. Ibid., p. 295; Reverend J. Ceredig Evan's *Report*.
57. Griffiths, *Khasis*, op. cit., p. 27.
58. Ibid.
59. Ibid., p. 58.
60. Jyrwa, *Reports*, op. cit., p. 183.
61. Morris, *The History*, op. cit., p. 197.
62. Ibid., pp. 197-8.
63. Robert Evans, *The Great Earthquake of 1897 in the Khasi and Jaintia Hills*, tr. Basil Morris, Shillong, 2003, p. 2.
64. Ibid., p. 21.
65. Ibid., p. 22.
66. Ibid.
67. Ibid., p. 23.
68. Evans Report in Jyrwa, *Reports*, op. cit., p. 496.
69. Jyrwa, *The Wondrous Works*, op. cit., see footnote, p. 34.
    Jones is the author of a book in Khasi concerning the history of the Presbyterian Church.
70. Jyrwa, *Reports*, op. cit., p. 432.
71. It is interesting to note that a small booklet containing *An Account of the Conversion and Persecution of Ka Nabon*, was published in English and created deep interest not only in Wales but other countries such as

Old Colabar, Africa, where the native converts sent their salutations to the Khasi Christians.

Morris, op. cit., p. 117.

72. The chewing of betel nut (*kwai*) and leaf mixed with the famous Khasi lime was and continues to be a habit prevalent among the Khasis of Meghalaya. In the past, distances were often estimated by the number of betel or *pan* leaves consumed on the way. At high altitudes and severe cold, betel nut and leaf mixed with tobacco and lime had practical uses as the body was kept warm and the digestion of food made easier. Khasi etiquette required, in the past and still does in the present, exchange of betel leaf and nut as mark of good breeding. Every chance meeting of persons was and is still followed by mutual offer of betel leaf and nut. A Khasi legend mentions that betel leaf and nut along with tobacco was given to them by God Himself as a cheap but efficacious means of hospitality after witnessing a tragedy where four lives were lost. Long ago there lived in a Khasi village two friends, the rich one (U Riewbha) and the poor one (U Baduk). U Baduk, unable to gather food to feed his rich friend, killed himself with the kitchen knife, and his wife too did the same. A thief lurking in the neighbourhood, afraid of being accused of murdering U Baduk and his wife did the same. When U Riewbha saw what had happened on reaching his friend's place, he also knifed himself to death.
73. J.H. Morris, *Christ's Ambassadors in Khasia William Lewis Jerman Jones*, Liverpool, 1939, p. 21.
74. Mr Evans Report in Jyrwa, *Reports,* op. cit., p. 335.
75. Sitimon Sawian, 'Is Khasi Society', in *SKSJV*, p. 85.
76. Attention must be drawn to the fact that marriage was regarded by the Khasis as a religious rite and was solemnized by a complicated ceremonial in which the High God, the goddess of the earth and the ancestor and ancestress of the clan, were involved. Three types of marriages existed, all of which took place in the bride's home. *Pynhiarsynjat*, 'The Burning of Rings', where the bridegroom and bride exchanged rings, involved sacrifice of pigs and was popular among the wealthiest Khasis; *Lamdoh*, 'Taking Meat' where there was no exchange of rings or sacrifice, pork being bought in the market for the feast; *Iadih*, 'Liquor Drinking' ceremony was the simplest form consisting of recitation of the marriage formula by the priest accompanied by the ceremonial drinking. See Shadap-Sen, *Origin and Early*, op. cit., pp. 221-3.

As for the naming ceremony, the custom was to be accompanied by libations of rice liquor poured from the gourd by the diviner on a plantain leaf, which has been previously covered with powdered turmeric. The three drops represented the three names chosen by the maternal grandmother or any other relative on the mother's side. The drop which took the longest to fall on the leaf indicated the name approved by the powers above. So, it is clear that no demons were actually involved!

77. Jyrwa, *Reports,* op. cit., p. 287.
    Today Meghalaya boasts of several sacred groves, mostly in the villages conserved by the Khasi rural communities. The largest grove is in Mawphlang, 22 miles from Shillong which is a watershed supplying fresh water to the population in Shillong. According to the residents of Mawphlang bad omens would visit anyone who picks up even a single twig from inside the forests. This was the way of the Khasi ancients to preserve the bountiful gifts of Nature.
78. Ibid., p. 182.
    The members of the Seng Khasi deny that the Khasi religion included any such thing like the demon. They point out that it was the result of misinterpretation and mistranslation by the Welsh missionaries whose reports and writings seem to be obsessed with what they saw as the worship of demons.
79. Morris, *The History,* op. cit., p. 152.
80. Jyrwa, *Reports,* op. cit., p. 18.
81. Nalini Natarajan, *The Missionary,* op. cit., p. 114.
82. Quoted from Herbert Jones' *Diary of the Khasi and Jaintia Hills, 1886,* in R.T. Rymbai, Babu Jeebon Roy, in *JRML*, pp. 21-2.
83. Shadap-Sen, *Origin and Early,* op. cit., p. 78.
84. Kharakor, Philemon, RNDM, *Biblical Influence on Pre-independence Khasi Literature*, New Delhi, 1998, p. 239.
85. Ibid.
86. Report of 22 June 1891, in Jyrwa, *Reports,* op. cit., p. 171.
87. Daniel O'Connor, *A Liberating Force and Friend?: Life and Work of Din Sevak Verrier Elwin*, Shillong, 1996, p. 9.
88. Cited in Sharmila Das Talukdar, *Khasi Cultural Resistance to Colonialism*, Delhi, 2004, p. 42.
89. Ibid.
    This was the feeling of U Tirahsing of the Malngiang (royal) clan.
90. Morris, *The History,* op. cit., p. 165.
91. Regarded as supernatural beings, partners with God, the ancestors were appeased with offerings of food and other material presents as they

were thought to possess powers that enabled their descendants to grow and prosper.

See Natarajan, *The Missionary*, op. cit, p. 50.

92. Hamlet Bareh, *A Short History*, op. cit., p. 39.
93. Ibid.
94. Talukdar, *Khasi Cultural Resistance,* op. cit., p. 84.
95. Bhattacharya, *Shillonger Bangalee*, op. cit., p. 39.
96. Ibid.
97. Talukdar, *Khasi Cultural Resistance,* op. cit., p. 95.
98. Griffiths, *Khasis,* op. cit., p. 52.
99. Morris, *The History,* op. cit., p. 211.
100. Talukdar, *Khasi Cultural Resistance,* op. cit., p. 94.
101. Some of the names were Kupardon Dkhar, Said Sing Dkhar, Rash Mohan Roy, Ram Charan Dympep, Nalak Sing Iangblah, Rotunmuni Roy War and Indromuni Jyrwa.

    For a detailed account of Jeebon Roy's role in counteracting missionary propaganda and uplift of Khasi society see my article, 'A Man with a Mission: Babu Jeebon Roy and his Works (1838-1903)', in *Journal of the Asiatic Society*, vol. LV, nos. 3-4, 2013, Kolkata, July 2014, pp. 95-106.
102. For more on Nilmoni Chakraborty's activities in the Khasi Hills and his observations about the Khasis, see my articles 'Health, Homeopathic Medicine and a Brahmo Missionary in the Khasi Hills (1889-99)', pp. 290-9 in A. Thakur, ed., *Proceedings of North-East India History Association*, Shillong, 2012 and 'Khasi Society: Through a Gendered Lens of an Autobiography, *Atmajibansmriti (1889-1916),* pp. 104-14 in A. Thakur, ed., *Proceedings of North-East India History Association*, Shillong, 2013.
103. Mary Pristille Rina Lyngdoh, *The Festivals in the History and Culture of the Khasi*, Delhi, 1991, p. 178.
104. Herbert Jones quoted in R.T. Rymbai and Babu Jeebon Roy, in *JRML*, p. 21.
105. Lyngdoh, *The Festivals,* op. cit., p. 178. Synchronizing with spring, marking the beginning of sowing and planting, this dance is where the Khasi people express their gratitude to the Almighty for his bounty. In this dance virgin girls, glorifying innocent maidenhood dance in the middle mutely seeking God's blessings to increase the tribe, whereas young men dance energetically around demonstrating that women are the keepers of the hearth and men the protectors. In the olden days men selected their brides from these maidens.

106. Dkhar, Phira Sing, 'Rash Mohan Jaid Nongrum: Should We Forget Him', in Abhijit Choudhury, ed., *The Cause of Netaji Subhas Chandra Bose Centenary Souvenir (1897-1997)*, Shillong, 1998, p. 25.
107. Ibid.
108. Ibid.
109. Ibid.
110. Jyrwa, *Reports,* op. cit., p. 380.
111. Jyrwa, *The Wondrous Works,* op. cit., p. 50.
112. Talukdar, *Khasi Cultural Resistance,* op. cit., p. 91.
113. Alexander MacKenzie, quoted in R.T. Rymbai, 'The Changing Pattern of Khasi Socio-Cultural Organization', in *Seng Khasi Souvenir 1964-1994*, Shillong, 1994, p. 56.
114. Talukdar, *Khasi Cultural Resistance,* op. cit., p. 29.
115. Griffiths, *Khasis,* op. cit., p. 48.
116. Ibid., p. 13.
117. Morris, *The History,* op. cit., p. 89.
   Morris writes: 'As soon as it became known that another Padre Saheb had arrived (Thomas Jones), his house was besieged day after day by a noisy crowd clamouring to be taught English, If we knew English, they declared, 'we could earn our living anywhere'.
118. Roger M. Keesing, *Cultural Anthropology: A Contemporary Perspective*, Japan, 1985, p. 403.
119. Fortis, *The Wondrous Works,* op. cit., p. 13.
120. Snaitang, *Christianity and Social Change,* op. cit., p. 63.

CHAPTER 7

Swarnakumari Devi

A Trend Setter in Colonial Bengal

Madhumita Mondal

Swarnakumari Devi (1856-1932) was born in a crucial phase of Bengal's history. The socio-cultural and political scene of Bengal was undergoing a process of gradual but significant change. Swarnakumari, who was five years older than her youngest brother Rabindranath Tagore, was born on 28 August 1856.[2] She was the eleventh child and fifth daughter of Debendranath Tagore and Sarada Devi.

Early Writings of Swarnakumari

Swarnakumari raised her voice in defence of women through her writings. During her lifetime, her novels were as popular as those of Bankimchandra Chattopadhyay, the most eminent litterateur of his time. The advent of Swarnakumari on the literary scene of Bengal heralded a new era for women. She was the first writer to demonstrate the strength of women's writing and use literature to address pertinent issues.

The eleven novels of Swarnakumari were widely acclaimed, viz., *Dip-Nirban* (1876), *Chinna Mukul* (1879), *Mibarraj* (1887), *Hooglir Imambari* (1888),[3] *Bidroha* (Revolt) 1890, *Snehalata* or *Palita* (1892-3), *Fulermala* (Fatal Garland) 1895, *Kahake* (To Whom?) 1898, and the trilogy *Bichitra* (1920), *Swapnabani* (1921), *Milanratri* (1925). The credit for introducing trilogy in Bangla literature can be accorded to her. In her social novels she broke away from the influence of Bankimchandra and proved her talent. *Dip-Nirban, Mibarraj, Hooglir Imambari, Bidroha,* and *Fulermala* were considered as socio-historical novels.

Swarnakumari's first novel *Dip-Nirban* focused on patriotism and nationalism which were relevant to contemporary times. Her second historical novel was *Mibarraj*. The context of the novel was 'love and war' between the Bhils and the Rajputs. This story, based on Todd's account, proved her ability to narrate a story in an attractive style. Though the style was quite similar to Bankimchandra's historical novel *Anandmath*, Swarnakumari made a good effort to develop a style of her own. After three years she wrote *Bidroha*. These two novels were based on tribal revolts against the Rajputs. *Hooglir Imambari* and *Fulermala* were two remarkable novels based on society and life of Bengal in earlier times. *Hooglir Imambari* was published in *Bharati*. Muhammad Masin (Mahasin) was the protagonist of the novel. His sister Munna's life, sufferings, pains and her efforts to overcome that and be free constituted the story. *Fulermala*[4] was based on the capture of Bengal by Prince Ganesh of Dinajpur. The novel was one of the best examples of Swarnakumari's capability to write a novel mingling reality with imagination. *Chinna Mukul*[5] was written against the backdrop of nineteenth century. The women were not the makers of their own fate at that time. The patriarchal society did not allow them to do so. The central character of the novel, Kanak, was a widow who did not have the freedom to spend her life as she chose. Her joys and sorrows were not a matter of consideration. Swarnakumari wrote the novel many years before establishing Sakhi Samiti. As an editor of *Bharati*, she gathered more experience from the outer world which helped her to understand the helpless situation of the widows. *Chinna Mukul* was a novel on the failed love of a woman that helps us understand patriarchal domination. Swarnakumari did not raise her voice against the patriarchal frame of society. She focused on the helpless situation of the women but did not explore the way one could change the situations.[6]

The protagonist of the novel *Snehalata* was extremely tolerant, forgiving, quiet and non-sentimental—qualities regarded as intrinsic in an ideal woman by the patriarchal society. The novel gives a lucid description of women in the second half of the nineteenth century. It brings out the issue of conflict between Hinduism and the practitioners of Brahmo faith; positive and negative effects of widow re-marriage; and the functioning of the inner quarters of the *antahpur*. The first part of the novel that deals with ideas of nationalism and patriotism reflects the general ambience of contemporary Tagore household. It also draws a portrait of a secret revolutionary organization that was akin to *Sanjibanisabha*. In the second part of the novel, she addressed questions pertinent to the conditions of widow. She narrates how society at large perceived them. Snehalata committed suicide at the end of the novel unable to bear her life any further. This brings out the author's sympathy for these hapless women in powerful language. Though her own years of widowhood spent within the confines of the Tagore household was nothing similar to that of her less fortunate sisters, she had a fair grasp of the reality that existed in contemporary society. The novel helps to understand the attitude of educated youths of Calcutta, the psychology of contemporary middle class society. The condition of women both in their paternal and maternal homes is sketched in lucid style. Swarnakumari raised her voice in favour of widow remarriage. She addressed the problems of widows but could not find a way to solve them. Her concern for female education and adverse effects of child-marriage was significantly expressed.

Swarnakumari's most significant novel was *Kahake?* (To Whom?). In the novel, she captures, for the first time in Bengali fiction, the ethos of the new urban middle class that was her milieu.[7] The novel depicts a young woman's growth into selfhood and independence through an understanding of what it meant to love. The female protagonist of the novel, Mrinalini or Moni Chotu and falls in love, a radical act for a middle class woman of that time. The novel surprised the readers of her time. She represented the changing role of women in society. It was an exceptional one that changed the image of the stereotypical Swarnakumari novel. Mrinalini was very concerned about her gender identity which was not very common in Swarnakumari's novels. She was confused about her object of love and could not understand who was more important in her life. *Kahake?* reflected perfectly the then *'Enga-Banga'* (Anglo-Bengali) society and its effects.

On Socio-cultural and Political Issues

Swarnakumari emerged as a notable essayist of her time and wrote on a number of issues, viz., socio-political and gender, educational and historical, travelogues and scientific essays and many others on burning contemporary affairs. There were some remarkable essays based on social-cultural and gender issues, viz., *'Strisiksha O Bethune School', 'Giltir Bazaar'* and *'Purusher Shresthatya', 'Bidhaba Bibaha O Hindu Patrika', 'Ekti Prastab', 'Aar Ekti Prastab' 'Sakhisamiti O Mahilashilpamela', 'Sat Batsare Sakhisamiti'.*[8] *'Strisiksha O Bethune School'*, was very significant as it intended to remind the readers of the contribution of the Bethune School in promoting female education. She used periodic tables to draw a comparative statement of the social and religious backgrounds of the students.[9] It may be considered as the most significant essay on female education. Among her other writings, *'Giltir Bazaar'* and *'Purusher Shresthatya'*[10] were very significant. She wrote these from a social viewpoint. The closeness between British officials and Indian higher classes and its impact on people was described in '*Giltir Bazaar*'. In '*Purusher Shresthatya*' she impressed the reader with its logic. She claimed that the 'manliness' of man owed a great deal to the nurture he received. His mother's guidance and the contributions of the women in the household also attributed towards it. Man, she says, was not complete without the woman. Swarnakumari concludes saying that if the women were provided with the same education and environment they too would develop a similar strength of character.

The results of her deep thinking on social issues, were '*Bidhaba Bibaha O Hindu Patrika*', *'Sakhi Samiti', 'Sakhisamiti O Mahilashilpamela'* and '*Sat Batsare Sakhisamiti*'. *'Bidhaba Bibaha O Hindu Patrika'*, dealt with the issue of widow re-marriage. She silenced the critics of Vidyasagar and widow re-marriage saying that the energy spent on criticism could be better used to mitigate the sufferings of women. She held that the rules of the Shastras were not unchangeable. Since ancient times, widow re-marriage had been practised. It was still in vogue among Hindus in different parts of the country. So there was no reason why it could not be practised in Bengal as Hinduism was not the sole prerogative of Bengali Hindus. Though she supported widow re-marriage, she was of the opinion that it should not be imposed. Besides, re-marriage would not automatically result in the betterment of the condition of women. She believed more in the viability of education and self-dependence for women. These two would primarily help in the emancipation of women. Her own activities were geared towards this end.

Her thoughts were reflected in her essays '*Sakhi Samiti*', '*Sakhisamiti O Mahilashilpamela*', '*Sat Batsare Sakhisamiti*'. In '*Aar Ekti Prastab*' Swarnakumari argued that law should be equal for both men and women. If a second marriage was permissible for a widower it should be allowed for widows. She also observed that child marriage should be stopped as it would ensure there would be no child widows. Swarnakumari portrayed the condition of the child widow in their paternal homes. She thought that education and self-dependence would free them from the sufferings they faced in their paternal home. Swarnakumari argued that the kind of education which while retaining the spirit of Hinduism instilled nationalism among women should be imparted. All children, male or female, received their early education from women. Child education constitutes the basis of all education. So, if women were inspired by nationalistic feelings it would have an impact on all people.[11] Her essays, viz., '*Ranabangshe Eranatya Arop*', '*Saralata Ki Nindapriyata*', '*Amader Samaj*', '*Bibidha Prasanga*' give an idea of her thoughts. Her political essays '*Rajnaitik Prasanga*', '*Rajyer Katha*', '*Amader Kartabya*', '*Kartabya Kon Pathe*', '*Kalpyabesh Sammilan*', and '*Bengalee*'[12] were expressions of her sense of patriotism and the philosophy of nationalism that she believed. Moreover, she was moved by the number of Bengali youth who were supposed to go to the battle field in South Africa to serve those who were fighting. They were volunteer workers with patriotic feelings and khaki dresses. She felt great pleasure that these healthy youth proved that Bengalis were not cowards.[13] She never supported violence and the politics of blood and death. However, she silently encouraged her daughter Sarala's radical activities. Sarala wrote:

When I opened a club for young men in the house, when I handed them knives and sticks, organized Birastami Utsav and so on, what did my parents and others say? Nothing at all—they did not put any constraints in my way. Their silent approval was the basis of my strength without this I would not have proceeded even a single step.[14]

Sarala emphasized on body-building and physical activities of the youth which included *lathikhela, kushti* and sword-play, etc. for developing ones' courage and self-respect. Swarnakumari too advocated the need for self-respect and self-strength being instilled in people. As a part of colonized mass she desired to overcome the colonizer in the battle of strength and knowledge. Literature was her battlefield and her literary talent was the weapon against the opponent. Contemporary political activities impacted upon her sensitive mind and she asked her countrymen to think passionately. In '*Amader Samaj*', Swarnakumari criticized the political techniques of the moderates. She believed not in the politics of begging but in strengthening oneself through self reliance and determination. She wrote: 'As political congress has been established for the purpose of political development, why don't we do something similar for social purpose?'[15]

Women's Organization

Swarnakumari Devi may be considered an early instance of someone who represented changing perception of home as well as gender. As an editor of *Bharati*, she was popular among her readers. She was quite aware of gender issues of her time. There was a regular space for women's issues in her journals.[16] All these helped her to think of an organization for helpless widows and needy women. *Mayar Khela* composed by her brother was performed in Bethune School in 1888. On that occasion, Mahila Shilpa Mela was inaugurated by Lady Lansdowne, the wife of the then Viceroy of India and Lady Bayley, the wife of the then Lieutenant Governor of Bengal. Bayley and Lansdowne also attended the fair and were two significant patrons of the Mela. Women from aristocratic families performed on stage for the first time in the history of Bengal. The audiences came mainly from the Tagore family. The Sakhi Samiti organized a fair every year named Mahila Shilpa Mela. It opened the door of recreation for the *zenana* (women) of that time. They eagerly awaited the fair. Avenues for their recreation were otherwise non-existent—*Ramonite Beche Ramonite Kene, Legechhe Ruper Hat* ('Ladies are the vendors, ladies are the purchasers, it was a gathering of beauty').[17]

The widows' home or Bidhabashram started by Sashipada Bandyopadhyay (1840-1925) at Baranagar, considered the first such venture, inspired Hiranmayee Devi. She had lost many of her children at an early age. That brought her close to the parentless children of Sakhi Samiti. She became their mother in a real sense. Then, she came to know about the Bidhabashram of Sashipada Bandyopadhyay. Hiranmayee took charge of Sakhi Samiti and re-named it Bidhabashram. She was extremely passionate about that. Her love and respect for her mother inspired her to serve its purpose. It was funded with the money deposited by Hiranmayee[18] and she was its director.[19] After the death of Hiranmayee, Swarnakumari became its sole organizer in 1925. In 1931, she donated the copy rights of all her books to the ashram.[20]

The main purpose of the ashram was to set up a shelter for widows and needy girl students. Initially, there were fifty students. They regularly visited the ashram for their education. It became popular among the women of Bengal. Once, Swarnakumari asked the readers of *Bharati* (Festival Issue, *Agrahayan*, 1317 BS) for financial help for the ashram. There was a tremendous response from the readers. Gyanadabala Mitra, a woman from Simla, sent Swarnakumari Rs. 100 along with a congratulatory letter.[21]

The samiti was centred round Hindu and Brahmo women but at the same time it was free from any form of communal bias. Most of the women's organizations in nineteenth century Bengal were restricted to upper caste and upper class women alone. Sakhi Samiti always encouraged the lower class needy women and was enriched by the participation of women from Muslim and Christian communities apart from the Hindu and Brahmo women. The Nawab Zaminder of Dacca, Faijunnesa Chowdhury, was one of the chief patrons of the Samiti. She donated a large amount of money for the Samiti on regular basis. The activity of Sakhi Samiti was highly appreciated by contemporary Bengali intelligentsia. A number of contemporary journals like *Bamabodhini Patrika, Education Gazette,* published articles on the Samiti and requested the readers to provide the Samiti financial help.[22] In the meantime, Sarala came back to Calcutta with the mission to promote female education in Bengal. Sarala's association and her activities became complementary to Sakhi Samiti and Bidhaba Shilpashram. For almost twenty years the Samiti served its purpose.

Swarnakumari set up organizations to help those women who matched her social class or were similar in status. The poor from rural areas, however, had no opportunity to send their daughters to school. Handicraft productions, especially sewing and embroidery, enabled only a handful of high class women to earn some form of living. They also needed a space of their own to work. Swarnakumari Devi started a non-political movement for women's emancipation by organizing Sakhi Samiti in Bengal. Her daughter Sarala enlarged its scope and introduced the movement at a national level by founding Bharat Stree Mahamandal. The mother and the daughter both were staunch believers in communal harmony. To quote Sarala, 'To join the party, to bring the several fragments together into one moral unity, to deepen the sense of sisterhood and common humanity of the women of all the races and parts of India is one of the main features of Bharat Stree Mahamandal.'[23]

By the middle of 1890s both the Bangamahila Samaj and the Sakhi Samiti lost much of their enthusiasm, not because women were becoming uninterested in social activities but possibly because there was none who could constantly look after the working of the association and thus, sustain their activities. In fact, these women were becoming more and more active and at the same time enlarging the sphere of their activities. They realized that they certainly had some roles to play outside the sphere of their families without which their lives would remain unfulfilled.[24]

The organizations did not survive long. It could not change the condition of the women from rural and undeveloped areas. Only the women from urban areas and upper and upper middle class society could get some benefit from them. It was, however, very significant that some women took initiative to promote the women's cause. Swarnakumari could not break away the image of the Bhadramahila of nineteenth century Bengal. In spite of these limitations, unquestionably her contribution towards the cause of women and their uplift was a bold step taken by her at that time. That was the start of a new beginning.

Involvement in the Nationalist Movement

Swarnakumari was one of the earliest Bengali women who took an active interest in politics in colonial Bengal. Throughout her career she formulated her own philosophy of politics. It was her surroundings that encouraged her. Within the boundary of Tagore family, nationalist projects were initiated by different members of Jorasanko. Swarnakumari lived in a period that saw significant changes in the political life of Bengal. She was well aware of the major political trends of her time. As the nationalist movement unfolded and anti-imperialist forces gained ground, her political perceptions evolved and her level of thinking attained maturity. Congress politics left an impact on her. Later, the Swadeshi and Boycott movement and then Gandhian politics attracted her daughter Sarala in particular. Their family connections brought them into direct contact with some of the leading political luminaries.

Dwarkanath Tagore, the grandfather of Swarnakumari, was one of the first who raised his voice for freedom of press in early colonial India. He was on good terms with the Europeans, though it never came in the way of his free thinking.[25] He protested against those government actions that he considered detrimental to the interests of his country. His successors imbibed his patriotism as their ancestral legacy.[26] His son Debendranath's *Tattvabodhini Patrika* encouraged free thinking and rationalism and national consciousness through publication of articles on indigenous education, culture and knowledge. Since mid-nineteenth century, newspapers and journals began to take significant initiative to spread the newly-resurgent patriotic sentiment. He began to patronize *Indian Mirror* to serve that purpose to enable expression of public grievances.[27] A national school was established to achieve indigenous education and promote body-building under 'National Society'. In 1867, the society organized Hindu Mela. The objective of this was neither religious nor material happiness but to serve the cause of motherland.[28] The Chaitra Mela or Hindu Mela was a nationalist project initiated by Gaganendranath Tagore and Nabagopal Mitra in 1867[29] and it played a significant role in promoting nationalism throughout Bengal. Swarnakumari was eleven years old when the Hindu Mela was held for the first time. It sought to promote physical activity and gave impetus to the advancement of national art and industry.[30] In the second half of the nineteenth century, there developed a tendency to use indigenous language and attires and feelings of patriotism were roused among an influential section of the society. The Tagore family played a significant role in that newly-born patriotism. The Tagores were believers in the practice of indigenous languages, dresses and cultures.[31]

Swarnakumari's brother Jyotirindranath established a secret organization called Sanjibanisabha. 'Hamchupamuhaf' was the symbolic name of the 'Sabha'. Rajnarayan Basu (1826-1899) became the chairperson of the Sanjibanisabha. Rabindranath in his younger days was also involved in the activities of the Sanjibanisabha. In *Jibansmriti*, he describes the activities of the sabha. Ambience of the *antahpur* in Tagore family was different from that in many other families. Women of the family had greater acquaintance with the outer world compared to other women of their time, of their class. Swarnakumari was deeply moved by the ambience. Since, she closely observed the activities of the Sanjibanisabha and the role played by the male members of the family, it inspired her in her later patriotic works. The Tagore family was so moved by the nascent nationalistic movement that they tried to become a part of it through the dress code they sought to adopt and their literary output. This had great impact on Swarnakumari. Her famous brother Rabindranath wrote: 'In the heart of our family a flashing pride for the motherland was seen. My father maintained true respect for the country in all events of his life. That inspired us to patriotic feelings.'[32]

Debendranath's Adi Brahmo Samaj was one of the chief centres that attempted to inculcate patriotic thoughts and feelings among educated people. Rabindranath observed, 'In the heart of the family patriotism, like pure, fire had been burning for years.'[33] Swarnakumari's elder brothers, viz., Dwijendranath, Satyendranath, and Jyotirindranath as well as younger brother Rabindranath were moved by this.[34] Swarnakumari inherited her father's patriotism.[35]

Swarnakumari's Attempts to Promote Nationalism

Swarnakumari's husband Janakinath was one of the earliest members of the Indian National Congress. He helped to organize some of the conferences held by Congress.[36] Swarnakumari attended the fifth (1889) and sixth (1890) sessions of Indian National Congress as a woman delegate from Bengal. She attended the fifth session in Bombay along with Kadambini Ganguly (1861-1923), Pandita Ramabai, Vidya Gorinikantha, Smt. Nikasawa and Ramabai Ranade, wife of Mahadev Govind Ranade.[37] It was Dwarakanath Ganguly (the husband of Kadambini Ganguly), whose non-tiring efforts made it possible for women to join the Congress session.[38] As a consequence, the 1889 session of the Congress party included six women, one of whom was Swarnakumari. Among other members from Bengal, Kadambini moved a vote of thanks in English and was hailed by Annie Besant as being 'a symbol that India's freedom would uplift India's womanhood'. In 1896, an exhibition was held in Calcutta during the twelfth session of the Indian National Congress.[39] In 1887, an industrial fair and exhibition was organized by Swarnakumari Devi's Sakhi Samiti, that was highly appreciated in contemporary society. The organizers of the Indian National Congress were perhaps inspired by Sakhi Samiti's exhibition. When Swarnakumari attended the fifth and sixth sessions of Congress, they exchanged their ideas in promoting *swadeshi* arts and crafts. Swarnakumari was an active partner in her husband's work.

Swarnakumari's close contact with Annie Besant and involvement with the Theosophical Society brought her closer to the national movement. Besant played a very significant role in the freedom struggle of India as well as in promoting the cause of women. At the request of Annie Besant, Swarnakumari took charge of the Bengal branch of Theosophical Society. Gradually, her activities as well as her literary world were inspired by that idealism. Swarnakumari held firmly that political movement was all about serving one's motherland and working for the benefit of the country.

Swarnakumari assumed an active role in the service of the motherland once she stepped out of the *antahpur*. Her respect and love for the nation is evident in the editorials of *Bharati* and in her essays, novels, verses, and other writings most of which were published in *Bharati*. She expressed her views through her literary works. The journal was named after the motherland. *Bharati* evoked some emotional attachment with Bharat or India. Rabindranath wrote: 'This was for the first time people earnestly began to realize Bharatvarsha as their nation.'[40] In an issue of *Bharati*, Swarnakumari wrote that 'Organizing movements on political issues is an objective of publishing *Bharati*'.[41]

There was a regular column in *Bharati* named '*Rajnaitik Alochana Ba Rajyer Katha*' (Discussion on Politics or News of the State) in which she published contemporary political and international news such as, the pathetic condition of Bengal, harassment of the Begum of Bhopal, Burmese War, war between Serbia and Bulgaria, Home Rule in England, problem of Burma's border with India, native states, violent agitation by the labour class in England, defeat of Gladstone and oppression of the women workers by the owners of the tea estates in Assam. *Bharati* regularly protested against any kind of political oppression and unlawful acts. Swarnakumari raised questions on inhuman politics and activities of the colonial authorities. She strongly criticized Lord Curzon for militancy in Tibet, the elaborate reception party for royal guests at Delhi court during a severe famine, increased expenditure, the University Act and so on.[42]

Swarnakumari's literary efforts were deeply motivated by her patriotism. Her patriotic feeling is quite evident in her novels.[43] Her first novel *Dip-Nirban* is a socio-historical work. She wished to dedicate her daughter Sarala to the welfare of the nation.[44] The central protagonist of her trilogy called Rajkanya Jyotirmayee resembled her daughter Sarala who dedicated her life for the welfare of the country, viz., setting up Byayamsamiti and formation of a group of volunteers who were ready to dedicate their life for their motherland. In those novels, rules of the Byayamsamiti were very similar to Sarala's organization, 'let your country's welfare be your welfare, do physical exercise to strengthen your welfare, do physical exercise to strengthen your body and mind, don't use strength unnecessarily, but don't hesitate to face any kind of insult'.[45]

What is significant is that Swarnakumari had a son too and being a conventional mother she could have asked her son to devote himself to nationalist work, following his father. Swarnakumari, however, asked her daughter to work for the country as a wholetimer. Possibly Sarala's own interest in patriotic work led Swarnakumari to desire so. In a greater sense, Swarnakumari wanted women in general of her time to come forward to serve the country. This is reflected in the fact that most of the characters of her novels, both male and female, were determined to dedicate their lives for the country. Swarnakumari broke away from the practice of creating stereotypical roles for women. Her characters were indifferent to material loss and gain in personal life, love and self-centred daily life. Rather, they were deeply involved in greater interest, working only for the country's welfare. National consciousness and a dream of constructing one nation were evident in the Bengali and Rajput communities in *Bidroha* and *Fulermala*. Swarnakumari's vision of nation and her feelings about patriotism were evident in her novels like *Snehalata, Vichitra, Swapnavina, Milanratri* and short stories like *Naba Dakater Diary*. Secret political organizations and their activities are realistically narrated in her triloy and *Snehalata*. Through the activities of Nabakumar, the central character of *Naba Dakater Diary*, Swarnakumari re-evaluated the Bengali sentiment about the 'Swadeshi dacoits'. She has recurrently blamed not the individual Englishman but the British who used to dominate and oppress Indian people.[46]

There was a great wave of political movement in Bengal during 1905. People were deeply shocked by the attempt at the partition of Bengal. Boycott and Swadeshi movement reached its peak. Lala Lajpat Rai commented, '*Swadesi* means the cult of home industries, i.e. the use of the article made in the country'.

It included boycott both economic and political, boycott of foreign, especially British goods, and of all honorary associations with the administration, national education implying a withdrawal of the youths of the nation from the officialized universities and government-controlled schools and colleges, and training them in institutions conducted on national lines subject to national control. National civic volunteering aiming at imparting a healthy civic training to the people economic and medical relief, popular education, preventive and police duties, regulation of fair and pilgrim gathering, settlement of civil and non-cognizable criminal disputes by means of arbitration committees should be promoted. Swarnakumari also nurtured the same opinion in her novels *Vichitra, Swapnabina, Milanratri* and *Naba Dakater Diary.*

In 1907, at the Surat session of the Indian National Congress, the division between the extremist and moderates became extreme and as a result revolutionary activities increased in Bengal. Revolutionary action began with Khudiram Bose and Prafulla Chaki's attempt to murder magistrate Kingsford in 1908. Gradually, secret killing and *swadeshi* dacoity became part of regular activities of the revolutionaries of Bengal. Swarnakumari was deeply shaken by these incidents. Reactions to all these political incidents were reflected in *Bharati*. Swarnakumari protested loudly against any kind of political oppression through *Bharati*. Some of her significant political essays were '*Kartavya Kon Pathe*', '*Amader Kartavya*', '*Rajnaitik Prasanga*', and '*Engrejer Sahit Surendra Prasanga*'. She never supported political violence and terrorism. In '*Kartavya Kon Pathe*' she suggested alternatives to the 'misguided extremist youth'. [47]

Addressing her countrymen she said that patience was necessary for successful *swadeshiyana*. She did not support use of force to stop traders selling foreign goods as it was not the way to achieve sustainable welfare. Swarnakumari rather emphasized on the inner strength of the common masses. She emphasized on increasing strength of the national spirit: 'We are untrue in the beginning. We have seldom tried to construct a national sprit. Real attempt to construct a nation lies in the attempt to increase the strength of the national spirit.'[48]

She rejected the politics of violence and thought that unity and integration could facilitate the development of a country. She rejected all kinds of superstitions and practice of untouchability. Swarnakumari was deeply moved by contemporary political events. She argued that any murder was unacceptable and using a bomb to kill someone must not be supported. She loudly expressed her anger at secret killings: 'Murder of both innocent and offences is obvious in throwing a bomb, on the other hand, such secret killings enormously terrify peoples' mind. That is indefinable fear, result is pathetic.'[49]

She regretted that the youth who were fighting for the independence of their motherland were choosing the 'wrong' path: 'Their objective is good, but they have chosen the way that is harmful for the country. To remove oppression they become one more source of oppression.'[50]

Dedicating one's life for the motherland was a matter of pride, she admitted and raised the question at the same time—'What should we do if that death causes failure instead of achievements for the nation's welfare?'[51] She reminded the extremist youth that working throughout life was more significant than the glory of accepting death for progress of the nation. She thought that accepting death in a moment of excitement was misguided heroism, whereas, real heroism lay in sacrificing one's life through working for the country till death with hard labour, sincerity and exemplary dedication. She addressed the patriots, 'You have so many works to be done. Completing so, you have to establish the base of *swaraj*.'[52]

She was sharply critical of British policies and activities in her essay *'Giltir Bazar'*. Political motivation behind Swadeshi and Boycott movements was protest against Bengal partition. *'Path o Patheya'* and *'Sadupay'* (1919) were two political essays written by Rabindranath Tagore, in which he expressed the necessity of preparation for the movements and also discussed the methods to be adopted. In the same year, Swarnakumari wrote an essay called *'Amader Kartavya'* that supported her younger brother's opinion about Swadeshi and Boycott movements.

A national level industrial gathering was held at Kashi where Romeschandra Dutta delivered a speech in the session as a president that 'the Swadeshi Movement is one which all nations on earth are seeking to adopt in the present day.... It will certainly foster and encourage our industries in which the Indian government professed the greater interest.'[53] Swarnakumari accepted Swadeshi as a constructive movement and supported the way it attempts national welfare in its early phase. She also encouraged industrialization, development of indigenous products, and use of *swadeshi* goods. In her *Swapnabina*, the king and the princess organized an art-exhibition and were successful.[54] This was reiteration of Swarnakumari's love for industry and industrial progress. She welcomed Priyanath Basu's efforts at promoting *swadeshi* circus and encouraged all Bengalis to watch the circus which had only Bengali performers.[55] Her message to the ones who dedicated themselves to their country was as follows:

Soldier and hero, O My Countryman!
In admiration of thee stands the world,
And I, though little, become great in thee,
My brother, and in thy proud state, forget
Myself the sorrows of my servitude.

Even as stars of burning beauty see
Merely to shoot and in the ethereal vast
To loose themselves, and none perceives the heat
Of dreadful fire intense that in their being.

Through every particle and atom breathes:
Even so thy sacrifice, but more splendid still
This death espoused, not for thyself, nor even
For Country, but for duty's sake alone:
Thy selfless death-pyre, holy warrior!

So long as bursts not yet the flood of doom,
And sun and moon within their orbits run,
Over her vesture thy great deeds shall earth
Blazen, thy glory's hymn proudly proclaim.
How shall we praise when speech to praise thee fails?

Thee, hope of Gods in this tremendous war!
I know not with what offering. I shall greet
Thee, in whose name, O hero, thy own land
Glories. and foreign lands feel blest indeed. [56] ('To the Brave')

A number of songs composed by Swarnakumari were intended to inspire the nationalist leaders:

Ek sutre ganthilam sahashrajeeban
Jeeban marane rabo shapatha bandhan
Bharat matar tare sapinu e pran…[57]

Travelogues written by Swarnakumari were rich in expression of her sensitive knowledge about the country and its heritage. She had her own vision of greater India and she constructed that with her patriotic mind. She thought *swaraj* could be achieved with self-strength and self-respect.

Rabindranath had criticized Bengali society thus:

> Wealthy people of this society do not contribute money to political movements. Reason is we are not truthful; we do not have faith on each other in any work. Before committing any work we must build our character properly. Begging for 'representative government' is odd if the nation does not have effort, self-sufficiency and courage.[58]

Swarnakumari disagreed with her brother in *Bharati.* She minutely observed the activities and limitations of Congress. She commented: 'Political movements in India are not like that what the essayist thinks. There is willingness to go forward to the national greatness through activities. Besides, he wishes to remove debris of thousand years in one day. How can he?'[59]

Swarnakumari also stressed on morality as one of the essential requirements of character building but did not agree with her younger brother's opinion about contemporary political movements. She was rather optimistic about the activities of the National Congress.

However, she criticized the limitations of contemporary political movements. She never forgot that women were doubly chained in a country that itself was under foreign rule. Women were bounded by the shameful chain both of *antahpur* and the outer world. She said that many people who were fighting for the independence of the country were not willing to give minimum freedom to the women of the country. She thought that as half of the population of the country was female both man and woman should participate in the freedom movement. That was why she felt women should be given freedom in the *antahpur* first.[60]

Idea of Sakhi Samiti was born out of the thought of nation and nation's welfare.[61] Swarnakumari Devi joined in the struggle for promotion of an independent scientific tradition and culture. She felt that development of India should be achieved through self-help only. She desired that India should cultivate science not only for economic betterment but also for its rebirth. She took the lead in publishing essays on scientific theories and concepts in easy language that could be understood even by people with little education. She made lucid exposition about the complicated theories of science for the benefit of the downtrodden and superstitious masses. In the colonial situation, studying science was simply not a way to enter into a knowledge system but another way for the colonized to become equal with the colonizer, to win independence and above all to build a nation that would be equal to the colonizers in its scientific progress. Her essays were not limited to mere analysis of science. Her mind mingled scientific thoughts with her nation; nationality and rationality were linked to serve a common purpose.[62] She wrote, 'India is the earliest home of science'. Even in the Vedic age there were several scientific propositions in India. Swarnakumari glorified the Indian tradition of scientific research. She reminded her countrymen that research both in mathematics and astronomy began in India, as also in medical science and chemistry. She thought Indians were the masters. Being a part of the colonial mass she took part in the rationalist movement through her writings. She analysed ancient Indian scientific text in the light of Western science with a scientific mind. She wrote: 'Scientific mind can drive any kind of superstition away … until, we, the Indians can understand the necessity of scientific education, there will be no progress at all.'[63]

By adopting the best wealth of the ruler, she combatted the arrogant pride of the colonizer. They domesticated whatever the West had to offer in the field of science, and also created a new consciousness that confronted the age-old darkness and led the nation towards modernity.

Swarnakumari was one of the few successful women who will be remembered for her contribution to the nation in the context of late nineteenth and early twentieth century India. She was unique for her works on politics, literature, patriotism and various social issues. Her political thoughts were motivated by the welfare of the countrymen and progress of the nation. That political ideology was evident in her works throughout her life. Later, Sarala played a significant role in the political movement.

Swarnakumari popularized her idea of nationalism through her writings. Swarnakumari campaigned for promotion of nationalist thought among people both through direct and indirect means.

She used literature as a tool to express her views on nation and its welfare. She was always opposed to the politics of bloodshed and violence. She spoke on how the welfare of the nation was possible through unity and integration going beyond superstitions and caste discriminations. There is a unique expression of nationalism in her writings. Perhaps Swarnakumari was not happy with her own standpoint about open politics. The then political world was also male dominated. Women seldom got importance in the field. That kept her away from direct politics and she engaged her literary skills as a medium to participate in the nationalist movement. Her writings were directed to her countrymen who she thought, needed basic education, health and rights.

Conclusion

Swarnakumari was an illustrious successor of Rasasundari Devi, the earliest woman writer of an autobiography in any Indian language. Not only did she introduce a number of literary genres like the short story, the dance drama, the saga poetry in Bangla literature, Swarnakumari also enriched the fields of novel, poetry, travelogues and essay. She participated in direct politics. Her Sakhi Samiti fought a long battle for empowerment of women in Bengal. Her sister-in-law Jnanadanandini introduced some changes in domestic life in the *thakurbari*. Swarnakumari came out of the *antahpur* and participated in literary discussions with the male members of the family and with scholars who were family friends. She and Kadambari were among the rare Bengali women who participated in such literary interactions in those days. *Bharati* was the outcome of such family gatherings. As editor of a literary journal Swarnakumari was very successful. The very notion of the woman's role in the 'home' thus began to change. Her essays on science and science-based subjects surprised the readers. She attempted to change the age old notion of gender. Her writings on the question of gender discrimination and emancipation of women impacted the society. Swarnakumari also represented the 'new mother' who inspired their children to become much more significant in society. She disliked child marriage and so was least bothered about the marriage of her daughters. Swarnakumari was a role model for dignified motherhood who inspired her daughters to serve the nation. She wished her daughters to be committed to the cause of nation. She formulated her own idea of patriotism and was involved in a number of events that prove her deep attachment to the nationalist movement. In India the nationalist movement over the years attracted a number of women. Swarnakumari was one of the earliest. Perception of home, gender and nation was changing and Swarnakumari was an active participant in this process.

She held herself up as a model of how a woman could serve her home as well as the nation. She admitted, repeatedly, the encouragement and help she received from her brothers and later her husband in enabling her to develop her talent especially, her literary faculties. She often extolled the help of her husband in moulding her in the way the world knew her. She was not averse to making men active partners in the venture to liberate women. The constant companionship of members of her highly talented family gave her an open mind and instilled the courage to question prevalent social norms, practices and conventions. The low status of Hindu women and the existing customs of early marriage, polygamy, *purdah* and denial of education to women attracted Swarnakumari's attention. Using her literary skills she spoke primarily to middle class Hindu society in Bengal. Her main focus was on providing education to women and making them self-dependent. These alone could facilitate the liberation and emancipation of women from the shackles of social practices geared to keeping them in captivity.

Swarnakumari emerged on the social scene of Bengal at a time when a handful of reformers were attempting to redress some of the social atrocities against women. The remarriage of widows had become a hotly debated issue. Swarnakumari was drawn into this. She emerged as a supporter of widow remarriage. Though she was against compelling widows to go in for second marriages by exerting any kind of pressure and felt it best left to choice, she was a strong advocate of law being made equal for both man and woman. She defended her attack against child marriage on the ground it would rid society of the tremendous burden of child widows. She argued that if second marriage was permitted for men who became widowers, it should be permitted for widows too. Here, she was talking in terms of gender equality. She epitomized the 'new' woman. The way she brought up her daughters and educated them bears testimony to her perception of what the position of woman should be in society. She advised women to develop their own selves first and then attempt to better their own society.

Swarnakumari skilfully used her pen to address pertinent issues relevant to contemporary times. For instance, in the textbooks for children she examined the question of child rearing and fulfilment of some of the basic needs of children. She highlighted the importance of regular physical activities, outdoor games, nutrition and components of a balanced diet.

Swarnakumari attempted to popularize scientific knowledge among the common people of late nineteenth century Bengal. She overcame the narrow confines of contemporary society and stepped into the sphere of science through her essays. She was the first woman who wrote essays on science. Her main objective was popularization of science education. However, she argued that even to familiarize children with basic scientific knowledge from an early age, women should be educated scientifically. She made lucid expositions about the complicated theories of science for the uplift of the superstitious masses. She raised her voice to emphasize women's role in society. She committed herself to making the unfortunate and illiterate women conscious through her excellent compositions on science.

Her essays were not limited to mere analysis of science. Her mind mingled scientific thoughts with her notion of motherland. Nationality and rationality were linked to serve a common purpose. Swarnakumari encouraged the Indian tradition of scientific research. She reminded her countryman that research, both on mathematics and astronomy, began in India. Swarnakumari was drawn into the nationalist movement through her writings. She analysed ancient Indian scientific texts in the light of Western science. She wrote that a scientific mind could drive any kind of superstition away. Until Indians could understand the necessity of science education, there would be no progress. Her scientific essays impressed the readers of her time. It was the early attempt of a woman to write on scientific themes and theories that was significant to understand the perception of gender of that time.

She argued for the betterment of the condition of women. All her life she struggled for their liberation. The fact that her own daughter Sarala did not get married till at a very late age and her son had an inter-caste marriage bears ample testimony to her strength of character. Her willingness to protest against injustice is evident in her claim that the *sastras* were for the good of mankind and so not unchangeable. Social norms should be made to accommodate changes keeping pace with time. Unlike any of her contemporaries she was well travelled which helped her to get acquainted with the diverse cultures of her country. Along with Kadambini Gangooly, Swarnakumari was one of the earliest women to participate in the session of the Indian National Congress.

Swarnakumari's notions of home, gender and nation were limited by the constraints of age and time. She attempted to promote women's empowerment through her own life, her activities and her writings. She believed in the inherent capabilities of women. She strongly adhered to the view that given the same kind of education and surroundings as her fellow women too would be able to give proof of their ability to serve their society and nation.

She focused primarily on the upper and upper middle class Hindu society. She concentrated on the betterment of the lot of women from these strata. Yet Swarnakumari's Sakhi Samiti did render substantial assistance to some poor and needy women. They were imparted education, trained to become teachers in the *antahpur*. Swarnakumari encouraged them to come out of the *purdah* and participate in active social life. She also tried to promote education among the women. However, on the whole, the poor and the needy were left out of the purview of their work.

Historically, Swarnakumari's contributions have great significance. She flourished and blossomed in the newly found freedom which literacy brought. It was access to the male preserve of learning which helped some women give expression to their feelings. She received recognition from her contemporaries for her work. Swarnakumari was widely acclaimed for her literary pursuits. She stressed on education and self-dependence for women. Only then she believed could their empowerment become a reality. She did not deny that women had an important role to play in the family and conjugal life. On the contrary, she gave a new meaning, a new dimension to the woman's position in society and in the work of nation building.

Notes

1. Referring to his childhood Rabindranath Tagore wrote: 'I was born in 1861. That is not an important date of history, but it belongs to a great epoch in Bengal, when the currents of three movements had met in the life of our country.'—*The Religion of an Artist*, Rabindranath Tagore, Kolkata: Visva-Bharati, 1988 (first delivered as a lecture in China in 1924), p. 7.
2. 14 Bhadra, 1263 BS (Bengali San/Era).
   Pashupati Shashmal, *Bangla Sahitya O Swarnakumari*, Santiniketan, 1378 BS, pp. 20-6.
3. 'Hooglir Imambari', *Bharati*, Year 8-10, 1291-3 BS.
4. Published in *Bharati O Balak* since 1299 BS and printed as a book in 1895.
5. The novel was based on relations between brother and sister. Perhaps Swarnakumari acquired the element of the novel from her own life. Her relations with Satyendranath, Jyotirindranath and Rabindranath are reflected in that novel.
6. Both were the female protagonists of Bankimchandra's popular novel *Bishabriksha* (The Poison Tree).
7. Susie Tharu and K. Lalita, eds., *Women Writing in India*, vol. I: *600 B.C. to the Early 20th Century*, Kolkata: Oxford University Press, 1991, p. 238.
8. Swarnakumari Devi, 'Strisiksha O Bethune School', *Bharati*, Shravan, 1294 BS.
   Ibid., 'Giltir Bazaar', *Bharati*, Baisakh, 1295 BS.
   Ibid., 'Bidhaba', *Bharati*, Baisakh 1318 BS.
   Ibid., 'Bidhaba Bibaha O Hindu Patrika', *Bharati*, Bhadra, 1316 BS.
   Ibid., 'Sakhisamiti O Mahilashilpamela', *Bharati*, Paush, 1298 BS.
   Ibid., 'Sat Batsare Sakhisamiti', *Bharati*, Ashar, 1315 BS.
9. Swarnakumari Devi, 'Strisiksha O Bethune School', *Bharati O Balak*, op. cit., 11th year, Sravan 1294 BS, pp. 224-9.
10. Swarnakumari Devi, 'Purusher Shresthatya', *Bharati*, Asar 1294, pp. 173-5.
11. Ibid., 'Ar Ekti Prastab', *Bharati O Balak*, 1293 BS.
12. Ibid., 'Amader Kartabya', *Bharati*, Vadra, 1315 BS.
    Ibid., Rajnaitik Prasanga', *Bharati*, Sravan, 1315 BS.

Ibid., 'Kartabya Kon Pothe', *Bharati*, Poush, 1315 BS.
Ibid., 'Engrejdiger Sahit Surendera Prasanga', *Masik Basumati*, Kartik, 1332 BS.

13. Ibid., 'Bengalee', *Bharati*, Ashar 1322 BS.
14. Sarala Devi, *Jibaner Jharapata*, Kolkata: Dey's Publishing, 2007 p. 174; Malavika Karlekar, *Voices From Within, Early Personal Narratives of Bengali Women*, New Delhi, 1993, p. 188.
15. Swarnakumari Devi, 'Amader Samaj', *Bharati O Balak*, Falgun, 1294 BS.
16. In the period of Swarnakumari's editorship, a number of articles were published in *Bharati* on contemporary women's issues, viz., the essay, '*Streelok O Purush*' (1296) by Krishnabhabini Das where she wrote, women were made only for men, this is not only wrong, but also very uncivilized and a hated practice.
17. Jogendranath Gupta gives an interesting description of the performance and the ambience in his book, *Banger Mahila Kabi*, Calcutta, 1337 BS, p. 46.
18. Indira Devi, the cousin of Hiranmayee, recollected the days how Hiranmayee tried hard to set up the home for the widows.
Ref. Indira Devi, *Smritisamput*, vol. I, Kolkata: Visva-Bharati, 2000, p. 22.
19. Sarala Devi, 'Hiranmayee Devi', *Bharati*, Falgun, 1332 BS, pp. 373-5.
20. Pashupati Shashmal, *Swarnakumari O Bangla Sahitya*, op. cit., p. 113.
21. Ibid., p. 110.
22. Swapan Basu, ed., *Sambad Samayikpatre Unish Shataker Bangalisamaj*, Paschim Banga Bangla Academy, Kolkata, vol. 1, 2000, pp. 70-2, 545, 547, 549; vol. 2, 2003, pp. 51, 668 and 701.
23. Sarala Devi, 'A Woman's Movement', *Modern Review*, October 1911.
24. Ghulam Murshid, *Reluctant Debutante: Response of Bengali Women to Modernization: 1849-1905*, Rajshahi: Sahitya Sangsad, 1983, p. 97.
25. Krishna Kripalini, *Dwarkanath Thakur: Bismrita Pathikrit*, tr. Kshitish Roy, New Delhi: National Book Trust, 2000; and Kishorichand Mitra, *Dwarkanath Tagore*, tr. Dwijendralal Nath, Kolkata, 1962.
26. Debendranath Tagore, *Aatmajibani*, ed. Sarishchandra Chakravorty, Calcutta: Visva-Bharati, 1962, p. 10
27. The editor was Monomohon Ghosh. Keshabchandra was also there with them till 1865. Later, because of a misunderstanding between Debendranath and Keshabchandra, the former left the project. He, thereafter, patronized *The National Paper* from 7 August 1865. The editor was Nabagopal Mitra.

28. Brajendranath Bandyopadhyay, 'Gaganendranath Tagore', *Visva-Bharati Patrika*, year 6, no. 2, p. 130.
29. Ibid.
30. *The National Paper*, 7 August 1872.
31. Rabindranath Tagore, *Jibansmriti,* Calcutta: Visva-Bharati, 1920, p. 56
32. Rabindranath Tagore, 'Swadesikata', in 'Jibansmriti', *Rabindra-Rachanabali*, vol. 17, Kolkata: Visva-Bharati, 1965, p. 348.
33. Ibid.
34. Debendranath Tagore, *Atmajibani*, ed. Satishchandra Chakravorty, Calcutta: Visva-Bharati, 1962.
35. Debendranath Tagore, *Patrabali*, no. 24, Calcutta, Magh 25, 1782, Sakabda, p. 30.
36. G. Paremeswaram Pillai, *Indian Congressmen*, 1899, p. 39.
37. Saumyajit Panja, *Freedom Struggle of India, Chronicle Events of India*, Kolkata: Ananda Prakashani, 2008, p. 150.
38. Karlekar, *Voices From Within*, op. cit., p. 178.
39. Dwarakanath Gangopadhyay was the initiator. The main intention was to promote indigenous products. Surendranath Bandyopadhyay was there to help him.
40. Abanindranath Tagore, *Gharoa,* Calcutta: Visva-Bharati, 1350 BS, p. 107.
41. 'Rajnaitik Prasanga', *Bharati*, Agrahayana, 1292 BS.
42. Madhumita Mondal, 'Rajnaitik Bhabna O Bhavnar Rajniti: Prasanga Swarnakumari Devi (1856-1932)', in *Itihaas Anusandhan-22*, Kolkata, January, 2008, pp. 844-8.
43. Pashupati Shashmal, one of the earliest and sincere researchers on Swarnakumari's writings, highly appreciates this novel in his book *Swarnakumari O Banglasahitya.*
44. Sarala Devi, *Jibaner Jharapata*, op. cit., p. 103.
45. Swarnakumari Devi, *Bichitra, Swapnabina, Milanratri.*
46. Mondal, 'Rajnaitik Bhabna O Bhavnar Rajniti', op. cit., pp. 844-8.
47. Swarnakumari Devi,'Kartavya Kon Pathe?', *Bharati*, Paush, 1315 BS.
48. Ibid., 'Amader Kartabya', *Bharati*, Bhadra, 1315 BS.
49. Ibid., 'Rajnaitik Prasanga', op. cit., Shravan, 1315 BS.
50. Ibid.
51. Ibid., 'Kartabya Kon Pathe', *Bharat*i, Year-32, Poush, 1315.
52. Ibid.
53. In an introduction of *Romesh Rachanabali*, Calcutta: Sahitya Sangsad, p. 100.

54. Swarnakumari Devi, *Swpnabina, Milanratri*, op. cit.
55. Ibid., 'Swadeshi Circus', *Bharati*, 1315 BS.
56. Swarnakumari dedicated her Collections of Shorts Stories to the soldiers and heroes of India.
57. 'Thousand lives are connected in single string.
    This bonding will remain throughout life,
    May end only in death.
    We are dedicating our life for mother India.'
58. Rabindranath Tagore, 'Nabyabanger Andolan', *Bharati*, 1296 BS.
59. As an editor, Swarnakumari commented on the above article in the footnote.
60. Swarnakumari Devi, 'Rajnaitik Prasanga'. It was published earlier in *Gurukul Samacharpatra*.
61. Commented upon by Amiyabhushan Basu in *Calcutta Municipal Gazette*.

    Padmini Sathianadhan wrote an essay, 'They Paved the Way: Srimati Swarna Kumari Devi', in *The Satesman*, 20 December, 1936, in which the above comment had been used.
62. Madhumita Mondal, 'Promotion of Science in Late Nineteenth Century Bengal: Swarnakumari Devi's Contribution', *Proceedings of the Indian History Congress*, Delhi, 2006, pp. 1209-13. The article was presented as a seminar paper in the session of 66th Indian History Congress, held at Santiniketan, 2006.
63. Swarnakumari Devi, 'Bignan Shiksha', *Bharati*, Shravan, 1289 BS.

CHAPTER 8

Family Health and Dissemination of Medical Knowledge in Nineteenth Century India

SUJATA MUKHERJEE

In nineteenth century India, urban centres such as Calcutta witnessed publication of numerous writings on home and family life. These included manuals addressed simultaneously to men and women and also books on health and hygiene and on the rearing of children, where the audience intended was unclear.[1] The aim of the present essay is to trace the growth of this genre of Bengali writings and analyse the context, content and impact of these writings to highlight certain aspects of medicalization of society in colonial India.

By far the largest numbers of books included in this collection were manuals written specifically for women. Between 1860 and 1900, more than forty advice-for-women manuals were written in Bengali (most in the 1880s) and thirty-seven women's magazines and journals came into existence between 1860 and 1910.[2] Whether published as separate books or within the pages of contemporary women's magazines, these works addressed a wide range of topics from purely medical discussions concerned with hygiene and disease, to discussions of household management, family relationships, child-rearing practices and so on. They show how the entire Hindu domestic life, from households' organization to family and gender relationships, became contested grounds. The Hindu woman and her domestic world were, in fact, at the centre of a debate over modernity and indigenous home and family life. To the colonized, the presence of colonial modernity as an alternative cultural system problematized all areas of indigenous life. The need to respond to both the civilizing mission of colonial ideology and to new conditions of life and work in British India had led Bengali and Indian men to construct new definitions of their own identities, roles, and relationships of the women in their homes.

Modernity had different connotations for indigenous reformers in nineteenth century India. Many scholars have explored its relationship to emerging nationalist discourses, its connections with the revitalizations of the Hindu Renaissance, its role in transforming traditions of music and art, so on.[3] I intend to focus on a less discussed subject and will seek to analyse the significance of the health advices contained in different manuals and other writings which became part of a new ideal of indigenous domesticity through which, the indigenous reformers sought to negotiate and reformulate the received notion of colonial modernity.

Domesticity and Colonialism

Scholars are generally agreed, domesticity, which essentially meant a set of ideas about the proper ordering of home and family relations, was a secular discourse produced by the nineteenth century European middle classes and was integral to bourgeois ideology and self-identity.[4] Central to this domestic discourse was a conviction that the 'natural' order of human relations involved a patriarchal family system with a gendered separation of spheres of activity and the husband at the head of the family unit.[5]

Bourgeois domestic discourse and the practices to which it gave rise were incorporated into the civilizing mission of colonialism itself.[6] In India, the British conceptualized the difference between Great Britain and India in terms of—apart from history and race—gender. Indian ideas of domestic life were described as 'barbaric' and demeaning for women when compared to Europe's 'civilized' notions about domesticity in general and women's freedom and equality in particular. In *The History of British India* (1826), James Mill stated: 'Nothing can exceed the habitual contempt which the Hindus entertain for their women. [They] ... are held ... in extreme degradation.'[7]

His view was an early, influential example of what would become a general theme in British writings on Indian civilization. The English-educated Indians in the city of Calcutta (mostly high caste Hindus with no prior tradition of manual labour were part of an all-India group, numbering perhaps fifty thousand by the late 1880s), as in other parts of India, had access to all the discourses of British colonial modernity and the 'civilizing mission,' and to colonialism's negative formulations of Indian identity and culture as 'decadent', 'weak' and 'effeminate'. Both in response to the colonial critique of Indian domestic practices and to changing demand of life under British rule, English-educated and/or Western-influenced Indian men increasingly saw the reform of women's social conditions—most particularly women's literacy and education—as the key to both India's progress and their own.

Majority of the vernacular literature on domesticity were written and published in Calcutta, the 'second city' of the British empire in the nineteenth century where the ideologies of British colonialism and structures of British power had come to dominate the public and working worlds of the city and where by the mid-nineteenth century, a substantial publishing industry had grown up in urban centres of the British Raj. Bengali writers initially produced advice literature for girls to use at home—for home education (the *zenana* system) and for home tutoring, both of which were popular in the 1860s and 1870s. Over the entire nineteenth century the number of girls attending schools continued to rise.[8] By 1881, government reports for Bengal listed the number of women's schools at 1,042 and of girls' students at 44,096. By 1891, the number of schools had doubled to 2,239 and the number of students had risen to 78,865. *Zenana* education also remained popular, at least, till the end of the nineteenth century.

New women, Domesticity and Health Advices

Behind the Indian middle classes' support for female education was an urge to create a compatriot wife. These new women were expected to develop as companions to men, as scientific nurturers, and as members of civil society, they were to remain a socially distanced class from the common or lower class women; inhabiting a world of unrefined, coarse, popular culture.[9] Thus, the main social utility of women's educational project was seen as lying in the constructive role expected to be played by the new women in bringing about moral and social welfare of family members.[10] As the discourse of domesticity made its appearance among the colonized, its central images, the well-ordered home and the skilful wife who ran it became tropes for progress and happiness that European civilization could bring. Punctuality, cleanliness, order, and discipline were seen as the inherent characteristics of European homes while dirt, disorder, and disease characterized the indigenous household.[11]

Large number of pedagogical texts written in this period, which produced a normative discourse on family, included guidelines for an ideal housewife for proper home management, scientific nurturing of children, regulation of dietary habits, creation of hygienic environment, etc. I will cite only a few examples from a large volume of literature on the subject. Conversations with the wife (*Strirsahitkathopakathan*) written by Dhirendranath Pal, a Brahmo (1883), taught details of hygiene, nursing, account keeping, and correct letter writing. The fact that this book lasted through more than twenty years and nine different editions indicates that its author's choices struck a sympathetic note with a wide range of readers. *The Duties of Women* (*Ramanir Kartavya*), composed by two authors—Giribala Mitra and Jayakrishna Mitra (1890)—contained sections on 'child rearing' where readers would learn what to feed a baby from infancy up to two years of age. It included, general advice on which food items were nutritious and also pointed out that every room of a house should be regularly and thoroughly cleaned for cleanliness to improve everyone's health.[12]

One noticeable feature of medical advices for women contained in manuals as well as periodicals was their heterogeneous nature. Women were expected to know a bit of all available forms of treatment, including folk medicine, allopathy, homoeopathy, *kabiraji*, and *hakimi*.[13] *Bamabodhinipatrika* (the longest surviving women's magazine), for example, included a regular feature on elementary home remedies called *Garhasthyacikitsapranali.* Other women's magazines including *Antahpur*, *Mahila* (both appeared in the 1890s) also published writings on treatment and medical advices. Women themselves were becoming aware of the importance of acquiring at least some basic knowledge of different forms of therapies and supported that. For example, one female writer advocated the 'common-sense' observance of certain rules of hygiene, with the use of Western drugs.[14] Satyacharan Mitra in his book *A Husband's Advice to His Wife* (*Strirpratisvamirupades*) wrote about the benefits of using neem twig instead of tooth powder for cleaning tooth.[15]

Why so much Emphasis on Health Advice?

The question arises why there was so much emphasis on medical advice. Another related question is why the educated women were advised to acquire skills in new medical knowledge as well as indigenous therapies. Undoubtedly, middle class Bengali Hindus were greatly concerned about the supposed continuous deterioration of the health of the Bengalis, and wrote a lot about the need to investigate the causes of this phenomenon and about different measures to be adopted to improve health conditions.[16] One way of improving health conditions was for mothers themselves to know something of different medical principles. Pratapchandra Majumdar, one of the early authors on the new role of women, remarked: 'Because of the flaws of the mother, the child is ruined; when the child is ruined, the family is ruined; when family life crumbles, society decays; and when society is polluted, no nation can advance.'[17]

It was pointed out that women who were ignorant of the rules of the body would not only harm themselves, but by producing weak and deficient children would also destroy the nation.[18]

One of the reasons behind advocacy of native remedies was their cheapness. Moreover, many believed that Western medicine was not always suitable for the Indians and, in fact, was harmful. Women were often criticized for having lost the expertise in native folk medicine held by women of previous generations and for harming children by giving them Western medicine. Rajnarain Bose, for example, pointed out that children of recent generations were weaker than in the past because their mothers treated them with Western rather than native medicines.[19]

At the same time, middle-class Indians were not averse to adopting Western medical knowledge because it was considered to be the vehicle of progress. It may not be irrelevant to mention that Dwarakanath Ganguly, a radical Brahmo reformer who among others supported medical education for women and who was the teacher, mentor and husband of Kadambini, the first qualified Indian lady doctor (1886), (a recipient of GBMC degree of the Calcutta Medical College), once wrote: 'Rather than learning the fine geographic details of various countries, it would be worthwhile to examine whether or not it is more relevant to have a basic knowledge of Physiology.'[20] The widely held view that Indian women patients would face death rather than accept treatment by male physicians, which gave a boost to promotion of medical education for women (this view was upheld by both Indian and British supporters of medical education for Indian women), also no doubt prompted many to write guide books and health manuals addressed to women and include health advices in writings on domesticity. A number of quasi-medical manuals were published on birth management, child care, etc., many of which were adaptations or translations of English language guidebooks. In 1857, the first of a continuing stream of mother and child care manuals, an adaptation of Andrew Combe's *Treatise on the Physiological and Moral Management of Infancy*, appeared under the title of *Sisupalan*: *Infant Treatment* authored by Shib Chunder Deb.[21] A manual of general instruction for women, published in 1862, stressed the importance of prenatal care.[22] The *bhadramahila* were encouraged to take up midwifery. In 1867, the *Bamabodhinipatrika* published a series of detailed and informative articles on midwifery, covering pregnancy, its symptoms and treatment, and delivery. Manuals on household hints and collections of essays for the purpose of female education generally contained sections on midwifery. Doctors wrote more detailed books of advice for expectant mothers. Jadunath Mukhopadhyaya, LMS of Calcutta Medical College wrote, *Dhatrisikshaebongprasutisiksha* or *A Guide to Native Midwives & Mothers* in two volumes (first published in 1867). *Saral Dhatrisiksha* written by Sundarimohan Das MB, Professor of Midwifery of Physician and Surgeon College, was published in 1308 BS.

With the institutionalization of medicine in nineteenth century and emergence and spread of the knowledge of a group of professional doctors, more and more families were becoming exposed to various kinds of expertise on medical matters, child rearing, etc. Parents, especially mothers, were expected to become the experts' allies, the supposed educators of the family and executors of the experts' orders. Parents were advised to follow the dictates of the experts and to prepare themselves by reading appropriate books and journals. Instructions like the following, for instance, were quite common: 'For the proper rearing of children, for proper knowledge about the child's nutrition and health, you should read appropriate books, you should take advice from expert physicians....'[23]

Thus, with the emergence of family as a site where nationalist restructuring was to be carried out, women were awarded a special, augmented status in remodelling the private domain of the nation. Undoubtedly, there was an economic dimension involved because the *bhadramahila* was expected to master the technique of becoming a *sugrihini* or good wife, by acquiring elementary knowledge of medical remedies as this would save the family a lot of expenses in doctors' fees.[24] In the new situation, mothers were advised to educate themselves to be able to understand and execute the medical experts' instructions to which the family had become exposed. At the same time, they were expected to act as repository of traditional knowledge.

Conclusion

It may be pointed out that the heterogeneous nature of health advices contained in domestic manuals as well as in articles, published in different periodicals addressed to women helps us understand the contested medical world which became influenced and the new world of domesticity. The educated middle class or *bhadralok* as well as *bhadramahila* in colonial India, tried to blend indigenous tradition with modern or Western medicine in reformulation of Western ideal of domesticity.

As pointed out by researchers, biographical evidence shows that some women did try to follow the advice given in the manuals. However, there is no direct evidence that would prove conclusively that the kind of knowledge disseminated here actually filtered down to the majority of the *bhadramahila.* The value of these manuals and other writings lie in the fact that they reflect the attitudes of the writers. As already pointed out, the family was becoming exposed to many outside forces, including the intervention of doctors or trained professional experts and the educated women were expected to assist them, and advises contained in manuals and other writings are partly intended to enable them to follow and execute the advices of medical experts. Theoretically at least, this created the possibility of augmentation of women's power through self-improvement and through acting under the guidance of outside experts along with development of their own skill by acquiring some degree of all available forms of elementary medical knowledge. The new, modern, educated women by simultaneously absorbing new health guidelines and knowledge of hygiene and treatment and also acting as repository of traditional knowledge would create the possibility of facilitation of women's empowerment.

Notes

1. These include books such as the Bengali translation of the English *The Parent's Friend* (1881), the 1895 *Diseases of Childhood*, or the enormously popular *The Body's Nutrition*, a Bengali language book that had reached its twenty-ninth edition by 1891.
2. Usha Chakraborty, *Conditions of Bengali Women Around the 2nd Half of the 19th Century*, Calcutta: Self-published, 1963, pp. 184-5, 190-1.
3. See for example, works like Partha Chatterjee, *Nationalist Thought and the Colonial World*, Minneapolis: University of Minnesota Press, 1986; 'The Nationalist Resolution of the Women's Question', in K. Sangari and S. Vaid, eds., *Recasting Women*, New Brunswick: Rutgers University Press, 1990; *The Nation and its Fragments*, Princeton, N.J.: Princeton University Press, 1993; Sumit Sarkar, *Writing Social History*, Delhi/New York: Oxford University Press,1997; Tanika Sarkar, *Words to Win*, New Delhi: Kali for Women, 1999, *Hindu Wife, Hindu Nation*, Bloomington: Indiana University Press, 2001; Brian Hatcher, *Idioms of Improvement*, New Delhi: Oxford University Press, 1996; Dipesh Chakrabarty, *Provincializing Europe*, Princeton, N.J.: Princeton University Press, 2000.
4. It is linked by most contemporary scholarship with the beginnings

of industrialization, industrial capitalism, and the new modes of production of the late eighteenth and early nineteenth centuries. See Carmen Luke, *Pedagogy, Printing and Protestantism*, Albany: State University of New York Press, 1989; Leonore Davidoff and Catherine Hall, *Family Fortunes: Men and Women of the English Middle Class, 1780-1850*, Chicago: University of Chicago Press, 1987; Jean Comaroff and John L. Comaroff, 'Home-made Hegemony', in K. Hansen, ed., *African Encounters with Domesticity*, New Brunswick: Rutgers University Press, 1992.

5. Davidoff and Hall, ibid.
6. Comaroff and Comaroff, ibid.
7. Quoted in Geraldine Forbes, 'Negotiating Modernities: The Public and Private Worlds of Dr. Haimabati Sen' in Avril A. Powell and Siobhan Lambert-Hurley, eds., *Rhetoric and Reality-Gender and the Colonial Experience in South Asia,* New Delhi: Oxford University Press, 2006, p. 225.
8. In 1862-3, the government's Report on Public Instruction published its first statistics on women's educational institutions in Bengal. It recorded the existence of 15 schools for girls and 530 attending students.
9. Geraldine Forbes, *The New Cambridge History of India, IV.2, Women in Modern India*, Cambridge University Press, First South Asian Paperback Edition, 1998, p. 41. Also see Sumanta Banerjee, 'Marginalization of Women's Popular Culture in Nineteenth Century Bengal', in *Recasting Women: Essays in Colonial History*, Kumkum Sangari and Sudesh Vaid, eds., New Delhi: Kali for Women, 1989.
10. Himani Bannerji, 'Fashioning a Self: Educational Proposals for and by Women in Popular Magazines in Colonial Bengal', *Economic and Political Weekly*, 1991, pp. 26, 43.
11. Dipesh Chakrabarty, 'Postcoloniality and the Artifice of History', in R. Guha, ed., *A Subaltern Studies Reader 1986-1995*, Minneapolis: University of Minnesota Press, 1997. It must be mentioned that concern for women's social conditions and the reform of home and family life were all-India phenomena in the late nineteenth and early twentieth centuries. Young, English-educated men from many regions wrote and spoke hopefully of the importance of women's literacy and education and despairingly of the possibility of happiness if married to an illiterate wife. In the colonial context, domestic and daily behaviour patterned on the European model was coded as evidence of (potential) civilizational superiority.

12. Judith E. Walsh, *How to be the Goddess of Your Home: An Anthology of Bengali Domestic Manuals*, New Delhi: Yoda Press, 2005.
13. Meredith Borthwick, *The Changing Role of Women in Bengal 1849-1905*, Princeton, N.J.: Princeton University Press, 1984, p. 219.
14. Lilabati Mitra, '*Grihaswasthyeramanir dristi*', *Antahpur*, 7, 9. cited in Borthwick, ibid., p. 221.
15. It was published in Calcutta in 1884. He wrote at least eight books in his lifetime; four were works of fiction. Among his seven Bengali books, four focused on women. *A Husband's Advice to His Wife* was self-published.
16. See articles like 'Indigenous Health Science', in *Swasthya*, Magh (January-February), BS 1307, (1901) in Pradip Bose, ed., *Health and Society in Bengal*, New Delhi: Sage, pp. 126-38; 'Precepts for Good Health', in *Vigyan Darpan*, Bhadra (Aug.-Sept.), 1289 BS (1882), P. Bose, ibid., pp. 120-2, 'The Revival of National Physical Health', in *Chikitsa Sammilani*, Baisakh (April-May), 1292 BS (1885), P. Bose, ibid., pp. 105-16.
17. Pratapchandra Majumdar, *Stricharitra,* p. 14, Calcutta, *Nababidhan*, 1891, cited in Pradip Kumar Bose, 'Sons of the Nation: Child Rearing in the New Family', in Partha Chatterjee, ed., *Texts of Power: Emerging Disciplines in Colonial Bengal*, Calcutta, Samya, 1996, p. 123.
18. Prasannatara Gupta, *Paribarikjiban,* Calcutta: Kuntaleen Press, 1903, p. 82 cited in Pradip Kumar Bose, ibid.
19. Rajnarain Bose, *Se Kal ar E Kal*, Calcutta: Bangiya Sahitya Parishad, 1976 (1874), p. 87, cited in Borthwick, op. cit., p. 220.
20. Quoted in Malavika Karlekar, 'Kadambini and the Bhadralok', *Economic and Political Weekly*, vol. 21, no. 19 (26 April 1986), pp. WS-25-31.
21. Shib Chunder Deb, *Sisupalan*, Part I, Serampore, 1857; part 2, Calcutta, 1862.
22. Mohendracandra Gupta, *Stribodh*, Dacca, 1862
23. Bose, 'Sons of the Nation ...', op. cit., p. 123.
24. In 1878, a native doctor's fee varied from Rs. 3 to 10; a European doctor charged Rs. 16. Lady Doctors charged Rs. 10 per visit. Borthwick, op. cit., p. 217.

CHAPTER 9

His Nest and His Sky

Rabindranath Tagore, Women and the Idea of the Feminine

SWATI GANGULY

> My mind must have a nest to which the voice of the sky can descend freely, the sky that has no other allurements but light and freedom.*

In his writing about the life of Leonardo da Vinci, Sigmund Freud suggested what a biographical study ought to do: 'If a biographical study really seeks to arrive at an understanding of the mental life of its hero, it must not—as most biographies do, out of discretion or prudery—keep silent about his … sexual individuality.'[1]

The educated middle-class Bengali has shown two tendencies regarding, the 'sexual individuality' of Rabindranath Tagore: the prudish and the prurient. The former regard as taboo any discussion of erotic-emotional life of Rabindranath, the 'Gurudev' who is to be respected, revered and deified. On the opposite end of the spectrum are those who are titillated by the possibility of new, more exciting material about Rabindranath's 'private life'. Indeed, these could be seen as the two sides of the same coin—stern custodians of sexual morality and those who derive pleasure from pursuing salacious gossip. Was it the sign of the repression of an entire linguistic community?

A section of the publishing industry thrives by focusing on his relationships with a chosen few: his sister-in-law Kadambari, the wife of his elder brother Jyotirindranath, the aristocratic Argentine feminist Victoria Ocampo; and Ranu Adhikary, a pretty, precocious young girl who began corresponding with Rabindranath when she was not even in her teens. The writings may roughly be categorized into two types: the avowedly academic and the flagrantly fictional.

The academic works are concerned with tracing the identity of the real woman/women who served as the feminine 'inspiration' behind Rabindranath's creativity, both verbal and visual. Thus, in a pioneering Bengali work, the poet's *manashi* (which translates as the muse in the European literary tradition), is most definitely identified as his sister-in-law, his brother Jyotirindranath's wife, Kadambari Devi.[2] A more recent work by a well-known historian explores the centrality of the notion of *jeebon debota* (Lord of Life) in Tagore's oeuvre, draws attention to its figuration to the image of a woman which recurs in his work and suggests that the roots of what is evidently a philosophical-spiritual notion can be traced to the real presence of three women in different phases of his life. It is not difficult to guess their identities: Kadambari Devi, Rabindranath's wife Mrinalini Devi and his Argentine friend Victoria Ocampo.[3] Such scholarship involves a close reading of Rabindranath's biography, memoirs, oral testimonies and letters against his oeuvre, spanning almost all literary genres.

There is enough evidence, most of these given by Rabindranath himself, about individual works—for example, poems or songs inspired by Kadambari Devi.[4] Tagore scholars have surmised that the young Ranu Adhikary was the inspiration behind several of Rabindranath's mature works, especially a play and a novel.[5] It was while he was at the Villa Miralrio, in San Isidro, Buenos Aires, as a guest of Victoria Ocampo that Rabindranath composed many of the poems of *Purabi*. The volume was formally dedicated to her. Thus, there are obvious instances of how knowledge of biography helps.

To suggest, however, that Tagore's entire oeuvre can be understood on the basis of inspiration and influence of individual women, to establish one-to-one equations, is to do injustice to a very complex process of creativity.[6] This is particularly misleading in the case of Rabindranath who inherited an ethical-philosophical tradition of the monotheistic Brahmo religion, a spirituality whose basis was the worship of God-the-Father. However, it is also true that the stern patriarchal nature of the inheritance underwent transformations through Rabindranath's deep reading and imbibing of alternative literary and philosophical traditions. The most important of these are the erotic devotional Vaishnava poetry in which the poet often assumes the persona of a women desiring her lover. Indeed, the emotion of *biraha*, a deep longing filled with melancholy (a leitmotif of many of Tagore's poems and lyrics), is traditionally regarded as a feminine expression. He was also influenced by the *bauls* of Bengal, whose thinking radically reformulates the patriarchal understanding of gender relations.

While academic or scholarly work may have a limited address, it is the works of fiction that enjoy immense popularity among a very large community of readers. Such fiction necessarily claims historical veracity.[7] There are Tagore scholars who tread the middle path and write well-researched essays that cater to the popular desire to know more about the secret life of the man whose iconic saint-like photograph adorns the walls of their living rooms. These writings thrive because readers flock to the book-stores as soon as a new book is released; the increasing re-prints or new editions testify to the popularity of these volumes.

It would be a mistake to dismiss this phenomenon merely as perverse voyeuristic delight. Read symptomatically, the undiminished interest surrounding the subject indicates Rabindranath's role in shaping the psycho-sexual coming of age of the Bengali community, its tryst with modernity.

By the first decade of the twentieth century, the amazingly prolific Rabindranath Tagore had not only established himself as a poet, but also as a novelist, a writer of short-stories, travelogues, letters, critical essays, and a song-writer. He proved himself indispensable as an editor of literary magazines/journals. The assessment of 'reception'—the various sources, both Indian and European—he drew upon eclectically is a specialized field of scholarship. What is pertinent is the recognition that Rabindranath Tagore could be regarded as truly *sui generis* as a creative artist—he not only perfected some of the existing literary genres, but invented new ones, created hybrid varieties, especially in the field of music and performances.[8]

There is a saga, at least a hundred years old, of the complex affect of Tagore's personality and more important his works, *Rabindra-Sahitya* as it is popularly known, on the middle-class cultural life of Bengal. The history of the affect is a largely unrecorded one. It is only in some fictions and memoirs that one can occasionally get a glimpse of how central Rabindranath Tagore was in the lives of individuals and of generations. Maitreyi Devi's autobiographical novel *Na Hanyate* (*It Does Not Die*) is one such work. The novel has long passages about the young, beautiful and talented Amrita's erotic relation with Tagore's poetry, most of which she can recite at will, from memory. These and the lyrics of certain *sangeet* of Rabindranath acquire new meaning when Amrita begins her passionate, secret affair with Mircea Eliade, the Romanian research scholar who came to read Indian philosophy with her father. On one occasion when Amrita visits the poet, she is overwhelmed with emotions and begins to weep uncontrollably, sitting at his feet. The saint-like poet, who understands her turmoil at once, places his palm on her head like a divine benediction asking her to calm down. This incident is no doubt singular/exceptional in its description of a young woman's feelings as if she were experiencing an epiphany; the fiction suggests that such heightened emotion would never have been possible without the textual presence of Rabindranath Tagore.[9]

It would not be an exaggeration to suggest that the popularization of his songs or *Rabindrasangeet* has had the greatest impact on the Bengali psyche. Rabindranath had once said that he would live on in his songs, a statement which seems prophetic. The average Bengali, who may not even have a nodding acquaintance with his essays and novels, has nevertheless listened to *Rabindrasangeet* with rapt attention being broadcast at regular intervals on the All India Radio; they have spent money buying the marvellous products of recording technology—the long-playing records, cassettes and of late compact disks, that have allowed him/her to listen to the renditions of Tagore songs by their favourite artistes. Bengali film directors, either mainstream or alternative have often turned to *Rabindrasangeet* to convey heightened emotions—either of love or loss, desire or death.[10] Tagore's songs have entered the unconscious, played a crucial role in shaping the notion of the famous Bengali romantic character, its 'refined', 'sensitive' approach to desire. It is likely that the educated middle-class Bengali audience-spectator continues to be captivated by the adaptations of Tagore's fiction because it allows him/her to express a 'superior' cultural taste. Cinematic adaptations have also shown a trend of focusing on representations of women characters, of suggesting that they constitute the crux of the narratives.[11] As in the case of contemporary production of his plays, cinema is a subject of controversy with purists hotly debating populists in staking a claim for their 'own' Rabindranath.[12]

Thus, it is hardly surprising that the educated middle-class Bengali should be forever curious to delve deep into the life of the mind of the man who shaped theirs. Unfortunately, there has been no attempt to write a complete psychological biography of Rabindranath Tagore, a work which would combine the critical tools of psychoanalysis, with a sensitive historicized reading of the main events of his life, in particular the life of the mind. Tracing the life of the mind of Rabindranath Tagore is a tough task. Biography alone can never be the sole resource in such ventures, but it can also be of assistance, especially when located in a historical context. The evolving relation between the sexes during the eighty years of his life-time constitutes one aspect of this history.

In *Civilization and its Discontents,* Freud suggested that in the context of the formation of the family and civilization the word love could be understood in two senses—the one concerned with sexual satisfaction and that which he calls aim-inhibited love (that for siblings, parents) or affection. He goes on to suggest that the aim-inhibited love, once fully sensual is still so in the unconscious; its drive, however is towards friendships, to non-exclusivity.[13] Using this Freudian, explanatory Model I would like to suggest that in Rabindranath was a man who was also highly self-conscious about his own calling—which he sometimes described as fulfilling a divine destiny, Rabindranath probably felt what Freud calls an aim-inhibited love which allowed him to form non-exclusive friendship like relations with men and also with women.

This returns us to the vexed question with which we began, why Rabindranath and Women. It may be worth expanding the scope of the question by asking is there any reason to suggest that Rabindranath had a special affinity for the feminine? A feminist

Tagore scholar once commented that Rabindranath must have been deeply affected by a remark made early in his adolescence, by one of his female relatives, that Rabi was not quite the Man. Tall, strapping, with fine facial features, a luxuriant beard, the handsome young Rabi was not overtly effeminate in so far as his looks were concerned. His reading was eclectic, but not overtly inclined to issues of gender. Yet his inclinations to certain modes of aesthetic expression—singing, writing lyrical love poems, could be regarded, within the dominant gendered mores of the society in which he lived, as feminized.[14] Evidently, it would be difficult to identify definite 'sources' for a peculiar admixture of the masculine and feminine in Tagore's personality and his work. Perhaps the affinity with women had roots in his intense emotional experiences in his adolescence and early youth.

Rabindrananth Tagore was born and came of age at a time when Bengali society was a sex-segregated, gender–hierarchized patriarchy. The famous Jorasanko household too had an *andar* (inner, private quarters) and a *sadar* (outer, public space) with a corresponding female/male gendering of spaces. It was not a custom of couples to meet at day-time or engage in any overt display of affection. Women were not part of the public space and sphere and those who did so were subjects of gossip or censure. It was also a time when one of the major debates was what historians term the 'women question', a broad rubric within which the 'bundle of reformist issues' concerning 'women's education, widow immolation, widow marriage, polygamy, age of consent, child marriage, and seclusion of women' were clubbed together.[15] So, the young Rabindranath inherited and was part of both these worlds—a largely tradition-bound world of daily habitation in the family and the social space and a continually evolving radicalized world of ideas and discourses. The latter existed not in isolation but in a dialectical relation with the former.

There was also a third world that Rabindranath inhabited; this was the world of his travels, both within the country and to foreign lands. He was sent to England in his early youth to pursue higher education. After his marriage when he had just begun to live with his family, Debendranath sent him to oversee the family estates in rural Bengal. In his later, mature years Rabindranath travelled to United States of America and Japan. This was followed by extensive tours of Europe (including Russia), Argentina, China and the many countries of South-East Asia. A man with a wanderlust Rabindranath received invitations across the globe, especially after the award of the Nobel. His travelogues are testimonies of his close observations, among others issues, of the differences of gender expectations, roles and modes of behaviour—in short, the ideas of the feminine as they have shaped in the West and in the East, in the country and the city.

To understand Rabindranath is to locate him in the interface of all these worlds. Such an interface does not always present a smooth surface of transition, i.e. from an older, traditional to a new-modern mode of thinking. There is a critical tendency to posit Rabindranath as pro-feminist or proto-feminist. Some of his short-stories and novels are often cited as instances of his radical thinking. Yet, the very same Rabindranath often expressed considerably conservative views about women's gender roles in his lectures, essays or informal conversation. These forms of writings reveal a mode of thinking in binaries, a tendency to use gendered tropes—to regard certain issues or subjects as masculine and feminine. Thus, a reader attempting to look for an upward curve of the graph, one which would reveal him to have become more radical with time, may be baffled. The problem lies with our expectations. Amazingly prolific, Rabindranath was also exceptionally diverse in his creative endeavour, moving among different genres not only of writing but those of performance and visual arts. He understood and responded to the demands of genre, to differences which occur in thinking and writing in a certain literary type, in ways which only an artist can. It would indeed be a disservice to his complexity as an artist to expect him to fit neatly into contemporary cartographies of gender.

II

How does Rabindranath Tagore's biography appear when seen through the lens of his relationships with the women in his family? Fortunately, the two memoirs that Rabindranath wrote—*Jibansmriti*

(1912) [*My Reminiscences*] and *Chhelebela* (1940) [*My Boyhood Days*]—contain vivid and poignant accounts which naturally lend themselves to such a reading.

Rabi grew up in a mansion which was divided into a *sadar* and an *andar.* As a child Rabindranath, like his other brothers, cousins and nephews, had little access to the inner quarters; he remained under the supervision of a strict man servant. As a sensitive boy, given to day-dreaming and musing it was likely that he craved for maternal affection. The patrician arrangement of the Tagore household deprived him of his mother's personal care. He writes of how on certain evenings he would go inside the house to find his mother playing cards with her aunt. The raucous behaviour of the boys would make his mother give up on her recreation and depart; in his memoirs it is never his mother Saradasundari who climbs on the large four-poster bed to cuddle up to the children and tell them a fairy tale.[16] Rabindranath recalls the night when his mother, who had been ailing for a long time, passed away. He was woken up from sleep by the lamentations of the old nurse with a sinking heart but was unable to fathom what had happened. The impact of her death happened in the morning when the body was being taken for cremation, when he felt a 'storm of grief pass through me at the thought that mother would never return by this door'.[17]

Kadambari, quite precocious for her age, probably realized the loneliness of his sensitive young *thakurpo*. She captivated the imagination of this sensitive romantic adolescent with an aesthetic of living that was unique to the Tagore family. Kadambari transformed the second floor terrace into a roof garden with plants that were famous for their sweet-smelling flowers: *chameli, gandharaj, rajanigandha, karabi*, and *dolon-champa.* It was in this enchanted enclosed garden that musical soirees were held, with Jyotirindranath playing on the violin and Rabi singing in his clear treble voice. It was Kadambari, with her unerring ability to spot literary talent, who patronized the budding lyric poet Biharilal Chakravarty. She was instrumental in shaping Rabi's taste for literature, and also inspire his poetic compositions. In many ways she was his muse, but quite unlike the stereotype of the distant, cruel beloved who the European poets imagined in their love lyrics. A close kin, Kadambari was also a care giver, a nurturer; she possessed remarkable ability to mould herself and others and transformed the quotidian into the magical. She probably held the keys to the young poet's heart. Much of Rabi's life revolved around Kadambari; yet he could hardly address the sufferings of this young woman from bouts of melancholy and depression which culminated in her suicide.[18]

Speculations have been rife about the exact nature of the relationship that Rabindranath shared with Kadambari. The questions seem to haunt critics and readers alike. Curious minds fail to grasp that two highly sensitive, creative and gifted young people belonging to different sexes may have an affinity which is difficult to classify within the middle-class norms of sex-gender relationship. Critics have argued that Rabindranath continued to mourn for her throughout his life in the best of his lyrics, poetry and stories of loss and longing. Hers was the face that surfaced from the depths of his unconscious in his paintings, which he began doing rather late in life.

Did the death of his beloved *natun bouthan* adversely affect his newly formed conjugal relations? There is no evidence to prove this. Critics and biographers have often hinted that Mrinalini (whose original name Bhabatarini was changed after her marriage to make it more 'suitable' to the Tagore family) was perhaps not the ideal partner for the immensely gifted Rabindranath. After all, she did not share his literary sensibility or creative talent and was intellectually incapable of understanding his genius. However, there is no reason to believe theirs was not a successful marriage. Rabindranath was deeply fond of his wife, who very soon became a mother. He encouraged her to adapt the *Ramayana* for children, and according to eye-witness accounts, gave her company, especially when she was in the kitchen, assisting, as he often jocularly said, in improving her culinary skills. Mrinalini was devoted to him and his ideals even if it may have interfered with her notions of a perfect family life. In fact, it must have been very difficult for her to live up to the expectation of being the wife of a genius. Mrinalini's willingness to participate in all his ventures bears testimony to her attempt to become a perfect helpmate.

The turn of the century boded ill for Rabindranath's personal life, even as he was trying to establish his dream project of a school in

Santiniketan. Rabindranath arranged for the wedding of his eldest daughter Madhurilata in 1901 and then fixed a match for his second daughter Renuka soon after. Around this time Mrinalini fell ill; Rabindranath's youngest daughter Mira has written about how her father spent entire nights nursing his wife, often fanning her with a palm-leaf fan since there was no electricity in those days. While Mrinalini was ailing his daughter Renuka, always a little pale and weak, was in a serious medical condition. While the exact reasons were not diagnosed, the doctors advised a change of climate. Rabindranath took Renuka to Almora via Hazaribagh in the hope that the cooler climate would improve her condition; when these attempts failed he brought her back to Calcutta, staying at her bed-side, reading to her. The deaths of his wife and daughter in quick succession, in 1902 and 1903 must have affected him deeply, but there was no outward expression of sorrow and bereavement. This unusual ability to contain his grief would become characteristic of Rabindranath, who witnessed many more deaths of his dear ones.

Around 1917, his eldest and favourite daughter Madhurilata or Bela who had been estranged from him for a long time was diagnosed with tuberculosis. Rabindranath spent long hours with his ailing daughter, even if he was an unwelcome visitor. Apparently, it was on the day she passed away that he walked to meet Ranu Adhikary, who had been corresponding with him. A straightforward psychoanalytic reading of this event might suggest that Ranu became a supplement, i.e. took the place of the daughter he lost. The affection that he may have felt for the pretty and precocious Ranu, his indulgent attitude allowed her to claim a special place in his life. Biographical criticism has made much of this relation. There have been suggestions, that for at least seven years, till her marriage in 1925, Ranu was not only a favourite but also in many ways central to his creative impulse.[19] The representation of women in works written during this period all bear the mark of this affective relationship.

It was during 1924 that Rabindranath met Victoria Ocampo, the aristocratic, charismatic Argentine who later became a major feminist. It was a chance meeting but a momentous one. Victoria had already read *Gitanjali* in the French translation by Andre Gide; this was a time when she was going through a crisis in her own life—

it was the dark night of the soul. The verses came to her as a solace, as the voice of faith. It was Victoria who took the initiative to meet Rabindranath; she suggested that he recuperate in the beautiful Villa Miralrio which she rented. At this time he was writing the poems of *Purabi,* translating some of these into English for *Vijaya* the name he gave to Victoria. It was she who suggested that his erasures or cancellations had immense potential as works of art. When Rabindranath left, it was a parting that affected them deeply.

The biographical-critical tendency to be obsessed with the erotic is exciting but limiting and fails the Freudian model of aim-inhibited, non-sexual love serves to explain the very interesting, engaging relationships that Rabindranath had with young women. Within the Tagore household, two young women who he was particularly fond of were his nieces, Indira (daughter of his brother Satyendranath) and Sarala (daughter of his sister Swarnakumari); both were very accomplished young girls, just slightly younger than his wife Mrinalini. Rabindranath, then a young man in his twenties who had just returned from his England sojourn, encouraged the musical talent of Indira and Sarala and also inculcated their taste in English literature. It seems that the bond with Bibi (as her family called Indira) was special; it is likely that the ethereally beautiful and elegant Indira, educated in the 'Western' mode, well read in literatures, was the model of the ideal feminine for Rabindranath. Sarala, as accomplished as her cousin was also a composer and a collector; in her memoirs she recalls the varied sources from which she collected songs and melodies for her Robimama to draw upon and transform in his own work. The rift between them occurred when Sarala, a young woman with very decided opinions and views about freedom struggle, began to champion what she regarded as a worship of the brave. This involved training young men in martial arts, to revive the lost glory of Bengal. Rabindranath was ideologically opposed to this strand of nationalism; though there were no overt ruptures the relationship was never as intimate as in its initial stages. One wonders whether this serves as a pointer to Rabindranath's discomfort with the idea of strong willed women who could be critical of his opinion? Was this linked to his ideas of femininity?

If Rabindranath had his notions of the ideal feminine, he also helped shape a certain idea of a modern Bengali woman often referred to as the 'new woman'. This is true primarily of his relations with young women who knew him through family connections: his daughter-in-law Pratima, who was also related to him as a grand-niece. Widowed at a tender age, Rabindranath chose the beautiful, talented Pratima as a bride for his son Rathindranath. Pratima became the closest companion of her *babamoshai* (the slightly quaint but respectful address for the father), taking care of his daily needs and also sharing with him a refined aesthetic taste. She also became the ubiquitous *bouthan* (sister-in-law) of the ashram community and many of the younger women who came to set up temporary residences in Santiniketan were taken care of and nurtured by her. Rani, the sister of the artist Mukul Dey, was one such young woman.

Rabindranath grew fond of the talented adolescent when she came to stay at the Santiniketan ashram. Rathindranath and Pratima were instrumental in arranging Rani's match with the eligible Anil Chanda, a talented, erudite and ambitious young man with Oxbridge education. The couple who lived in the ashram premises, close to Rabindranath's residence, would visit Tagore regularly. It was with Rani that Tagore engaged in regular *tete a tete*; some of these have been captured in the several memoirs written by the former. The memoir *Gurudev*, for instance, is loosely strung, primarily thematic in nature, highlighting certain events or issues that evidently left a mark on Rani Chanda's mind. He was similarly fond of another Rani—Nirmalkumari Mahalanobis, the wife of Prasanta Mahalanobis—a young man who impressed him immensely with his learning, sharp intelligence and ability. Rabindranth liked spending time in their spacious residence in Baranagar when he visited Calcutta. Both Prasanta and Nirmalkumari accompanied Rabindranath on his Europe trip in 1926; accounts of this exist in Nirmalkumari's travelogue *Kabir sangye Europe e* (In *Europe with the Poet*). The intimate relation that Maitreyi Devi shared with Rabindranath has already been mentioned. Maitreyi Devi's memoir of Rabindranath's visits to her house tucked away in the beautiful cool Himalayan hill town Mongpu, titled *Mongpu te Rabindranath* is a favourite of Bengali readers for its ability to convey the witty conversations of the poet.

These are invaluable insights into mind of the creative artist, the ethical philosopher, thinker, educationist and a man who had drunk deep at the fountain of life. One might expect an occasional tone of adulation and hero-worship what comes across so memorably are his ready wit, humour, tenderness and affection, aspects which seldom come across in official biographies. Similarly, invaluable are the series of exquisitely evocative letters addressed to his favourite niece Indira Devi. She copied them in a *khata* or exercise book and gave it to her Robikaka, who made a selection and published them as *Chhinnapatra* (*The Torn Letters*) in 1912.[20] The appendix to the volume has a few letters in which Rabindranath states unambiguously that he could have only written these letters to Indira; she was the ideal recipient of his letters because of her ability to elicit and also comprehend the sensitive outpourings of his heart.[21]

Much later in life he developed a unique epistolary relation with Hemantabala Devi, a woman who belonged to a middle-class orthodox Hindu family. It would be difficult to imagine anything in common between the two, yet, in spite of his continual warning that she should not expect regular replies, there is a steady flow of letters from Rabindranath culminating in more than two hundred. The letters range from the quotidian to the philosophical. Rabindranath writes of his ailments, his work at Visva-Bharati, of his travel plans as well as of serious contemporary political issues like the British firing on the prisoners at Hijli, a satirical critique of Gandhi's response to the earthquake in Bihar, sensitive issues like Hindu idolatry, or response to the virulent criticism of his novel *Ghare Baire*. The epistles bear testimony to Rabindranath revealing his thoughts and ideas to his women companions, not only of his private inner self, but the public persona that he had cultivated over years. They were crucial to his self-fashioning, as a creative artist, as an ethical philosopher.

III

No article on the issue of Rabindranath and the feminine can be complete without a reference, albeit brief, to the unique space that had opened up for young women in Rabindranath's ashram school and community in Santiniketan.

The *brahmacharyashram* was set up in 1901 as an exclusively boy's school. In 1908, Rabindranath added to it a separate section for the girls. In a letter to Manoranjan Bandopadhyaya he referred to how he had always wished to do this but had hesitated out of apprehension; he added an enigmatic explanation about the bold step 'but now that the deity has come of her own, worship I must'.[22] Unfortunately, the venture for a girl's hostel folded up by 1910 and there was a temporary break in Tagore's wish to include girls and young women in his experiment of an alternative pedagogic community. Women were inducted into ashram once again when Rabindranath's idea of an international centre for pursuing culture, aesthetics and languages, took shape and Visva-Bharati was formally inaugurated in 1921; the motto of the Visva-Bharati, *yatra vishwvambhabatye ekneedam* (where the world makes its home in a nest) rang true with the active participation of young women in the life of the community.

This was a radical experiment in its time. Though women's education in Bengal had a history of more than half a decade, this did not involve women staying away from homes. In a later mature phase, in the second decade of the twentieth century, Rabindranath was not merely a poet or an artist; he became a revered figure, a spiritual guardian, a *Gurudev*, especially among a section of the educated Bengali community. Families began to entrust him with the responsibility of their daughters, and agreed to send them to the ashram community. Santiniketan was a semi-rural, secluded place which took pride in its unostentatious lifestyle. Most importantly, it meant that the girls would be part of a co-educational system (though of course, there were strict rules of conduct and the wardens of *Sreesadana* the women's hostel, were formidable matrons whose regimes of strict regulations had turned them into legends).

At Visva-Bharati, education was not restricted to the received sense of class-room teaching in humanities or sciences; the subjects offered included visual and performing arts. Talented young women received training in singing and dancing—the focus was on *Rabindrasangeet* or Tagore's songs and the particular mode of dance he evolved. At Kala-Bhavana, women students were encouraged in 'feminine' decorative arts like *alpona* and *batik*, though they also learnt the techniques of tempera or murals. They participated with their teachers and other male students in this unique collective form of public art.

Rabindranath also took the initiative to give the girl students training in martial arts like *jujutsu* and quite a few of the young women became adept at it. Young women participated in dance-drama and theatrical performances and were part of the troupes that travelled to various parts of India. There is little doubt that was made possible because of Tagore's towering personality that acted as a shield to protect the 'reputation' of young women from respectable middle-class families. The aesthetic curriculum at Visva-Bharati allowed young women an opportunity to hone the artist in themselves; many of the alumni became famous singers, dancers and artists. It is true that Rabindranath believed that men and women had distinct roles to play in family and society; some of his notions about women's roles were linked to traditional ideas of care and nurture as naturally feminine; the ashram sought to inculcate these traditional feminine traits. At the same time, the ashram provided a space in which young women could explore their self-hood without the restrictions imposed on them in a largely conservative society.

The photo archives of Rabindra Bhavana have a photograph of the girl perched on the branches of a tree, absorbed in reading a book. This photograph seems a perfect visualization of Rabindranath Tagore's dream of the nest, not so much as a closed cocoon but a resting place which was open to the embrace of the sky.

Notes

* Rabindranath Tagore's letter to Victoria Ocampo, 13 January 1925.

1. Sigmund Freud, 'Leonardo da Vinci and a Memory of his Childhood', in *The Uncanny*, tr. David McLintock, London: Penguin Books, 2003, p. 50.
2. Jagadish Bhattacharya, 'Kadambari: Dhrubatara', Chapter VI, *Kabimanashi,* vol. II, Kolkata: Bharabi, 2000, pp. 147-377.
3. Rajat Kanta Ray, ed., *Jeeban Debata: Rabindra Rachana Sankalan,* Kolkata: Visva-Bharati, 2010.
4. For a concise account see Subrata Rudra, *Kadambari Devi,* Kolkata: Papyrus, 1384 BS.

5. Ranu was chosen by the poet-playwright to play the girl-heroine Aparna in the play *Bisarjan* (Sacrifice) for a performance in which Rabindranath cast himself as Joysingha, the young hero, whom she deeply loves. Rabindranath was then in his late sixties. Ranu may have been in Rabindranath's mind when he created the spirited, vivacious Nandini of *Raktakarabi* (Red Oleanders).
6. This is the argument advanced by Sankha Ghosh for instance in his book *Kabir Abhipray*, Kolkata: Papyrus, 1994.
7. The references are to the phenomenally popular books by Ranjan Bandopadhyay, *Adorer Upabash*, Kolkata: Gangchil, 2007, *Kadambarir Suicide Note,* Kolkata: Patra Bharati, 2012.
8. In the initial phases of his writing career, Rabindranath had to face hostility and harsh uncharitable criticism. It was only with time that he earned the respect, admiration and adulation of his countrymen.
9. While, this may be a rare instance of a very self-conscious narrative, one could think of other instances of Bengali writings, which indicate the crucial role of *Rabindra-Sahitya* in the realization of one's romantic/erotic drive. Buddhadev Bose's *Tithidor* (reference details), comes to mind.

10 Some of the most famous instances are those by Satyajit Ray and Ritwik Ghatak. Ray makes the eponymous heroine of his film *Charulata* (an adaptation of Ranindranath's novella *Nashtaneed*) sing 'phule phule dhole dhole kahe ki ba mridu bai' (the flowers sway and murmur in the breeze) when she is on a swing and Amol plays on the piano and sings 'ami chini go chini tomare, ogo bideshini' (I know you o dear foreign maiden) even as his sister-in-law, the eponymous heroine walks into the room to convey the unstated erotic tension between the two; Ghatak famously used the song 'je ratey mor duar guli bhanglo jhore' (The night my doors were broken in the storm), with a background music of whiplashes in his film *Meghe Dhaka Tara* to convey the mute agony of his heroine Neeta who has come to know of the infidelity of her lover. Rituparno Ghosh also used Rabindrasangeet in his two Tagore films, *Chokher Bali* and *Noukadubi.*

11. Satyajit Ray, the acknowledged maestro, renamed *Nashtaneed* as *Charulata*; his *Teen Kanya* (Three Maidens) brought together three short stories of Tagore with an evident 'gender' focus. Rituparno Ghosh regarded his Tagore film *Chokher Bali* as the passion play of its heroine Binodini.
12. After Satyajit Ray it is Rituparno Ghosh who fulfilled the *bhadralok* Bengali's desire for film versions of Rabindranath Tagore's fictions.

13. Sigmund Freud, *Civilization and its Discontents*, tr. David McLintock, London: Penguin Books, 2002, p. 38
14. Scholars believe that the contempt expressed by Tagore's slightly younger contemporary, Swami Vivekananda for the Bengali males given to coyness, poetic utterances, and other 'feminized' forms of behaviour was perhaps a veiled attack on Rabindranath.
15. Sumit Sarkar, *Beyond Nationalist Frames: Relocating Postmodernism, Hindutva, History*, New Delhi: Permanent Black, 2002, p. 3, fn. 3.
16. Rabindranath Tagore, *My Boyhood Days,* tr. Marjorie Sykes in Uma Das Gupta, ed., *Rabindranath Tagore: My Life in My Words*, New Delhi: Penguin/Viking, 2006, p. 21.
17. See Uma Das Gupta, ed., *Rabindranath Tagore: My Life in My Words,* New Delhi: Penguin/Viking, 2006, p. 36.
18. Rabindranath narrates a telling incident of the intense emotional relation shared with his beloved *bouthan* which took place in the garden house on the bank of the Ganga, a place he used to frequent with Jyotidada and his wife. It was a day of monsoon when young Robi, still in his teens, sat watching the gathering clouds and its shadow on the ripples of the stream; evidently on days like this he would be visited by his muse and be inspired to compose his own songs. However, that day he was reminded instead of a famous poem by the great Vaisnav poet Vidyapati, 'e bhara badar maho bhadaro sunya mandir mor' and set it to tune. He sang it and Kadambari sat and listened to it in pensive silence.
19. It has been suggested that the triangulated relation between Rabindranath, Ranu and Leonard Elmhirst was the impulse for the play *Raktakarabi, Red Oleanders*, written in 1924. In this play about fascist totalitarian regime in a town called Yakshapuri, an ageing but very powerful king has an unrequited desire for the young and vivacious Nandini who is in love with the young rebel leader Ranjan.
20. An English translation of a selection made from *Chinnapatra* was done by Surendranath Tagore and published as *Glimpses of Bengal* in 1921 by Macmillan Co.
21. Rabindranath Tagore, *Chinnapatra*, Kolkata: Visva-Bharati, 1912.
22. Rabindranath Thakur, *Chithipatra*, vol. 13, Kolkata: Visva-Bharati, 1992, p. 9.

CHAPTER 10

Too Long a Prelude?

The Formative Century of Bengali Theatre

SUBHAYU CHATTOPADHYAY

Introduction

There is no denying the fact that Western influence played a pivotal role behind the evolution of modern Indian theatre. The experiments with modern theatre in tune with Western concept and technique were first felt in two opposite parts of India, i.e. Bombay and Bengal. But there were two very significant differences between the experiences of these two regions. Whereas theatre activity in Bombay always received generous financial support from the Parsi capitalists of the region, Bengal's public theatre at its initial phase never got such support from the moneyed members of the society in an organized form. On the other hand, as the theatrical producers in Bombay always considered the financial viability of those, they chose to stick to the safe path of traditional as well as familiar themes, mostly religious and social, and punctuated with songs, dances and music. But it was a slightly different story in Bengal. Apart from the private theatre of the wealthy Bengalis, there developed slowly but surely a new, stronger trend where there had been a conscious effort to make a perfect blending of the latest Western techniques with that of a new genre of scripts addressing the issues of contemporary political and social life and practices.

East and West

A performing art form carries a tendency to blend together different components like written scripts, speech-acting, performance, songs, music, dance etc. It can be in any other art form, also involving more than any two of these elements. But so far as theatre was concerned, there had always been an effort to put together all the elements to make it a meaningful one. It was almost on the same track that the different traditional folk forms of entertainment in Bengal like *keertan, tarja* and *kabi-gaan* in general, and *jatra* in particular, used to be produced in the region, prior to the introduction of European proscenium theatre into the cultural life of Bengal. It was mainly because of the absence of regular availability or circulation of written scripts in those traditional *jatras*, the other elements started to gain prominence, thereby, creating an aesthetic imbalance as well as gradual absorption of obscenity in the content which finally led to these folk forms being pushed to the periphery. The vacant cultural space, thus created in and around Calcutta, was captured by the European style of theatre during the second half of eighteenth century. Earlier, in the traditional form of *jatra*, performances used to take place in the open space either on a flat marked ground or on slightly elevated platform where people used to sit or stand surrounding the performers at the centre. There was hardly any separation of physical space between the viewer and the performer, thereby, creating more scope for imagination and cooperation on part of the viewers; finally leading to a perfect joint-project of the viewer-performer.

But the introduction of European style of proscenium theatre initiated a disjuncture into that cultural space with a concept of height and distance. It introduced the concept of proscenium stage, where the performance was to be on an elevated platform while the spectators would sit in a dark closed auditorium in front of the stage. According to the norms of the proscenium stagecraft, production would be enhanced with usage of light, sound, stage props like drop scenes, songs and dance (if the script demanded it). In contrast to the traditional form of *jatras*, the proscenium stage could immediately create an attraction for the distant, a reverence for the newly-introduced technical elements as well as an aura of mystery where the spectators and the performers are segregated by a physical distance. The elevation of the stage for the performances perfectly accomplished the feat where the spectators were compelled to give importance to the performers in that dark, closed auditorium, where the acting zone was supposed to be the only lit zone. The absence of the viewers on all sides of a production, as was in the case of the *jatras*, added to this element of unfamiliarity, and thereby to glorification and finally the popularization of the format.

The earliest known English theatre in Bengal, a proscenium playhouse known as 'The Theatre', was built in Calcutta in 1753 and was closed following Nawab Sirajuddaula's attack on the city in 1756.[1] In 1775, during the time of Warren Hastings, 'The New Playhouse', also called 'The Calcutta Theatre', came up. Until 1808, when it went out of business, the theatre performed plays written by William Shakespeare,[2] Philip Massinger,[3] William Congreve,[4] Richard Brinsley Sheridan[5], etc. A host of other proscenium playhouses soon followed, of which the Chowringhee Theatre (1813-39) and the Sans Souci Theatre (1839-49) were most noteworthy.

Early Response to Proscenium

The people of Bengal had three options to get associated with this new cultural trend—as a viewer, as an owner or as an actor; and it is interesting to note that they played all the three roles over the time.[6] As the entry fees were quite steep, only the affluent section of the Bengali society could see those productions. However, with Dwarkanath Tagore purchasing the Chowringhee Theatre on 15 August 1835, by quoting the highest price at the auction, the owner's role was also executed by a Bengali. The performance of Baishnab Charan Auddy, in the role of Othello on 1 August 1848, ensured a Bengali's participation in the capacity of an actor. It goes without saying that the Bengali association with the theatres were of a very limited character as there were no more instances of a Bengali Theatre owner or a Bengali actor enacting the main character. However, Bengali viewership of these English theatres increased over the time, signifying a genuine interest for these proscenium productions. This interest for European theatre could develop because of inclusion of English plays in the curriculum of English medium schools and colleges of Calcutta. Even the genuine interest that some of the teachers took in the skill of acting, like Richardson and Derozio as is evident in the writings of the members of the Young Bengal group, also could have mattered. It is learnt that in 1805, sixty pieces of Shakespeare's works came to Calcutta from London, second highest after the Bible.[7] The students of the Hindu College, Metropolitan Academy, Oriental Seminary, and David Hare's Academy started to produce and perform Shakespearean plays like Julius Caesar, Merchant of Venice, Othello, and Henry the Fourth on a regular basis. It was evident that an urge to portray different facets of life through realistic performance on stage was slowly but surely taking control of the imagination of the people, but they were no more satisfied with performance or content of the plays of foreign origin, which were surely beyond their own socio-cultural understanding. They wanted plays to be written and performed in their own language.

Bengali Theatre: Hesitant Beginning

It is now a well-known fact that the first performance of a play in Bengali, on a proscenium stage, by an 'all-native cast' (both male and female), was made by a Russian named Gerasim Stepanovitch Lebedeff (1749-1817), on 27 November 1795. The second production took place on 21 March 1796. The play, *Kalpanik Sangbadol*, a Bengali translation of Richard Jodrell's comedy, *The Disguise*, performed at the Bengali Theatre, was surely a surprise event in the history of Bengali theatre. Though it is known that Lebedeff had an intention to perform in Calcutta as well as in the countryside, and own a permanent theatre hall and stage, he could not fulfil his dreams because of circumstances beyond his control.[8] It is obvious that Lebedeff got little scope to initiate the process of creating original Bengali plays and to perform those on the stages, but it is equally true that he, for the first time, thought of modifying the content and language of the play, trying to make it much more acceptable to the people of Bengal. There was another less famous attempt at Chandannagar in 1808, where a French play, *L'Avocat,* was translated into Bengali and staged.[9] It should be interesting to note here in this context that following the early proscenium performances in Bengali language, the Bengali intellectuals, from the early decades of the nineteenth century slowly and steadily started to take interest in theatre, from a creative point of view, mainly in two forms; either by taking part at the organizational level and/or by translating original Sanskrit and English plays in to Bengali.

Theatre of and for the Affluent

For the affluent section of the contemporary Bengali society, starting from landed magnets to the new middle-class, emerging following the Permanent Settlement, to owners/editors of newspapers; the proscenium form of theatre production with an Indian content, and preferably in Bengali language gradually became one of the main cultural activities apart from their commitment elsewhere. The trend, commonly being termed as *Babu Theatre* or *Baganbarir Theatre* started to develop centring the private spaces owned by these new patrons from around mid-nineteenth century. Those productions were mainly staged in the private residences or farm houses (*baganbari*) of the babus on specific occasions. This new area of activity opened for the *babus* new avenue to show off their wealth as well as to come close to English officials for their favours. However, exceptions were there where a genuine interest for the development of a distinct form of Bengali theatre could also be found. But, as the invited guests to these productions belonged to the same class as of the host, the opportunity for the common people to watch those productions was minimal.

'Hindu Theatre', owned by Prasanna Kumar Tagore, in 1831, is regarded as the first theatre established by a Bengali intellectual.[10] The first production of the house was the English translation of Bhababhuti's *Uttar Ramacharita* on 14 December 1831. Horace. H. Wilson[11] was the translator, director and one of the main actors in the play. The next production, *Nothing Superfluous*, based on an Indian content, was staged by the Hindu Theatre on 29 March 1832. This new trend, subsequently and substantially was enriched by Nabin Basu's theatre at Shyambazar, Pyarimohan Bose's Jorasanko theatre, Asutosh Dev's (Satubabu) theatre at Beadon Street, Ramjoy Basak's theatre at Natun Bazar, Gadadhar Seth's theatre at Bara Bazar, Kaliprasanna Singha's 'Bidyotsahini Ranga Mancha', Belgachhia Theatre, the Rajas of Paikpara,[12] Metropolitan Theatre at Ramgopal

Mallick's palace at Chitpur, 'Pathuriaghata Banga Natyalaya' at Jatindra Mohan Tagore's residence, Shobhabazar Private Theatrical Society by Radhakanta Deb and others. They made several experiments with techniques and formats like introduction of quality orchestra as background score, fine perspective backdrops, gas-lanterns, and limelight. However, it seems that the *babus* were more comfortable either with translated works from English masterpieces or plays based on traditional themes from the Puranas. The plays reflective of contemporary social issues, which generally found them at the centre, were naturally not promoted by them. However, with time, when people of the region were no more satiated with mere translation works or Indianization[13] of Western plays because of their thin connection to the indigenous socio-cultural scenario, incorporation of contemporary social issues in the content of the plays became inevitable, leading to the gradual fading away of private theatre towards the end of 1860s.

Parallel to the existing practice of translation of Sanskrit or English plays, a new form of play-writing, much more conscious and committed to the age, began to flourish. It was in 1854 that a large section of Bengali audience were moved to see Ramnarayan Tarkaratna's *Kulin Kula Sarbasva*, as they could relate it to a contemporary social evil of polygamy. Though it had some influence of Sanskrit dramaturgy, the play was contemporary and hence, very near to a 'true' Bengali theatre, at least from the angle of the content. If one looks at the list of the plays produced or written during this time,' the mere names of them would suggest that they dealt with contemporary social evils as their theme.[14] Apart from this, farces and plays based on ancient Puranic themes were also written during this time.

Bengali Theatre: Facing the Raj

The consecutive occurrence of Sepoy Mutiny and Indigo Rebellion immediately after it pushed the reformist zeal of a self-confident Victorian liberalism of the British to a back seat, as many of them in the administration started to believe that the Indians were beyond reform. A new mood of 'conservative brand of liberalism', as observed by Thomas Metcalf, was initiated which rested upon the 'solid support of the conservative and aristocratic classes and upon the principle of complete non-interference in the traditional structure of Indian society'.[15] This conservative reaction evidently made the empire more autocratic and denied the socio-politico-cultural aspirations of the educated Indians for sharing equal space. The offshoot was the rise of a feeling of frustration among the educated middle-class, which finally led to the formation of different political associations in different parts of the country to voice their grievances, centring different issues.

In Bengal, during this time, parallel to the formation of political associations, one of the dominant cultural expressions, apart from literature, was the theatre activity, initially started in the region under the European influence. It was also undergoing some fundamental changes, be it in the form of content, or technology and most importantly in the approach, and much more concerned and reflective of the contemporary time. The playwrights of the region felt the need to address to their time; and gradually the performances on the stages of Calcutta started to show more maturity by taking on contemporary social evils. The middle class intelligentsia as well as the moneyed members of Bengal, the *babus*, who were also sometimes linked with the rise of political associations, were largely connected, directly or indirectly, with the theatre activities. It was either under their influence or under the influence of British legitimization of India's rich heritage, that a trend of patriotism, through glorious portrayal of heroes of the country, also started to feature in the themes of contemporary plays. However, a play like Dinabandhu Mitra's *Neel Darpan* (*Neeldarpanang Natakam*), which was published from Dhaka in 1860, dared to alter the scenario, hinting at a potential where plays and theatres can reflect the mirror image of contemporary social condition and practices. While the playwrights belonging to other parts of the country were still engaged with translated works or satires or themes reflective of age-long scriptural tradition,[16] Dinabandhu Mitra's *Neel Darpan* was certainly a marked shift on stage towards actual reality.

The dominant trends during this period included a definite shift of Bengali plays towards more maturity in form and content, based on the individual talents like Madhusudan Dutta or Dinabandhu Mitra. Social plays occupying the centre stage, attempted to organize public theatre on the financial support of the common people. The British were increasingly apprehensive of Bengali 'social plays that gradually slipped into making political statements through theatrical means'.[17] There was a new shift in production of theatre under the leadership of Girish Chandra Ghosh. There was also an unmistakable reflection of middle-class mentality of cynicism, ensuring their class interest and choosing a safe option of criticizing their own society that started to be reflected in the theatre productions towards the end of the century.

Michael Madhusudan Dutta (1824-73)

Dutta was one of the stalwarts among the Bengali dramatists who wrote some of the earliest original plays in Bengali. His composition of blank verse, sonnet and epic only enriched Bengali literature. That he was aware of the demand of original plays in Bengali is evident from his writings on the issue. He wrote:

> The friends who wish that our countrymen should possess a literature of their own, a vigorous and independent literature, and not a feeble echo of everything Sanskrit, will rejoice to hear that a taste for the Drama is beginning to develop itself rapidly among the highest classes of Hindu Society. I am fully convinced that the day is not far distant, when the princely munificence of such patrons as the Rajahs of Paikparah will call onto the field a host of writers who will discard Sanskrit models and look to far higher sources for inspiration.[18]

Dutta's most productive years were between 1858 and 1865 and he penned some brilliant pieces like *Sharmistha* (premiered at the Belgachia theatre where he made his debut in 1859), *Padmavati* (published 1860, premiered 1865) and a historical tragedy titled *Krishna Kumari* (published 1861, premiered 1867). Madhusudan shines most brilliantly with his farces, where the language is easy, the attack is sharp and relevant, and the characters are drawn distinctly. In *Ekei Ki Bale Sabhyata* (published 1860, premiered 1865), he ridiculed the ultra-progressive members of the Young Bengal group who blindly copied European culture and in *Budo Shaliker Ghade Ron* (the original name of the play given by Madhusudan was *Bhagna Shibmandir*, but it was renamed by the Rajas of Paikpara; first published 1860, premiered 1867), he exposed the hypocrisy of the affluent class of the society, which may be relevant for any country in modern age.

Dinabandhu Mitra (1830-73) and *Neel Darpan*

Dinabandhu Mitra, as a playwright, was most modern in his approach as he completely discarded the Puranic themes and concentrated on depicting the evil aspects of society of his time. It is interesting to note that his given name was Gandharba Narayan, but he took the name of Dinabandhu Mitra, a man dear to the destitute. Whether to do justice to the name that he took or as a playwright with different approach, Dinabandhu created a stir with the publication of his play *Neel Darpan*, published in 1860, immediately after the outbreak of indigo revolt. For the first time a Bengali play struck the chord of history and *Neel Darpan* secured its place in the same bracket with *Oliver Twist* by Charles Dickens (related to reforms of the jails) or *Uncle Tom's Cabin* by Harriet Beecher Stowe (related to abolition of bonded labour).[19] The play was published from Dhaka and soon after its publication it ignited a major argument concerning the issue, with many contemporary Bengali intellectuals sharing Mitra's views through publication of editorials in newspapers on a regular basis.[20] His first hand experience of the indigo cultivators, while on the job as the post master in rural Orissa and Bengal, were reflected in the drama. Michael Madhusudan Dutt translated the play into English and Reverend James Long published it. *Neel Darpan* got wide publicity even in Europe where it was translated into many other languages. No other Bengali book at that time got such publicity at such a large scale. A lawsuit was filed against Revd. Long by 19 July 1861 for libelling the indigo planters. Revd. Long was fined a sum of Rs. 1,000 and a month of time in jail. On the other hand, the revolt had a strong effect on the government, which immediately appointed the 'Indigo Commission' in 1860.

Neel Darpan holds a unique place in the history of Bengali theatre for reasons more than one. Although because of the weak portrayal of some of the central characters like Nabinmadhab, Raicharan, Sairindhri or Bindumadhab, it is alleged that the peasant characters of the play display more urban *babu*-like behavioural attributes than anything else;[21] *Neel Darpan*, apart from being first of its kind with a strong stance against the European oppressors, became also a trendsetter. More plays of so-called social protest, a large number of them in the *darpan* (or mirror-) style, were written; plays that purported to hold up a mirror, as it were, to the ills of society. Most notable among them were Mir Masarraf Hossain's *Jamidar-darpan* (The Mirror of the Landowner, 1873), which was about a peasant rebellion against the land-owning *babus*, *Cha-Kar-Darpan* (The Tea-Planter's Mirror, 1875), by Daksinaranjan Chattopadhyay, that dealt with the poor working conditions at the British tea-estates in north Bengal and *Jail-darpan* (The Mirror of the Prison, 1876) that dealt with the terrible life of prisoners in the jail houses of Bengal, also by Chattopadhyay. All three plays protested against the atrocities by colonial authority directly or indirectly through some of its agencies, targeting mainly the lower tier of the society.

Era of Public Theatre and State Apprehension

'The emergence of the public theatre was, in fact, an early instance of the appearance of a class conflict within the *bhadralok*, between a more conservative and loyalist landlord elite and a group of lesser men who by the 1870s were to lay claims to be of "*madhyabitta*" (middle class) status with patriotic aspirations.'[22] The content of *Neel Darpan* suited the mood of the time as associations in different parts of the country started to voice their grievances on different issues against the colonial rule by this time. The younger generation of theatre enthusiasts of Calcutta, outside the aristocratic ambit of the city, also felt the mood and decided to do their part of the job through theatre. On 7 December 1872, history was made with the opening of the first public playhouse in Bengal, the National Theatre, formed by a group of theatre-crazy youths of Baghbazar Amateur Theatre (1869-72),[23] some of whom like Ardhendu Sekhar Mustafi, Amritalal Basu and Girish Chandra Ghosh were to become stars of professional theatre in the next few years. Among the patrons, they got people like Sisir Kumar Ghosh, editor of *Amrita Bazar Patrika*, Nabagopal Mitra, editor of *National Paper* and founder of Hindu Mela, Manmohan Basu, the noted playwright and journalist. Dinabandhu Mitra's *Neel Darpan* was the automatic choice for the premier. 'The playhouse with its proscenium stage was a temporary construction in the courtyard of the private residence of Madshusudan Sanyal in the Chitpur area of Calcutta. The National Theatre took another important decision of introducing ticket system for the viewers. It is known that first class ticket cost Re. 1, second class 8 annas, reserve seats Rs. 2 and 4 annas to sit on the flight of steps. The ticket sale for the first show of *Neel Darpan* was Rs. 200 and it was so well received that the sale jumped to Rs. 450 for the second show of the play.[24] There were several shows arranged for *Neel Darpan* with all the tickets sold off, but the demand for the next show was still high. Ardhendu Sekhar Mustafi was so emotionally motivating in portraying the role of Mr Wood, the planter, that during one of the shows, Iswar Chandra Vidyasagar, taken in by the realism of the performance of Mustafi, threw a shoe at the actor on the stage. National papers reported on the success of staging *Neel Darpan* as 'of national importance'. *Amrita Bazar Patrika* suggested that the play should not be restricted to Calcutta, but should venture beyond Calcutta to such places as Krishnanagore, Berhampore, Jessore and other such areas where the issues addressed in the play would be more relevant. The proscenium public theatre in Bengal reached very near to a truly democratic experience where low prices of tickets as well as addressing to the contemporary social and political issues and producing it places in and outside Calcutta involved a larger number of common people, sharing the same chord of sentiment through appreciation of the theatre.

Reaction of the State

The staging of *Neel Darpan,* however, earned the displeasure of the *Englishman* which, in its 20 December 1872 issue, condemned the play for having had damaging effects on the dignity and prestige of the British government and ordered that the performance of the play be immediately stopped. It wrote:

Considering that the Revd. Mr. Long was sentenced to one month's imprisonment for translating the play, which was pronounced by the High Court as a libel on the Europeans, it seems strange that the Government should allow its representation in Calcutta, unless it has gone through the hands of some competent censor, and the libelous parts excised.[25]

Neel Darpan also travelled to other parts of the country, mainly north Indian cities. Towards the end of May 1875, some earlier members of the National Theatre (that had now become the 'Great National Theatre') went on tour. In Lucknow, during a scene of *Neel Darpan*—the scene where Torap, an Indian ryot, holds down the European Mr Rouge, who assaults the helpless woman Kshetramoni—British soldiers among the audience, enraged, rushed onto the stage and began behaving violently, which led to the breaking up of the play.

The following year, Edward, Prince of Wales, visited Calcutta. Soon after his visit, the Great National Theatre presented the play *Gajadananda O Jubaraj* (or *Gajadananda and the Crown Prince*), which sought to target Jagadananda Mukherjee, a well-known citizen of Calcutta, Junior Government pleader and member of the Bengal Legislative Council. The man had invited the Prince to his Bhowanipur residence on 3 January 1876 and had taken him on a tour of the ladies' apartment of the house where he was given a traditional Bengali welcome by the female members of the family. This incident enraged the orthodox Bengali society for it appeared to them that Jagadananda had sacrificed his ethics and culture in a bid to placate the British masters and win favours from them.[26]

The satirical play *Gajadananda O Jubaraj* was penned by playwright and director of Great National Theatre, Upendranath Das. It was first staged on 19 February 1876, followed by another show on 23rd of the same month. The wide public appreciation irritated the British government and the play was stopped by police order, yet it returned the following week on 26 February under a different name, *Hanuman Charitra*. It was again banned by the British government.

On 1 March, Upendranath Das's play *Surendra Binodini* was followed by a satire called *The Police of Pig and Sheep*, mocking Sir Stuart Hogg, Commissioner of Police, and Mr Lamb, Superintendent of Police, for their hostile behaviour towards the common people.[27]

After the show, Das gave a speech in English to the audience where he attacked the government.

It is interesting to note in this context that on the previous day, on 29 February 1876, Lord Northbrook, Governor-General of India, promulgated an ordinance. The *Indian Mirror* of 1 March 1876, reported:

> A Gazette of India Extra-ordinary was issued last evening containing an Ordinance to empower the Government of Bengal to prohibit certain dramatic performances, which are scandalous, defamatory, seditious, obscene, or otherwise prejudicial to the public interest. The Ordinance shall remain in force till May next by which time a law will be passed by the Vice regal Council on the subject.[28]

On 4 March 1876, when the play *Sati Ki Kalankini* was being performed on the stage of the Great National Theatre, the police stormed in and arrested the director Upendranath Das, the manager Amritlal Basu and eight others on the charge of immorality for an earlier play, *Surendra Binodini*. On 8 March Upendranath and Amritalal were sentenced to one month's simple imprisonment while the rest were released. Later, however, the high court overruled the order of the police court and released the duo on 20 March 1876.[29]

On the same day, the draft of the *Dramatic Performances Control Bill* was introduced in the Viceroy's Council and despite strong public opposition the Bill was passed into law on 17 December 1876. While the immediate provocation for the promulgation of the ordinance was the play *Gajadananda o Jubaraj*, the actual motive of the government was to silence such nationalistic plays as *Neel Darpan*, *Bharat Mata*, *Puru-Vikram*, *Bharate Yavan*, *Banger Sukhabasan*, and *Beer Nari*. This Act also served as a weapon for the British government to ban plays like *Anandamath*, *Chandrasekhar*, *Mrinalini*, *Chhatrapati Shivaji*, *Karagar*, *Palashir Prayaschitta*, *Matripuja* and among others. The Dramatic Performance Act (DPA) was a clear hint that the British government became apprehensive of the potential of Bengal public theatre. The protest mood or the exposition of patriotic sentiment on the stage irritated the British government whose mood by that time got tuned with James Fitzjames Stephen's assertion on inferiority of the Indians as subjects. It is noteworthy in this context that within fifteen months of DPA, the British government introduced two more Acts, the Vernacular Press Act and the Arms Act, both of which were vehemently protested against by the Indians. However, it is surprising that the Indian protest was half-hearted in case of DPA,[30] the reason for which is still not clear. A trend of commercialization of theatre immediately emerged to fill up the space that got vacant following the sudden closure of patriotic plays being staged in Bengal. The sole objective of making material profit gradually overshadowed the trend of hosting 'meaningful theatre'.[31]

Girish Chandra Ghosh (1844-1912)

It is said that Bengali theatre in the nineteenth century reached its pinnacle under the leadership of Girish Chandra Ghosh, the most famous playwright, director, actor, innovator of different stagecraft and last but not the least, an able organizer of Bengali theatre of the contemporary time. He is credited with writing most number of plays in Bengali, which is numbered at around eighty-six. Among the most famous plays written by him mention may be made of *Daksha Yajna* (1883), *Chaitanya Lila* (1886), *Billvamangal* (1888), *Prafulla* (1889), and *Sirajuddaulah* (1906). He was deeply influenced by his predecessors Dinabandhu Mitra for his social plays, Jyotirindranath Thakur for historical plays and Manmohan Basu to Rajkrishna Roy for writing Puranic plays.[32] He left the job of a clerk of a mercantile office and joined Star Theatre as its manager. With him came a decisive turn towards mythological and Hindu religious themes, along with domestic melodramas. In addition to all these, Girish Ghosh undoubtedly initiated a new age in the stagecraft. It was a time when people wanted realistic representation of the events to be depicted on the stage, and Ghosh successfully catered to that demand.[33] But one should take note in this context that all those stagecraft of Ghosh was introduced not to show his talents regarding stagecraft, but to enhance the blooming of his poetic genius to the fullest. But Girish himself criticized in his later life the exaggeration of this stagecraft by saying that it overpowers the aesthetic elements of the scriptural content. He later on tried to look for an alternative where the acting skill along with the aesthetic value of the script would gain predominance over the technical issues like stagecraft or light; and it is here where he thought that there was not much of a difference between traditional forms of *jatra* of Bengal and the Shakespearean plays, so far as the production format was concerned.

Bengali Theatre and the Middle Class

It would not be out of context if one takes note at this juncture of the experience of theatre in the Western world in general and England in particular. If one takes a closer look at the evolution of theatre in England, it would be clear that theatre had to traverse a very rough path there also, mainly because of the opposition from the newly-emerged bourgeois elements, led by the puritans. The monarchy in England had always been a great patron of theatre, and that became instrumental in the clash between the monarchy and the bourgeoisie, where theatre was inevitably brought into the middle. In 1577, Bishop Thomas White in his speech at London accused the theatre halls as the symbols of collective sin, which led to the outbreak of plague in the city. That was the dominant mood among the newly-emerged bourgeois class, which was further carried forward by people like Bishop John Northbrook of Glauster, or dramatist-cum-Bishop Stephen Gosson. However, in 1595, Sir Philip Sydney's famous article on 'In Defence of Poesy' was published, where he fought against the all-pervasive bourgeois criticism targeting the theatres. Thomas Nash in his work 'Peers Pennyless' also argued in favour of theatre production. However, the interesting part was that both of them agreed on the basic bourgeois criticism that until and unless the theatres are not the centres for sermonising moral lessons for the spectators, they are short of their social responsibilities. Finally, on 6 September 1642, theatre was banned in England, including the plays of Shakespeare, Marlow or Johnson, with the reason being maintenance of 'sad and pious solemnity' to pacify God during the time of Civil War. It is interesting to note this contradiction of attitudes, where they could think of altering the economic and social order, but maintaining a middle-aged, intolerant attitude towards performing arts in general, and theatre in particular. The performance of plays were banned for nearly two decades, and lifted only after the

Restoration of the monarchy in 1660. In this phase, theatres had to take permission from the censor, police and the mayor before any performance. The earlier openness about the human potential in the scripts was lost to a great extent, and a new genre, i.e. Restoration Comedy, came into place.

As soon as the Indians were introduced to the Western form of theatre they were also oriented to the idea of a moralistic role of theatre that it was supposed to play content wise, apart from its new technical newness related to the stage craft to add to its entertainment value. But it is to be remembered that moral lesson could any time become immoral, if it didn't fit in with the rulers' notion of morality. Theatre activity in India in general, and Bengal in particular, went through almost the same experience during and after passing of the DPA, an intervention on the freedom of art form, similar to what England had experienced. With the passing of the DPA, there was a clear shift in the productions which became more focussed on the commercial viability, rather than igniting people's mind about any contemporary social or political injustice. A host of commercial theatre houses like Star Theatre, now owned by the non-Bengali businessmen like Pratapchand Jahuri, sprang up within no time, hosting social and mythological plays, with a sprinkle of historical plays, safely set in the pre-colonial times, written by Girish Chandra Ghosh, Dwijendralal Roy and others in between. But plays addressing to contemporary issues, social or political, remained absent from Bengali stage till the turbulent forties, which experienced the post-war syndrome, mass movement, famine, transfer of power, Independence, Partition, the related displacement and migration of common people and the growth of Indian Peoples Theatre Association as a witness of all these.

Conclusion

If one wishes to study the growth and development of theatre activity in Bengal there is no doubt that nineteenth century would constitute the formative period of it. Starting from the traditional form of *jatra* down to the introduction of proscenium stage; from the private theatre of the wealthy class to the public theatre of the lesser *bhadraloks*; from staging Shakespeare, Sheldon to the translation of English and Sanskrit works and finally to staging Bengali plays; from one time trend of depicting the true realities of contemporary time down to the trend of realistic portrayal of insignificant domestic issues; from exposing the oppression of the Indigo planters and creating a stir among the common people down to the portrayal of valour and tragedy of a historical figure, confined within the safe pre-colonial times; from participation of the high English officials in the private theatre of the *babus* of Bengal to the passing of the Dramatic Performance Act; the theatre in Bengal faced through many currents and cross-currents only to get enriched day by day. Alongside, it was also emboldened by the contributions of some able individuals, who by might of their pen, continued to enrich the tradition of Bengali plays.

However, the unfortunate part of the whole story was the shift in the character of the plays during post-DPA era. There was hardly any play written, staged and well-received by the common people, which addressed the contemporary political turmoil. With the turn of the century, colonial India saw many concepts and ideologies, starting from 'passive resistance' to 'swadeshi' down to 'non-cooperation' and 'civil disobedience' associated with the ongoing political struggle for achieving Indian independence. But it is interesting to note that neither the radical protest mood of the people nor the constitutional or politico-philosophical concepts or ideologies could accommodate or give place to the cultural expression of the common people as a medium for voicing grievances. As a result, with no dearth of talent in any quarter, the first forty years of Indian theatre in general and Bengali stage in particular, remained defunct to a great extent, in mirroring the concerns of the society.

Notes

1. Roy Chowdhury, ed., *Bilati Jatra Theke Swadeshi Theatre,* Kolkata, 1972, p. 14.
2. William Shakespeare (1564-1616) is widely regarded as one of the greatest writers in the world in English language.
3. Philip Massinger (1583-1640) was an English dramatist. His plays

were famous for its satire and were reflective of contemporary social and political issues.

4. William Congreve (1670-1729) was an English poet and playwright. Some of his famous plays were *Love for Love* and *Double Dealer*.
5. Richard Brinsley Sheridan (1751-1816) was an Irish poet and playwright. *The School for Scandal* or *The Rivals* were some of his noteworthy works.
6. Pabitra Sarkar, 'Unobingsho Shatabdir Bangla Natak O Tar Proyogkala', in Swapan Basu and Indrajit Chowdhuri, eds., *Unish Shataker Bangali Jibon O Sanskriti*, Kolkata, 2003, p. 513.
7. Ibid.
8. Lebedeff had to face stiff opposition from his contemporary European owners of the theatres of Bengal. He did not get permission for staging his production in any of the theatre halls in Calcutta. Therefore, he built his own theatre stage at 25, Dhormotollah (present Ezra Street) and staged two productions successively there. His language teacher Goloknath Das was his chief source of inspiration. It is known that Das took the responsibility of arranging the actors and actresses for the play. Lebedeff decided to curtail the price of tickets for his plays. All these might have led to a sense of apprehension among his competitors. His arch rival Thomas Roworth, owner of Calcutta Theatre, conspired against his group and Lebedeff finally had to return to his own country empty handed leaving a disbanded group behind. [Subir Roychowdhury and Swapan Majumdar, eds., *Bilati Jatra Theke Swadeshi Theatre*, Calcutta, 1999 (rpt.), pp. 14-15
9. Ibid. p. 18.
10. Darshan Chowdhury, *Bangla Theatre-er Itihas*, Kolkata, 1995, p. 62.
11. Horace Heyman Wilson (1786-1860) was one of the early English orientalists, who came to India as a medical professional. He learnt Sanskrit and in 1927 published *Select Specimens of the Theatre of the Hindus,* which contained, apart from a detail study of Indian drama tradition, translation of six complete plays from Sanskrit to English.
12. Belgachhia Theatre is considered to be the first permanent proscenium stage in Bengal.
13. One may cite, as example in this context, Hara Chandra Ghosh's *Bhanumati Chitta Bilas,* a translation of *Merchant of Venice* or *Charumukh Chittahara,* which was based on Romeo and Juliet.
14. One may cite in this context *Bidhaba Bibaha* by Umesh Chandra Mitra (1856), *Bidhaba Manoranjan* by Radha Madhab Mitra (1856), *Sapatni Natak* by Tarak Chandra Churamani (1858) and *Balya Bibaha Natak*

by Sripati Mukhopadhyay (1860) etc. [Pabitra Sarkar, op. cit., p. 516.]

15. Thomas R. Metcalf, *The Aftermath of Revolt: India, 1857-1870*, Princeton, 1965, p. viii.
16. A study of the plays written in different languages of India till the 1880s suggests that playwrights were either focussed on contemporary social evils or took shelter in the Puranic storylines. There is hardly any example where a dramatist has come out openly to criticize the foreign rule through his works. The works like Hem Barua's *Kania Kirtan* (1861) or Ramakanta Chowdhuri's *Sitaharan* (1875) in Assamese; Narmada's *Krishna Kumari* (1869) or N.T. Marfatia's *Gulab* (1862) in Gujarati; Bharatendu Harishchandra's *Vaidiki Himsa Himsa Na Bhabati* (1873) or *Satya Harishchandra* (1875) in Hindi; Karki Venkatraman Shastri's *Iggappa Heggadeya* (1887) in Kannada; C.V. Raman Pillai's *Chandramukhi Bilasam* (1885) in Malayalam; Vishnudas Bhave's *Sita Swayambaram* (1843) in Marathi; Ramshankar Roy's *Kanchi Kaberi* (1880) in Odiya; Sundaram Pillai's *Mana Vijayam* or *Kalavati* (1880s) in Tamil; Korad Ramachandra Kavi's *Manjari Madhukariyam* (1860) in Telugu are some of the noteworthy examples in this regard. However, a Hindi play, *Nil Devi* (1881) by Bharatendu Harishchandra was an exception where, along with the issue of women emancipation, an urge for freedom from the rule of the British India government had also been reflected.
17. Sudipto Chatterjee, 'Performing (Domi-)Nation: Aspects of Nationalism in Nineteenth-Century Bengali Theatre', in http://www.lib.uchicago.edu/e/su/southasia/TESTold/Sudipto.html, last accessed on 20 April 2014.
18. Madhusudan Dutta, *Madhusudan Rachanabali* (ed.) Kshetra Gupta, Kolkata, 1982, vol. XXVII, cited in Sudipto Chatterjee, ibid.
19. Sarkar, op. cit., p. 519.
20. *The Englishman* and *The Hindu Patriot* published regular articles on the issue. However, according to Ranajit Guha, the middle-class attitudes towards peasants in this context were 'a curious concoction of an inherited, Indian-style paternalism and acquired Western-style humanism'. Ranajit Guha, 'Neel Darpan: The Image of a Peasant Revolt in a Liberal Mirror', *Journal of Peasant Studies*, 2:1, 1974, reprinted in David Hardiman, ed., *Peasant Resistance in India, 1885-1914*, Delhi, 1992, pp. 64, 92.
21. Chatterjee, op. cit.
22. Sumit Sarkar, *Modern Times: India 1880s-1950s, Environment, Economy, Culture*, New Delhi, 2014, p. 391.

23. Chowdhury, op. cit., p. 96.
24. Ibid., p. 97.
25. Binodini Dasi in her memoir mentioned about the incident which took place in an area called Chhatrmandi in Lucknow in the month of May 1875.
26. Renowned poet Hemchandra Bandopadhyay wrote on this occasion,
    ami swadeshbasi amai dekhe lajja hote pare
    bideshbasi Rajar chhele lajja ki lo tare.
    [You might be ashamed of me, your fellow citizen;
    But why should you be ashamed of the King's son,
    Even if he is from an alien land!]
27. Chowdhury, op. cit., p. 119.
28. http://en.wikipedia.org/wiki/Dramatic_Performances_Act, last accessed on 20 April 2014.
29. Chowdhury, op. cit., pp. 119-20.
30. Jatindra Mohan Tagore from British India Association protested against this Act, while Raja Narendra Krishna Bahadur supported the Act.
31. It should be of interest to note that the clauses, charted out by the British authorities way back in 1876, were prevalent in independent India also. Though Allahabad High Court in its ruling of 1954, declared it as unconstitutional, many state governments, including West Bengal, could not afford to abolish it.
32. Ajit Kumar Ghosh, *Bangla Nataker Itihas*, 2nd edn., Kolkata, 2010, p. 146.
33. Girish Chandra Ghosh, in his play, *Kamale Kamini,* installed a life size huge boat on the stage and created a successful portrayal of the sea-voyage of Srimanta Saudagar, with a moving background, created by adequate drop-scene and light projection. He even took the help of a stüdent of chemistry of Calcutta University to create a storm sequence on the stage. People were spellbound to see his play called *Jana* where a tree on the stage suddenly caught fire and within few minutes it was a thoroughly scorched tree standing on the stage.
    Utpal Dutta, 'Bangla Nataker Adi Parbe Europeo Probhab', in Arup Mukhopadhyay, ed., *Epic Theatre: Subarna Jayanti Sankalan*, vol. 1, rpt., Kolkata, 2015.

CHAPTER 11

Revisiting a Marginalized Community
The Bone-setters of Bengal

ARABINDA SAMANTA

It has been argued in recent years that under the compulsion of maintaining health of the troops, a new 'medical market' was created in the nineteenth- and twentieth-century India, and that it impelled the colonial government to restructure the variety of 'indigenous' medical practices[1] prevalent in the country. While some research has been undertaken on the fate of the principal medical 'systems' of *Ayurveda* (Hindu) and *Unani* (Islamic/Greco-Arabic), that of 'folk' practices such as bone-setting, laments Mark Harrison, has been largely neglected.[2] Indeed, the impact of colonial intervention in indigenous medical practices seems to have been highly complex, and changed considerably over time as the relatively open and informal 'dialogue' between the Western and Indian practitioners gave way to scientific scepticism of the nineteenth century. While some amount of research on the bone-setters of Madras and Rajasthan has been done recently,[3] Bengal still remains a relatively less addressed area with regard to this practice.

This paper is a tentative attempt towards retelling the story of a little known community of health providers in Bengal. I would like to address in this paper the socio-cultural trajectory of the bone-setters. The bone-setters, as we all know, are traditional orthopaedics specializing in treating broken bones using indigenous medical knowledge, but due to lack of patronage from both the government and the patients, they are marginalized. Their art of setting bones is not considered a science, nor is their scientific approach to orthopedics valued as art. They are not practising magic, nor do they invoke religion directly into their profession. Setting of broken bones brings them money, but it hardly constitutes their professed livelihood. They are all part-time professionals and irregular farmers; tilling land and joining bones at times, these people belong to a zone of liminality and maintain a narrow identity.

It has been argued that the actual art or science of bone setting has trickled down the silk route.[4] The Mughal armies seemed to have brought this technique with them as they came to India invading from the north. The knowledge of manipulation and healing was well known for centuries. When the British occupied India, they found a well-reinforced orthopaedic system in perfect practice. Medical practitioners attached to the English East India Company picked up this art from local bone setters and took it with them back home.

Bone-setting is, in fact, an indigenous 'popular culture therapy' practised in India since time immemorial. Many interesting facts have been stated in ancient Ayurvedic texts on the management of fractures. They also allude to different kinds of bandages and slings to be employed. The science of bone-setting has been addressed by Ayurveda, which calls it *bhagna*. Ayurveda enumerates bones into major five categories: *kapala,* i.e. flat bones, *ruchaka,* i.e. small cubical bones, *taruna,* i.e. cartilage, *valaya,* i.e. curved bones like rib bones, and *nalaka,* i.e. long tubular bones. The impacts of trauma on these various types of bones are varying. For instance, *ruchaka* or the cubical bones can get fragmented while the *valaya* or curbed bones generally break or crack under minor fall or trauma.[5]

Bone injuries have also been classified by Ayurveda[6] into two major categories: *savrana*, i.e. open or compound fracture and *avrana,* i.e. closed or simple fracture. *Avrana* is further classified as *sandhimukta* or dislocations and *kandabhagna* or fractures. Again, dislocations can be subdivided into six more types, and fractures into twelve types. This indicates that India's traditional knowledge about human anatomy was profound.

The six types of dislocation are also of six types: *utpista* or fracture dislocation; *vislista* or dislocations of joints due to ligamental tears; *Vivartita* or anterior-posterior dislocation of the head of the humerus;

avakshipta or downward displacement of the head of the humerus; *atikshipta* or marked displacement of any articulation surface usually found in the knee joint and *tiryakshipta* or oblique dislocation in one of the articulating bones.

Khanda bhagna or fractures in general, show swelling, twitching, rotational deformity, tenderness, crepitus, and various types of pain, continuous restlessness and loss of function of the affected part. All these features were mentioned by Susruta three thousand years ago and are still found as definitions in any standard modern textbook on orthopaedics.

Twelve types of fractures have been mentioned and fully described by Susruta. They are *karkataka,* i.e. depressed fracture; *aswakarna,* i.e. oblique fracture; *curnita,* i.e. comminuted fracture; *piccita,* i.e. fracture due to compression; *asthichallita,* i.e. usually due to sudden passive flexion, for example in interphallangeal joints if hit by a ball, *khanda bhagna,* i.e. spiral fracture; *majjanugatha,* i.e. impacted fracture; *atipatita,* i.e. complete compound fracture usually due to severe injury; *vakra,* i.e. green stick fracture; *chinna,* i.e. incomplete fracture; *patita,* i.e. comminuted fracture on the flat bone where it may be difficult to bring about permanent repair and *sphutita,* i.e. fissured fracture.

The surgical treatment of *bhagna* and *vislista,* or fractures and dislocations, involves various processes depending upon the location and nature of the case. Susruta enumerates four successive measures of first-aid followed by convalescence.[7] The four first-aid measures are: (a) *anchana*, i.e. lifting to the surface. This measure helps the hanging or distorted limb get restored to its original shape; (b) *pidana,* i.e. digital or other form of local pressure. This process helps bring back the broken and disjointed parts together; (c) *samksepa,* i.e. shortening or opposition and stabilization. This is the actual operation of resetting the fracture or dislocated parts to fit them together; (d) *bandhana,* i.e. bandaging or immobilization. Detailed explanations on each of the above steps are given. He also stresses that the splinting should be proper. The splint should not be too loose or too tight. All these processes are executed in such a way that the actual movements of the affected parts are reduced to a minimum.[8]

After the resetting is over, the part is covered with a piece of linen soaked in clarified butter. It is then covered with jute stow, the necessary splints placed in position. Then a firm but not too tight bandage is applied. If the bandage is too tight, pain and swelling might follow; if it is too loose, the affected parts might not adhere. Such bandages should be replaced at a regular interval of four to seven days, depending upon the weather. Medication, if needed, is also recommended. The diet during the healing period should be free from salt, acids, alkalis and pungent substances.[9]

Susruta has also given due consideration to the age factor in deciding the prognosis. According to him, skeletal injuries take one month to heal in young patients, two months in middle-aged patients and three months in old people. Special techniques like management of compound fractures have been dealt with separately. The wounds are dressed before immobilizing the fracture.

There is an indication of the use of practical physiotherapy in the traditional texts. An interesting feature in Susruta's technique of dealing with fractures is the method of immobilizing the injured limbs by using a fracture bed. It is important to mention that Susruta has treated fracture and dislocations of cervical spinal bones correcting the deformity. After the actual treatment is over, Susruta also defines a properly united fracture like absence of gaps between the broken fragments, shortening deformity and return of painless, easy movements.

Only when a surgeon is satisfied that these four features exist clinically, should the bone injury be declared as ideally healed. Susruta's bandaging techniques are also interesting. He has described fifteen types of bandages for use in different parts of the body: *kosa*—sheath bandage for limbs and fingers; *dama*—sheath bandage for thighs; *swartika*—cross bandage for joints; *anuveellita*—spiral bandage for limbs; *pratoli*—bandage for soft parts like neck and male genitalia; *mandala*—circular type for thoracic region; *sthagika*—sheath bandage for fingers and toes; *yamaka*—bandage to cover two wards at a time; *katra*—four-tailed bandage used on the chin and face; *cina*—four-tailed bandage for the eyes; *vibandha*—bandage for the trunk to be tied at the back; *vitana*—cephaline bandage for head injuries; *gophana*—T-shaped bandage used on the perineum and anal region; *panchangi*—five-tailed bandage employed around the neck and chin and tied above the head; and *utsangi*—a sling bandage used for immobilizing the upper limbs.

Sasruta has also described treatment for wrongly set bones. Faulty setting should be disjointed by a surgeon, and then treated like a case of general fracture or dislocation. If, in a case of untreated compound fracture, a bone is found sticking out, dried or forming the focus of an ulcer, it should be removed by a surgical saw before other treatment. The mode of preparing a special embrocation, termed *gandhataila*, is described in details. It is said to be very efficacious in fractures and dislocations which fail to heal normally.[10]

II

According to World Health Organization, 'Traditional medicine refers to the health practices, approaches, knowledge and beliefs incorporating plant, animal and mineral based medicines, spiritual therapies, manual techniques and exercises, applied singularly or in combination to treat, diagnose and prevent illness or maintain well-being.'[11] Unlike many other countries which possess only oral traditions of health knowledge, India and China have two types of traditional medical systems: one, codified system with written literature spanning over three to four millennia, as in the relatively formal systems like Ayurveda or traditional Chinese medicine, and the other, more localized, non-codified, folk traditions, which are far more diverse and draw from varied local ecosystems.[12]

In developing countries like India, traditional orthopaedic practices are found predominantly in rural areas. They include a wide spectrum of practices such as management of fracture, dislocation, and primary care of patients suffering from chronic musculoskeletal conditions like arthritis, post-polio residual paralysis and congenital deformities. These practices often involve a special understanding of anatomy, such as the concepts of vital points in the body as also special types of massaging techniques and herbal medicinal preparations to promote the healing of wounds and to strengthen bones. In many developing countries, these practices have been formally recognized, as in the case of Osteopathy and Chiropractic treatment.

According to one estimate, between 10 and 40 per cent of

patients with fractures and dislocations in the world are managed by unorthodox practitioners.[13] In a developing country like India, this type of bonesetters are one of the largest specialist groups practising this type of medicine, and their numbers are superseded only by the traditional birth attendants or *dais*.[14] It has recently been estimated that there are approximately 60,000 traditional orthopaedic practitioners in rural India.[15] The *Census of India, 2001*, records that there are as many as 6 lakh inhabited villages in India. This means, that for every ten villages there is one orthopedic practitioner. Another estimate records that there are about 70,000 traditional healers and bonesetters and they treat 60 per cent of the trauma.[16] Their practice includes management of fracture and dislocation, management of injuries and their complications, management of congenital anomalies like club foot and treatment of post-polio paralysis, etc.

Bone setting or traditional orthopaedic practice is a crucial domain of local health knowledge. These traditional bone setting measures are practised even today in many centres in south India. The well-known ones are Puthur in Chittor district, Mamsapuram in Kamarajar district and Olakkade in Kanyakumari district. Other than these are centres in the heart of the city very near the Ayurveda College in the Triveni Hospital at Thiruvananthapuram. Each centre has its own special oil or medication which they claim is the cause for the successful healing. Plants used in traditional bone setting are *Ampelocissuslatifolia*, *Anetemisla lacniata* and *Banbase ceiba* and a red coloured powder (which they call a disinfectant) and cover it with a thick layer of cotton over which splints are placed and kept in place by another bandage.

III

Bosipur, a tiny hamlet at Gurap in Burdwan district of West Bengal is widely known for housing a large number of bone-setters. The art and science of bone setting is very much alive here as are traditions, superstitions and folklores that surround it. These bone-setters are neglected in official health care programme for a variety of social, economic and political reasons. And consequently, there is an evident lack of sufficient data on health seeking behaviour, demographics of traditional orthopaedic practitioners, and the quality, safety and efficacy of their practices. A survey was conducted in December 2010 in and around Bosipur to explore some of these aspects of traditional orthopaedic practice and practitioners. I have recorded some key findings from the study reflecting on broader questions around the role of this popular and varied group of health providers.

The astonishing thing about this treatment is that these healers have neither any institutional medical knowledge nor do they know any charms or magic. The bone-setter is not a qualified physician from an institution. They are ordinary persons having no formal training of any kind. They are not recognized as *vaidyas,* nor are they respected as doctors. Most of them have passed out primary school examinations, but could not acquire formal education beyond the tenth standard. But their hands work as magical instruments. They carry on the hereditary service of their ancestors. Such healers come from a family of traditional bone-setters. No female practitioner, however, could be found. But more recently it has been observed that these families do not allow their children to practice bone setting, as they treat people on contract, like a business. Most of the bone-setters interviewed are in the age-group of 21-54.

The treatment process is bafflingly simple. When a patient approaches the 'clinic', the bone-setter first tries to ascertain the nature of the injury. He feels the affected part of the body to locate the fractured bone or the dislocated joint. In most cases the bone-setter will, all of a sudden, twist, pull or poke the arm or leg to set it right. He then ties up the affected part with medicinal herb and a sling around the neck is fixed to immobilize the area of injury. The entire process takes no more than 10 to 15 minutes. The specialty, however, rests not much with herb but with the expertise in manipulating the bones and setting the alignment in right order.[17]

In some other cases, after aligning the broken bone, for which no radiological aid is needed, they only touch the swelling and feel the fracture gently. They apply a paste liberally and bandage it firmly; they put paste on every layer of the bandage. Finally a creeper of a plant, botanically known as *Cissius quadrangularis linn*, is tied around the affected part 'to prevent any chance of movement of the limb'. This bandage is kept like that for at least three days. This plant happens to be a real doctor, bone-setter, and is known as *Asthisamharaka* in Sanskrit, meaning setting or repairing bones. It is also known as *vajravalli,* which is celebrated for its vast curative and therapeutic properties. In Hindi it is called *Hadjod,* in Tamil *Pirandai,* Bengali—*Harjora* and Malayalam—*Changalam Piranda.* The English name is perhaps Verdt Grape Vine, Winged Tree Vine or Edible Stemmed Vine. The plant is anti-bacterial, anti-inflammatory, and anti-osteoporotic and has all the properties of an analgesic pain killer. The fleshy stems and scanty leaves contain phytochemicals, flavonoids and rich anti-oxidants. And most important, the stems have the miracle properties of healing and joining fractured bones. Cissius is a proven Ayurvedic remedy for sports injuries of muscle over exertion, injuries to tendons, bones, nerves and cartilages.

Unlike their southern counterparts, who are mostly drawn from the Kshatriya community in Andhra Pradesh and Tamil Nadu, almost all the bone-setters interviewed in Bosipur hail from Bagdi community. A few pertinent questions perhaps are in order. Elsewhere, in my study on the *tikadars* or smallpox inoculators in Bengal, I have shown that initially all of them were drawn from the Brahmin family, but gradually, however, as the demand for *tikadars* rose, so did the number of persons afflicted, and people from the marginalized section of the society took to this calling.[18] The question is: did it happen to the bone-setter community too? Did these people coming from the so-called untouchable Bagdi community take over this profession from the more knowledgeable Brahmins at a distant past? This is not yet clear.

Generally speaking, traditional bone-setters do not undertake medical service as a full time vocation. A typical healer may be a farmer, a barber, a shopkeeper, a blacksmith or even a wandering monk.[19] But here at Bosipur, their primary occupation is bone-setting, but all of them do possess some amount of cultivable land where they could work and produce crops over the year. For them, bone setting is not a full-time job. The question that seems to perplex is: were they originally farmers or did they purchase land with the savings from their calling and turned cultivators later? Land is not certainly abundant in this area, and as such its prices are reasonably high which scarcely warrant wanton purchase by anybody. Or do they purchase land to ensure livelihood of the members of the next generation, who are much less interested in the profession of bone-setting and opting out fast for white collar jobs? Land is admittedly a marker of social prestige. Did they purchase land to uplift their status and climb up the social ladder?

The number of patients they draw daily varies from one bone-setter to another. But on an average each bone-setter can boast of having treated 30 to 40 patients daily. They are also called out to patients' houses if the affected person is incapacitated by his/her fracture injuries. The fees for such occasional calls depend upon the distance they need to travel.

In Andhra Pradesh and Tamil Nadu the consultation charge is free for the poor, and all other patients generally pay anything between Rs. 50 and 100 at the end of the treatment.[20] Bosipur seems to have no prescribed pattern of fees. Almost a decade ago, they used to take Re. 1 paise 25 as their usual fees. Recently it has been increased to Rs. 5. Considering the present market condition, the amount seems to be a bit trifle. Is it because of a role reversal of the patron-client relationship? For, these people had long been at the receiving end, sustained with financial doles from their wealthy patrons. So, are they paying back the patronage in this pittance? Rs. 5 is not a service charge *per se*, it can very well be dubbed as *dakkhina*, an acknowledgement that they are now patrons. Benefaction or benevolence might be a convenient plank for social service for just one bone-setter or two, but it can hardly be a reason why all members of a community shall go in for such an agreed benevolence. Each patient gives what he or she can afford as offering. However, true to their claim, most of the patients are poor. Labourers at construction sites, maid servants, and poor children are very often found to be their regular clients. Only a few of them are from the middle class. But patients from affluent families are not always a rare sight. If the fracture is serious and the patient is wealthy, bone-setters will demand more money for the treatment. Otherwise, they are quite generous and do not take any fee from a poor person. But if a wealthy person does not pay adequately, the treatment may be defective. In that case, it is not possible for the patients to approach another such healer, because, according to their professional ethics, no one can interfere with a case which is dealt with by another traditional healer.

Their income from practice also varies considerably. The minimum, they admit, is Rs. 5,000 and maximum Rs. 20,000 per month. They claim their success rate to be 100 per cent. After successful healing of the fracture, the bone setters advise their clients to perform *puja* in a manner they please.

The method they employ for setting bones may be unorthodox, but seem effective. I saw a young girl brought on a makeshift stretcher. The bone-setter pushed and pulled her fractured leg. She was evidently in terrible pain, but she somehow bore it with patience. The bone-setter then told her to return after a fortnight. The process lasted about 25 minutes. By the time she left the room, another had taken her place. People attending the chamber confided that fear of heavy plaster, prolonged period of immobilization and possible amputation weighed in favour of visiting the bone-setter.[21] There are other considerations as well. The modern medical management, the cost of diagnosis, medicine and surgery are quite enormous compared to that of bone setting through traditional methods.[22]

The concern on the faces of the new patients was telling. Some bit their lips, some just turned away as if to muffle their ears, others stared wide-eyed, more so the parents of children, wondering why they failed to rob the pain. In sharp contrast were the attendants of patients who were here for the second or third time. They were happy and said the wound had healed.

But the bone-setters are not a happy lot. They are trying hard to stick to their profession, but in vain. The decline of indigenous medical practice, such as bone setting, can be ascribed to so many historical circumstances. The Buddhist doctrine of *ahimsa*, which is said to have caused dissection to be abandoned with the subsequent deterioration of surgery and anatomical knowledge might be one reason. Decline can also be attributed to Muslim conquest and support of a rival medical system, followed by British conquest and patronage of yet another rival system. In addition, it can also be attributed to Hindu customs of over-valuing authority as a method of validation, and of treating knowledge as a secret. The techniques of bone setting have had few takers. Thus, traditional-culture medicine is described as being in an abject state. Over-grown with superstition, only a few elements remain from antiquity, like ruins that testify to a glorious past.

Notes

1. Leslie would prefer to call it 'popular culture medicine'. Charles Leslie, *Asian Medical Systems: A Comparative Study*, Delhi: Motilal Banarsidass, 1998, p. 359.
2. Biswamoy Pati and Mark Harrison, eds., *Health, Medicine and Empire: Perspectives on Colonial Medicine*, Hyderabad: Orient Longman, 2001, pp. 9-10.
3. M. Radhika, 'A Tradition of Bone-Setting', *The Hindu*, Chennai, Special Issue with *Sunday Magazine, Indian Health Traditions*, 8 October 2000. www.hinduonnet.com/folio/fo0010/00100380.htm.
4. Amitabha Mitra, 'Ramblings of a Bone Setter', www.boloji.com/ramblings/181.htm

   The Silk Route is a convenient name for the Trans-Asia trade routes. The route that linked Middle East Asia, i.e. Arab countries, with its far eastern regions that included China during the ancient and middle ages, came to be called the Silk Route. Silk, a Chinese invention, was a coveted item traded for the exotic goods of Arabia. Arab contact with the West facilitated exchange of goods, thus extending the influence of this link. The route passed through inhospitable terrain with formidable mountains and punishing deserts. India played a vital role in the trade, virtually by its position at the centre of the route as well as its unique products such as spices, precious stones and hand-crafted goods. Besides, India had a reputation as a hub of learning and treasure house of scriptures, particularly of Buddhism. References to Chinese silk are seen in *Arthashastra,* a treatise in politics written by Chanakya, the mentor of Chandra Gupta Maurya.
5. For this section I have heavily drawn on Dr. M. Radhika, 'A Tradition of Bone Setting', op. cit.
6. Ayurveda (the science of life) or Ayurvedic medicine is a system of traditional medicine native to India and practised in other parts of the world as a form of alternative medicine. In Sanskrit, the word *Ayurveda* consists of the words *āyus*, meaning 'longevity', and *Veda*, meaning 'related to knowledge' or 'science'. Evolving throughout its history, Ayurveda remains an influential system of medicine in south Asia.

The earliest literature on Indian medical practice appeared during the Vedic period in India. The *Susruta Samhita* and the *Charaka Samhita* were influential works on traditional medicine during this era. Over the following centuries, Ayurvedic practitioners developed a number of medicinal preparations and surgical procedures for the treatment of various ailments and diseases.

7. *Susruta Samhita*, ed., Priyadaranjan Ray, Hirendranath Gupta and Mira Roy, Indian National Science Academy, New Delhi, 1980, p. 96.
8. Ibid.
9. Ibid.
10. Fractures of bone are set right by bone-setters in *Siddha* tradition as well. It is a separate science also known as *Varma* Treatment. It deals with the various kinds of fractures and their cures.
11. WHO fact sheet on Traditional medicine (revised May 2003), www.who.int./mediacentre/factsheets/fs134/en, accessed on 1 December 2010.
12. P.M. Unnikrishnan, H.P. Lokesh Kumar and Darshan Shankar, 'Traditional Orthopaedic Practitioners' Place in Contemporary Health: A Case Study from Southern India', in Kabir Sheikh and Asha George, eds., *Health Providers in India: On the Frontiers of Change*, New Delhi: Routledge, 2010, p. 182.
13. S.A. Green, 'Orthopaedic Surgeons: Inheritors of Tradition', in *Clinical Orthopedics and Related Research*, 1999, no. 363, pp. 258-63.
14. A. Agarwal and R. Agarwal, 'The Practice and Tradition of Bonesetting', in *Education for Health*, vol. 23, no. 1, 2010, www.educationforhealth.net
15. D. Shankar, 'Field tested participatory methodology for rapid assessment of the community's therapeutic use of medicinal plants', in the proceedings of the workshop on approaches towards evaluation of medicinal plants prior to clinical trials' conducted by the foundation for medical research. November 2006. Cited in Unnikrishnan, Kumar and Shankar, 'Traditional Orthopaedic Practitioners' Place in Contemporary Health', op. cit., p. 184.
16. J. Church, *Regional News: World Orthopaedic Concern Newsletter*, January 1998.
17. The setting skill of the bone setter is comparable with the *puttur kattu* (bandage) in south India. Vide Asok Kumar Panda and Suvendu Rout, '*Pattur Kattu* (Bandage): A Traditional Bone-setting Practice in South India', in *Journal of Ayurvedic and Integrative Medicine*, 2011, vol. 2,

no. 4, pp. 174-8, www.jaim.in/xt.asp2011/2/4/174/90766, accessed on 7 July 2012 .

18. Arabinda Samanta, 'Smallpox in the Nineteenth Century Bengal', *Indian Journal of History of Science*, vol. 47, no. 3, June 2012, pp. 220-4.
19. D. Shankar, Abdul Hafeel, Unnikrishnan Payyappapallimana and Suma Tagadur, 'Reviving Local Health Traditions', FRLHT, India www.compasnet.org/blog/wp-content/uploads/2011/03/ARNS/arns 07.pdf, accessed on 7 July 2013.
20. Asok Kumar Panda and Suvendu Rout, 'Pattur Kattu (Bandage): A Traditional Bone-setting Practice in South India', in *Journal of Ayurvedic and Integrative Medicine*, 2011, vol. 2, no. 4, p. 176.
21. L.O. Thanni, 'Factors Influencing Patronage of Traditional Bone-setters', *West Africa Journal of Medicine* (PUBMED), 2000: 19, pp. 220-4.
22. Mathar Sahib Abdul Razak, 'Traditional Bone-setters and Rural Health Status in India', Paper presented at the 12th World Congress on Public Health, 27 April-1 May 2009, Istanbul, Turkey, wfpha.confex.com/wf[ha/2009/webprogram/paper4803.html, accessed on 8 July 2012.

CHAPTER 12

On Identity, State and Conflict in North-East India

Sajal Nag

Identities are constructions. They are constructed according to political expediencies. An argument can be presented on 'construction' *versus* 'formation' of identity. What about shared cultural traits, traditions, history that determines an identity? It is said that what we inherit from our parents are genetics like physical attributes and what we inherit from our society is culture, tradition and customs and so on. The social inheritance facilitates the formation of an identity on the basis of its history, culture and traditions. But this identity may not have political relevance. For that this identity has to be re-fabricated, altered and even reshaped to render it politically relevant. This is construction. Hence, identities do not create conflict. But when they are constructed and used for political objectives it might create conflict situation.

Pre-Colonial Identity

Like most identities the Naga identity was exogenous to themselves. Most Nagas or Mizos identified themselves by their village/subtribal names and the Naga name was given to them by their neighbours. This name was popularized and enforced by the British during colonial rule. But the markers that were used by colonial anthropologists to identifying Nagas were more confusing. For example, common characteristics that help to identify a Naga were as follows: Head hunting, bachelor's dormitory, dwelling houses built on post or pits, disposal of dead or raised platform, betel chewing, trial marriage system, aversion to milk and milk products, tattooing by pricking, absence of peaceful political organization, the double cylinder vertical gorge, the loom for weaving clothes, a large quadrangular or hexagonal shield, abode in the hills and crude form of agriculture.[1]

In the pre-colonial period most of the tribes were not conscious of their tribal identities[2] and their world was confined to their family, clan, *khel* and village. Terms like Nogas, Kuki, Abor, Lushai, Garo, Chulikata, Banferia, Kapur-shor and so on were given to them by non-tribal plains' people.[3] Even the major tribal groups in Naga Hills such as Ao, Angami, Lotha and Konyak, got their names from other tribes.[4] There was, however, a general awareness that a group of villages living in a particular geographical area were somehow related to each other in a way they were not related to each other. There were similarities of myth, religion and social custom and language, but the differences in these same areas were even greater. An examination of the north-eastern scenario will amply illustrate it. For example, the Nagas and Mizos, two of the major tribes of north-east India, which are in conflict with the state now, were unaware of their identities.

The Nagas, based on certain characteristics among themselves, came up with sub-tribal names, viz., the Aos, Angamis, Chakesangs, Konyaks, Sangthams, Yimchungers and so on. Each of the village was a state (*ang*) or *khunbao* (chieftaindom) or *tatar* (Ao Naga council of elected headmen) and was sovereign and often compared to Greek city states of the ancient world. Most interestingly, many of these were at war and often committed violent raids on each other taking a heavy toll on its demographic strength. They were called Nagas (pronounced as Noga) by the neighbouring plainsmen of Assam. It is not known why they were called Noga but existing theories advocate that the word Noga came from the Sanskrit word Naga meaning naked, or because the nature of violence they perpetrated (Naga Gha or Naga Jalakiya) have been falsified. Interestingly, most Nagas cannot pronounce the alphabet 'G'. For them Naga is Naka. In fact, even the Assamese people who coined the description Naga, very rarely called the Nagas as Nagas. They were referred to as Khamjangias, Aitonias, Tablungias and Namchangias. Sometimes they were mentioned not by the name of the Naga tribe or clan but by the names of several villages against which an expedition was sent. Commencing from the west between Dayang and Dikhow rivers, the Naga tribes were known to the Assamese as Panihatias (those who come by water), the Torhatias (those who come by land) or Dayangias, the Hatigorias, Assyringias, Dupdorias and Namchangias. The first two were subdivisions of the Lotha Nagas and the rest that of the Aos. Between the Dikhow and Buri Dihing, the Naga tribes were known as the Tablungias Jaktoongias, Mooloongs, Changnois (also known as Bhitor Namchangias), Jabokas (Abhaypurias) Banferas, Mutonias (or Kooloongs). Paniduarias, Barduarias and Namchangias (or Jaipoorias) who were not connected with the Namchangias (division of Ao) who inhabit the low border hills on the left bank of Dikhow. Some of these tribes were more extensively placed spreading over several villages (Tablungias over thirteen villages while other tribes inhabited a few villages (Jobokas, Banferas and Mutonias, each with four or five villages only). These Naga tribes were the Konyak and Nocte tribes who lived between Dikhow and Buri Dihing bordering plains. The names of these Naga tribes originated either from the *duars* or passes through which they descended into the plains or from the important Naga villages or places of the plains situated at or near the entrance of the passes. In fact, the Ahom state appointed some officers to control and deal with each of these tribes.

Similar was the case of the Mizos who lived along the Bengal frontier. They were known generically as Kukis to the plainsmen irrespective of their sub-tribe or any other identities. Despite their periodic raids on the plains which were economically necessary, the relationship was amicable and mutually dependent. The pre-British literature of Bengal does not mention the Kukis as any hostile group. In fact, they were frequent visitors to the *haats* and *melas* of the plains where they often traded their products for the commodities of the plains. It was the British who first distinguished between Kukis and other Chin tribes into several ethnic groups and ascribed an identity.

Construction of Identities in North-East India: The Colonial Project

The construction of identity of the tribal started with the British. But the nature of construction shifted according to political necessities. In the first phase, the British, deeply disturbed by the violence in the north-east frontier and the regular tribal raids and uprisings, decided to put a stop to all these with a strong hand and bring stability to these frontier areas which was needed if the growing tea industry was to prosper. It was done by fixing territorial boundaries of each of the tribe and sub-tribes, reducing the so-called sovereign tribes to subjecthood by subordinating them to the administration, binding them to colonial laws, and schooling them into subjecthood by opening schools to stop the tribal practices. Thus, the Naga hills was constituted into a district; a district administration was inaugurated, laws were formulated to which tribal were compelled to adhere, and territorial boundary was fixed beyond which Nagas could not venture. Through these measures raids were stopped, Naga chiefs were absorbed into the administration as lambardars and tax collectors. Some of them were made intermediaries between the Nagas and British as Dobhashis, schools and health care centres set up to make the people look up to and depend on the administration. Officers were instructed to learn the language and culture of the tribes and write monographs about them. A fixed territorial unit, an enumerated language, a constructed past, an apparent sense of unity made the people conscious of an identity. These were then consolidated by Census Reports, Linguistic Survey and Churches (Missionaries organized churches as Ao church, Angami Church, etc.). In Mizoram, T.H. Lewin, Shakespeare, and Parry were also part of this endeavour, who, through ethnographic efforts, ascribed an identity to the Kuki Chin tribes.

Christian missionaries, through their efforts, strengthened the process of identity formation in various ways.[5] The missionaries contributed towards identity consciousness through standardization of language that was required for proselytization. A dialect was chosen as a tribal language and endowed with a written form; in the absence of a script, Bengali or Roman alphabets were used. This written form of the language was accepted by the government, and became the language of education and administration throughout the area inhabited by a tribe. This standard language gradually displaced other dialects, especially among the literates. Closely related to the formation of a standard language was the American Baptist Mission and Welsh Presbyterian Mission and church-controlled educational system, and the creation of an incipient literature. While there were certain government schools at major centres of the Naga Hills, Lushai Hills, Manipur and the Khasi-Jaintia Hills, the responsibility for education was largely entrusted by the government to the Mission, especially the Baptist and Presbyterian Missions. These schools spread knowledge of the standard language, thus, making meaningful communication possible among the various dialect groups. They also established an educational network based on village primary schools, from which the best students went on to middle schools located in the Mission centre. For the first time, tribal students from different areas came into contact with one another. These schools created the nucleus of the tribal elites who were to become the future leaders of the solidarity movements. But even then identities remained at sub-tribal level. As the nationalist movement grew stronger in the rest of the country, colonial effort at othering the major tribes of north-east gained momentum.

This was part of an agenda in the second phase that given the violent nature of the tribes, if they were allowed to be a part of the intensified nationalist movement, it would become uncontrollable. Hence, politically the British tried to keep them excluded from reforms through which the tribes could be brought under political participation by declaring them as excluded area, or backward area and at the same time banned Indian political parties from entering and operating in these hills to pre-empt such a situation. On the theoretical side, they tried to construct an identity for the tribals which would prevent them from identifying with the rest of the Indians. In fact, the much celebrated Naga Club memorandum, which famously stated, 'we the Nagas' for the first time, submitted to the Simon Commission, was a handiwork of Harry Blah, a Khasi officer of the colonial administration, under the instruction of J.H. Hutton, the Deputy Commissioner of Assam. The result was the declaration that north east India was backward and partially backward by which concepts the tribal region was kept out of political reforms.

In the third phase was the Montagu-Chelmsford Reform, which was examining the question of representative government and provincial autonomy for the Indians as was later envisaged in the 1935 Act. Again, the fear was that tribals of north east India must not be allowed to demand reform or take part in the nationalist movement lest the whole movement go out of control. It was in this phase we see that the colonial officers were trying to create a separate identity for the tribals. This was done by telling the tribals that they were not Indians and, therefore, they should refrain from participating in the nationalist movement led by the Indians. True to their agenda, the Government of India Act 1935 declared North East as Excluded Area, Partially Excluded Area and so on. The identities that were created for the tribal to legitimize these concepts were as follows: J.H. Hutton, the Deputy Commissioner of Naga Hills, argued that the tribals of north east India, particularly the Nagas and Mizos, were not Indians in any sense of the term. They belonged to the Mongoloid race and were akin to the Chins of Burma. Nagas belonged to the Indonesian stocks of Mongoloids and were closely connected with the Pagans of Malay, Borneo and Philippines. They spoke a language which was Tibeto-Burman while Indians spoke largely Indo-Aryan. They became a part of the Indian subcontinent only after the British occupation of the area. Although they lived in contiguous areas, the neigbouring Bengalis or Assamese had never been able to subdue them and nor were they influenced by any of the Indian faiths. The tribals practised their own brand of animism. In fact, the Hindus and Muslims ostracized them for eating beef and pork, respectively. The tribals did not observe the caste system and had they joined the Indians they would have been relegated to the lowest rungs of the caste hierarchy. Unlike the Indians the tribal did not have child marriages, restrictions on widows or evils like prostitution in their society. Hutton went on to argue that not only was there nothing common between the Indians and these hill tribes, there actually existed a deep-rooted antipathy between the two.

N.E. Parry, the Superintendent of Lushai Hills, also asserted that the Lushai tribals belonged to the Mongoloid races and were affiliated to Kuki-Chin tribes of Burma. They were not only distinct from the Indians but there was also mistrust between the two. Even the colonial administration of Assam supported this view before the Simon Commission. The Governor of Assam, Robert Reid (1937-42), felt that:

the tribal of north east India were not Indians in any sense of the word... neither in origin nor in appearance nor in habits nor in outlook and it is by historical accidents that are tagged to an Indian Province. Therefore, we have no right to allow these great body of non-Indian animists and Christians to be drawn into the struggle between Hindus and the Muslims which is now and will be in future with ever increasing intensity the dominating factor in Indian proper.

The superintendent of Lushai Hills A.G. McCall wrote:

We have come to see very clearly that the Lushai is bound to the Mongolian than to the Aryan races. This begs the whole question as to whether it would not be better for the Lushai to seek shelter under the colonial or dominion offices. While still remaining within the spheres of Mongolian influences by a closer association with the hills of Burma, the Shan states, the Karen and others with whom the Lushai would find so much in common.

Reginald Coupland, who formulated the plan to have a separate autonomous state for the tribals, went a step ahead and asserted that these tribes were not even Burmese, 'the inhabitants of both (Nagaland and Lushai Hills are alike in race and culture. They are not Indians or Barmans but of the Mongol Stock. In no sense do they belong to Indian or Burman nations.'

The logical conclusion of this construction was to advocate a separate sovereign state for the tribals of north-east India. When the British were about to withdraw from India, they wanted to separate the tribal from India and continue to keep them under their authority. Several proposals were formulated like North-Eastern Frontier Province and Crown Colony which would comprise all the tribals of north-east India and Burma and would be administered directly from Whitehall.

Nationalist Construction

When the tribals themselves constructed their identity they obviously borrowed from colonial construction as the political expediency could not afford any other construction or reliance on history. Such construction also went through several shifts according to the phases of their struggle. In its earliest phase, the Naga intelligentsia emphasized the merger of disparate and even hostile tribes living in the designated area of 'Naga Hills' into the generic Naga identity. In the second 'liberal' phase, the Naga intelligentsia not only included neighbouring non-Naga tribes, like the Dimasas and Karbis, into the fold but also incorporated their traditional 'enemy' tribes, like the Kukis, against who they had been engaged in prolonged warfare over land and habitat. In this phase we find the Nagas willing to accommodate even the migrant Nepalis or Gorkhas, who settled in their area as ex-servicemen of the British army, and were subsequently co-opted as members of their nationality.

Thus, we can surmise that Naga nationality, at this stage, privileged territoriality over ethnicity or tribal ideology. In the third phase, during which the Naga 'nationalist' movement had been launched from the 1950s, the thrust was on the consolidation of a regional identity by including more and more tribes who were willing to adopt and accept the generic Naga identity. In this period, the Naga movement expanded across the administrative boundary of Naga Hills to extend to neighbouring Assam, Manipur, North-East Frontier Agency and even Burma, where a large number of affiliated tribes lived. The inclusion of these tribes expanded the purview of Naga identity and enlarged their territorial claims. In the fourth phase, the Naga identity movement assumed an aggressive posture and an authoritarian character. A number of small tribes who were unaffiliated to any of the large tribes of the region like the Kuki, Mizo or Naga, were targeted and mobilized into the fold of Naga identity through the agency of the Naga church or through tacit coercive tactics. The Naga nation-making process mentioned above apparently unified various tribes into a strong Naga identity and presented this identity (internally and externally) as a viable national formation.

Yet, I argue that the Naga identity only constructed an enumerable and presentable national identity for a political objective of 'Naga nation state' that was separate and independent from the Indian nation. On account of its unstable structure, I propose that it also rendered itself fragile and dependent on favourable historical conditions for its sustainability. The first organization, which attempted to manifest a pan-Naga identity, was the Naga Club, formed in 1918 in Kohima and Mokokchung. Its members were government officials and a few leading headmen of neighbouring villages. In Mizoram it was the Mizo Union, founded in 1946.

Origin of Conflict

There is a misconception that the origin of conflict between the tribal like the Nagas and Mizos and the Indian State was over conflicting identity. There was no identity issue at all in the early phases of struggle. In reality, it was over the issue of retaining pre-modern social formation and modernity. With the advent of the British elements of modernity made its inroads into these hills as well. The introduction of modern education had produced modern elite who wanted to change the social structure of these societies from 'chiefly' oppression.

Both the Naga and Mizo society was deeply oligarchic where chiefs not only ruled but owned all the assets. The liberal elites wanted to free these societies from chiefly oppression and transform them into modern republican, egalitarian societies. The declaration of Indian National Congress that after independence India would abolish all medieval system like the princely states, *zamindari* and chieftainship encouraged them to imagine its implementation in their areas as well. In Nagaland the new elite was led by leaders like Aliba Imti and T. Sakhrie who wanted to be part of India, while in Mizoram the Mizo Union was divided into two factions, one right wing—which wanted independence, and the left wing, which wanted to remain in India. The chiefs, however, feared that it would deprive them of their power, privilege and hegemony. Hence, they were hopeful of the colonial idea of a sovereign unit out of India. In Nagaland, this faction was led by people like Phizo.

Such profusion of tribes, ethnic groups, languages and dialects were suggestive of the degree of complexity of and the consequent implication in the political economic and socio-cultural relation in the region. Both the Naga and Mizo movements in this period was restorative, who like some of the Princely States of India wanted to be restored to their pre-British status. They wanted the old order be restored where the old chiefs would retain their hold and control over resources like land and power over the people. The new middle class wanted to do away with them which was why they wanted to merge with India, which promised a republican egalitarian social order. It was a conflict between modernity and its adversaries, medieval order and its opponents who wanted to make a transition to modern times. It was not a crisis between Indian nation and the Nagas or Mizos. It was an internal crisis where nationalist discourse was used as an instrument to achieve that goal. India's involvement in the crisis was the way it negotiated the crisis.

Autonomy Movements

The North-Western Frontier formed the gateway of the Indian subcontinent for the numerous migratory waves of Central Asian people, the north-east India formed the other gateway from the opposite direction through which, similar migration from East and Southeast Asia took place. Such profusion of tribes, ethnic groups, languages and dialects were suggestive of the degree of complexity of and the consequent implication in the political economic and socio-cultural relation in the region.

However, big or small each of these indigenous tribes or communities was, they had their own evolved polity. The Khasis had their Hima, the Jaintias, Dimasas and Tipperas had their own monarchy, the Ahoms and the Meitheis had a full fledged state, each of the Naga and Mizo sub-tribes had their polity in the form of chieftaindom. Such numerous and petty polity formation in a relatively narrow space has been described by Stanley Thambiah in anthropological terms as the 'galactic polity' in the context of Southeast Asia.[6] It was compared to a political galaxy formed by several principalities and dependencies within a small territory. The north-eastern situation in pre-colonial times could be profitably seen as a similar galactic polity—in a continuous state of migration, polity formation, and varied stages of political evolution. Such state formation remained in a fluid state for long spells of time. Each of these polities was autonomous in some form in pre-colonial times and most of them even were at war with the neighbouring tribes or plainsmen.

The post-colonial situation was a continuation of this situation which has to be understood because the colonial system did not touch them much and the colonial administration did not interfere with the structure. The autonomy demand that arose in north-east India was on the basis of these pre-colonial polity formations which explain the profusion of such demands. The demands arose because the tribes/communities in question were wary of the nationalist discourses and the nation state's power of submerging smaller and marginal communities. Since the federal polity allowed them some sort of autonomy these groups wanted autonomy on the basis of their pre-colonial status, which the Indian state could not afford as it would mean virtually every village would have to be granted a province, district or autonomous council. The result was a stalemate in which there was a confrontation between these communities and the Indian State. This was the beginning of the conflict which developed into a secessionist movement due to the nature in which Indian State negotiated the problem.

Oppositional Approach

The oppositional approach originated by Edward Spicer seeks precisely to do that.[7] This approach emphasizes the following proposition: The greater the opposition (the circumstantial component) between groups, the deeper the intensification of primordial sentiments (the primordial component) and hence, the greater the ethnic solidarity.

It has to be put in perspective that secessionist movement was not only restorative, which wanted to revert to their old status after British withdrawal from India, an attempt to put the clock back, it was also led by the traditional chieftains who wanted to retain their hegemony over the people.[8] The new middle classes, which emerged out of modern education, had actually opposed this move. This was true of all the Naga and Mizo movements. In doing so they often imitated nationalist discourse stating each of these tribes was a nation by themselves. But since there was multiplicity of tribes in each of these hills who had their inner contradiction, there was a move to constitute a generic tribe resembling a nationality in terms of demography and political strength. The identity projected was national but since it drew from its pre-modern roots and composition it actually was an ethnic identity, more than a tribe but less than a nation.

Moreover, post-colonial experience proved the apprehensions of the constituent communities. Nationalism had emerged as a legitimizing ideology of modern nation state. The imagination of Indic civilization in modern India was consolidated by differentiation with the Western civilization. Sanskritic culture and Brahmanic order were its essential features. In this imagination Hindus were seen as symbol of composite culture. The communities of north-east India were to fit into the framework of the cultural imagination of India. Despite the fact that north-east India did not really figure in this imagination any resistance to assimilation was seen as a threat to its composite cultural ethos. Hence, autonomy demands were seen as threats to national integration. Force was used instead of governance. Development was seen not as an independent enterprise but as something related to peace and tranquillity. Interrogating the nationhood of India and demand of restructuring of the polity is seen as secessionism.

Notes

1. W.C. Smith, *The Naga Tribes of Assam*, London: Cambridge University Press, 1926.
2. Frederick Downs, 'Indentity: The Integrative Principle', in M. Sangam and D.R. Syiemlieh, ed., *Essays of Christianity in North East India*, Delhi: Indus, 1994, pp. 222-36. The following discussion is based on his research.
3. See for details, Laxmi Devi, *Ahom Tribal Relations*, Gauhati: Lawyers Bookstall, 1992.
4. S.M. Dubey, 'Inter-Ethnic Alliance, Tribal Movements and Integration in North East India', in K.S Singh, ed., *Tribal Movements in India*, New Delhi: Manohar, 1982, p. 4.
5. Frederick Downs, 'Study of Christianity in North East India', in *NEHU Journal of Social Sciences and Humanities*, July-September 1991, pp. 203-14.
6. Stanley Thambiah, 'The Galactic Polity in South East Asia', in *Culture,*

Thought and Social Action: An Anthropological Perspective, Cambridge: Mass: Havard University Press, 1985

7. Edward Spicer, 'Persistent Identity Systems', in *Science*, vol. 67, no. 4011, 1971, pp. 795-800, cited in D.V. Kumar, 'Explaining Mizo Ethnicity: The Relevance of Oppositional Approaches', in *Man in India*, vol. 89, nos. 1 & 2, 2009, pp. 37-50.
8. A detailed discussion on this is available in my 'A Comparative Analysis of Naga, Mizo and Meithei Insurgencies', in *Faultline: Writing on Conflict and Resolution*, vol. 14, July 2003, pp. 67-79.

CHAPTER 13

'What, Drawn, and Talk of Peace!'

Security, Development and the Autonomy Question in the Indian North-east*

ATIG GHOSH

Subcomandante Insurgente Marcos, the iconic ski-masked leader of the Zapatista movement in México, tells the camera in the documentary *Zapatista!*—perhaps, a little too dramatically—that the rebels rose up against the Mexican government in 1994 only to discover that the Mexican government did not exist; instead, they found themselves confronted by the structures of global capital.[1] The case may not have been as dramatic for the autonomy movements in the Indian north-east (henceforth, simply the north-east), but progressively, and especially in their post-1990 *avatar*, these movements too have found themselves fighting against what the Zapatista leader described as the structures of global capital. If we take the last 15-odd years of uneasy ceasefire as a heuristic 'phase' in the war-and-peace continuum of the north-east, then it would indeed seem that the region is experiencing a changed nature of engagement with the powers that be. The earlier, possibly more clear-cut opposition between the state and the autonomy groups has given way to a more complicated template where increasingly the market has come to play a pivotal role.

Market Matters

Commentators have written copiously on this de-escalation of conflict in the region, even though most of them agree that this has been the result of pacification.[2] That is to say, the apparent peace that prevails today is 'governed' peace which does not completely rule out conflicts but makes a convenient mix of war and peace—convenient to most parties and stakeholders involved in such conflicts.[3] Be it as it may, the commentators tend to praise this de-escalation of conflict and draw our attention to the newly emergent concern for rights, justice and democracy in the north-east. This development, says Samir Kumar Das, is playing a critical role in triggering off a series of new social movements in the region. 'Insofar as the public agenda is being redefined,' he avers, 'a new citizen seems to be surfacing in the region—a citizen who harps less on her distinctiveness from the outsiders or the foreigners as seen in the course of the Assam Movement (1979-85) but more on the three key issues of rights, justice and democracy.'[4] Das feels that the process is likely to be a trendsetter for peace in future, given that the region has until recently been witness to ethnic schism, occasionally erupting into acute xenophobia, violence and insurgency.

Das's point is moot, however. He was making these observations about the north-east in general, and Assam[5] in particular, in a tract published in July 2012. That very month would see the western districts of Assam erupt in an ugly wave of xenophobic violence perpetrated by the ethnic Bodos against the Muslim cultivators. By 8 August 2012, 77 people had died[6] and over 400,000 people were taking shelter in 270 relief camps, after being displaced from almost 400 villages.[7] The Bodos—who had for many decades been clamouring for autonomy vis-à-vis Assam and the Indian State, emphasizing their non-belonging, so to speak, to the mainstream Indian body politic—swiftly turned around to rephrase their identity in terms of Indian nationality in this period and branded the Muslims—some of whom had been settled in agriculture in these parts for many generations—as outsiders, as infiltrators from Bangladesh. The north-east, therefore, is not a region about which general predictions can be made and sustained. Having pointed this out, it must also be conceded that Das is making a number of germane observations here: he is introducing key (f)actors of an unmistakeable change that has taken place in the region. The 'revolutionary' focus on fracturing the Indian state's sovereignty—which only in ahistorical, juridical terms is indiscerptible—and seizing autonomy has transformed into newer, more innovative organizing, one strand of which Das has described as the concern for rights, justice and democracy.

One way of understanding the general cessation of violence in the autonomy movements of the north-east (or the new social movements, as some would prefer to define such movements in their contemporary *avatar*) is to describe this as a secular trend. This explanation, of course, is quickly confirmed by the comfortable clichés of the periodic waxing and waning of the moon, the ebb and flow of tides. Conflicts, that is, have hit a trough. Once the new political economic factors have been sorted out by the actors in question, it would crest again. However, this leaves unanswered the query regarding what is 'new' about the political economic situation: what is the nature of this 'newness'? With this we arrive at another, though not unrelated, way of understanding the downswing in conflict. This second mode of understanding harks back to Marcos's observation at the beginning of this essay and is related to the impact of neo-liberalism in the north-east. With neo-liberalism, the older muscular Indian nation-state (as envisaged by, among others, Sardar Vallabhbhai Patel[8] in the years after Independence) has disappeared from the limelight. Privatization and economic liberalization has resulted in the contraction and redeployment of the state, shifting the locus of political struggles away from direct contestation for state power and opening new spaces to contestation (by new movements and old) over whether they will be controlled from above or below. The state acts increasingly as broker for global capital as it attempts to re-regulate the conditions for accumulation on a global scale. To be sure, neo-liberalism involves not simply a headlong retreat of the state but a renegotiation of state-society relations. As such, the attempted recomposition of capitalist hegemony in the north-east too has included targeted social-composition programmes. There is almost no ministry in New Delhi that does not have a dedicated north-east window, and then there is the Ministry of Development of North-East Region (DoNER) to coordinate various welfare schemes, development projects and sundry governmental policies[9] and also to guide the decisions of the Northeastern Council.[10] Immense quantities of money are being pumped into the region in the name of grants-in-aid, infrastructural development, and so on and so forth, to forge a new clientele sold on the rationale of the neoliberal market. Yet, paradoxically, for this strategy to work smoothly the neo-liberal state has had to depend more and more heavily upon age-old strong-arm tactics of colonial provenance. For state 'largesse' to have its desired impact the success of counter-insurgency must be guaranteed. This in turn implies that government officials and counter-insurgency forces must enjoy absolute impunity. In the north-east, the draconian Armed Forces (Special Powers) Act, 1958, or AFSPA has been the chief instrument for guaranteeing such impunity.[11] However, these somewhat contradictory efforts to create a reformulated clientele for the neo-liberal era—one more selective and flexible than the old muscular-corporatist structures had allowed—did not entirely succeed in shielding the dominant state from political challenge from below. These efforts, as shall be argued later in some detail, produced new restive, resistive subjectivities. The shift from state-orchestrated to market mechanisms of distribution overlapped with new forms of social movement-based struggles in which the old autonomy question was merely reformulated, not abandoned.

Before we turn to a discussion of the exact contours of this reformulated autonomy question in the north-east, it merits asserting that this market-driven reorientation of governance—one which makes 'social conflicts disappear or at least manageable, contradictions a matter of imagination or at least temporary, and schisms of society a guide to or at least an occasion for social development'—has been evocatively termed by Ranabir Samaddar as the 'government of peace'.[12] Not a peace-ingeminating governance this, but a mode of effecting 'governed peace' which is a potent cocktail of securitization, on the one hand, and developmentalism, on the other. This heady mix is the pith and marrow of the statist counter-insurgency *mantra* in India in the age of globalization. More prosaically, but no less demonstratively, Samaddar also calls this 'social governance'.[13] However, here an argument for novelty is not being made, either in terms of the time of occurrence of this type of governance or in terms of its site of occurrence, i.e. the north-east. Even as the Mexican military was attempting to encircle and close the noose around the

Lacandón Jungle region of Zapatista core support in December 1994 (no doubt a security measure), targeted social compensation programmes such as the National Solidarity Programme, or the PRONASOL, were already at work. The hide-bound corporatist and clientelist mechanisms once controlled by the PRI party-state was giving way to a recomposition of capitalist hegemony through social governance.[14] The PRONASOL later segued into PROCAMPO and PROGRESA, the latter reconfigured as the 'Oportunidades' programme by President Vincente Fox in the twenty-first century. What was true of late twentieth-century México was, in the same period, true, mutatis mutandis, of Guatemala, Ecuador and many other states of Latin America and also true of the Indian north-east.

Again, the market-driven reorientation of governance was already evident in Europe at the end of the Second World War with the initiation of the European Recovery Programme (ERP, April 1948-December 1951), better known as the Marshall Plan after its promulgator George Marshall, war 'hero' and US Secretary of State from 8 January 1947. Marshall shared with the world the concept of the eponymous plan, crafted with the expertize provided by George F. Kennan, William L. Clayton and others, in a speech on 5 June 1947 at Harvard.[15] The Plan, he proposed, was intended to rebuild the economies and spirits of Western Europe, primarily. It was his conviction that the key to restoration of political stability lay in the revitalization of national economies. How was this to be achieved? The road to revitalization of national economies was through international (read US) economic aid. With administrative and technical assistance provided through the Economic Cooperation Administration, or ECA (under the stewardship of Paul G. Hoffman, a former head of Studebaker), which was later succeeded by the USAID, sixteen European nations, including Germany, became part of the ERP and received nearly US $13 billion in aid.[16] It has been suggested that the trade relations that the programme engendered led to the formation of the North Atlantic alliance and the subsequent economic prosperity led by coal and steel industries helped, among other factors, to shape what today we know as the European Union. However, many experts have challenged—even rejected as unreliable—such sweeping assertions.[17] In any case, once fully woken up by war, the so-called giant, lulled into non-interventionist 'sleep' by the Monroe Doctrine (1823), took quick steps to assume control of the emergent global economic order.[18] The rules of the old game changed decisively with the Marshall Plan and the incipient globalization it unleashed: the US would never again be a state that harboured imperial designs; it conclusively became an economic empire that behaved like a state.[19] The developmentalist agendum of the Plan with a view to fostering political stability in western Europe was, as Marshall unambiguously stated, a part of combating the advances of communism in that region. The other complementary part consisted in the parallel securitization of the world order—the Cold War, the so-called nuclear race and, more historically specifically, the opening of the 'ratlines'.[20] The latter were a system of escape routes for Nazis and other Fascists fleeing Europe at the end of the Second World War, sometimes with the active support of US intelligence and even the Vatican. These escape routes led towards havens in South America but also to the US, Great Britain, Canada and West Asia. The US intelligence's involvement in at least one 'ratline'—the Draganović 'ratline'—has been established by historical research.[21] The point here, however, is not so much to pass value judgements about the US's dubious role in post-War 'recovery', but to demonstrate the coupled nature of securitization and developmentalism even in these early manifestations of 'government of peace'. Noam Chomsky wrote about this security-development complex in 'The Umbrella of US Power'. The amount of US dollars given to France and the Netherlands under the aegis of the Marshall Plan equalled the funds these countries used to finance their military actions against their colonial subjects in Southeast Asia—in French Indochina and the Dutch East Indies. Further, the Netherlands was forced into joining the Korean War in 1950 after threats that the project would end if it did not comply. Simultaneously, the Plan 'set the stage for large amounts of private US investment in Europe, establishing the basis for modern transnational corporations'.[22] However, in different geopolitical contexts, the security-development complex of social governance can produce very different consequences. And the Indian northeast is a case in point.

The market-mandated retraction and redeployment of the state poses a critical Foucauldian aporia: the state becomes 'at once that which exists, but which does not yet exist enough'.[23] And there is much a slip betwixt the cup and the lip. As the turn to the market leaves state authorities in control of fewer resources for cooptation, newly constituted social subjects confronting neo-liberalism throughout the north-east formulate a discourse of rights by simultaneously claiming indigenous and other collective rights that markets deny and the citizenship rights that the neo-liberal state pretends to offer equally to all.[24] This double strategy is evident in the recent Bodo-Muslim conflict of Assam. While the Bodos stridently assert their ethnic exclusivity in terms of non-belonging to the mainstream body politic, they can at the same time claim citizenship rights and privileges vis-à-vis Muslim agriculturist neighbours whom they brand as aliens. Simply put, the forces of globalization and concurrent social governance that affect class relations are experienced and resisted through a variety of locally relevant 'identities', including ethnicity and gender.[25] In the context of the north-east, let us now look at these two 'identities' in succession and at how social governance, and the entwined peace building efforts, interact with them.

Ethnic Encounters

It has been suggested that the neo-liberal project implies atomization and loss of control to global market forces, posing dilemmas for movements seeking to reassert community identity and grassroots empowerment—that is, in other words, for autonomy movements. On the one hand, what Hellman terms the 'fetishism of autonomy'[26]—eschewing affiliation or engagement with any political structure for fear that it might absorb the newly asserted identity—can be a *cul-de-sac*. On the other hand, negotiating a share of power with existing political institutions runs the risk of replicating dominant hierarchies (serving global capital) and distancing the 'autonomous' representatives from their social bases. Taking advantage of this dilemma, the state, in India at least, has been seen to set up two interrelated kinds of snares, to use a stern metaphor.

The first is to grant regionally based self-governance to autonomy-demanding groups that would amount to a kind of territorial decentralization negotiated with the state. This strategy in some ways predates the emergence of the neoliberal Indian state, harking back to colonial times, and may be loosely termed as a containment policy. The British began administering the north-east region through a series of Acts such as the Scheduled District Act of 1874 and the Frontier Tracts Regulations of 1880. In 1873, the British passed the Inner Line Regulation. According to Joysankar Hazarika, the logic behind this regulation was that the 'unrestricted movements which existed between the British subjects in Assam and the wild tribes living across the frontier frequently led to quarrels and sometimes to serious disturbances'.[27] However, an equally important reason was that the British administration also wanted to control the rubber trade that was still in the hands of the hill people and that caused frequent skirmishes between the groups. It must be understood that the inner line did not in any way give sovereignty to the hill people; rather it was a means by which administrative zones of the hills and the plains were separated ostensibly because the 'civilized' faced problems cohabiting with the 'wild'. The Government of India Act, 1935, classified the hill areas of Assam into excluded and partially excluded areas. The excluded areas were not demarcated to protect regional autonomy. This was done mainly to exclude hill areas of Assam from the jurisdiction of the Reformed Provincial Government that included the Brahmaputra plains and the Barak Valley. These successive administrative measures, however, had somewhat unpremeditated consequences. Firstly, it resulted in a separate political evolution of the hills and the plains, thereby paving the way for autonomy movements. For the Nagas, for instance, identity claims consolidated into a powerful secessionist movement. The Naga National Council (NNC) was formed in 1946 under the leadership of Angami Zapu Phizo. Under its banner, the Nagas declared their Independence on 14 August 1947. The Indian State, of course, quashed this claim brutally with military action, whereafter it adopted the two-track policy of securitization by clamping on the Armed Forces (Special Powers) Act, on the one hand, and initiating a dialogue-based peace process, on the other. This dual process has continued till date. 'Dialogues and wars in the Northeast with alternative regularity,' observes Ranabir Samaddar, 'demonstrate in this way the governmental logic of treating war and peace as a continuum'[28]— a series, if you will.

The second consequence of the British administrative measure is evident from, and flows out of, the above discussion. Territorial demarcation/reorganization became a dominant template of social governance in post-Independent India, and more so in post-liberalization India.[29] Territorial reorganization, grant of statehood and introduction of the model of peace accords went hand in hand with military operations. Each major military operation was followed by major administrative measures of territorial reorganization and regrouping of villages. There is the example of the creation of Nagaland in December 1963 as the sixteenth state of India; there is also the North-Eastern Areas (Reorganization) Act of 1971.[30] Sajal Nag has written about the regrouping of villages in Mizoram.[31] In Tripura, too, villages were regrouped, though the formal justification in this case was economic: 'cluster villages' were being formed to improve the condition of the indigenous population.[32] Recently, there has been the deliberate policy of introducing rural decentralization in the form of the *panchayati raj* (local self-government).[33] More importantly, territorial autonomies along ethnic lines have been created throughout the last twenty years within the states of the region.[34] Today, the autonomous arrangements have reorganized the states internally while the Northeastern Areas (Reorganization) Act of 1971 has externally reorganized the states. Of greater importance has been the introduction of autonomy as a result of the many successive peace accords.[35] These autonomous arrangements have been part of the governance structure in the north-eastern states of Assam, Mizoram, Tripura and Meghalaya. They influence the patterns of conflict; they give an idea of the governmental resources to be available for cornering and sharing (an aspect we shall return to later in this essay), the size of the territory to control, and the volume of population to govern. As such, they form a major dimension of the 'government of peace'.

Territorial decentralization/reorganization may be called a parochial interpretation of autonomy. One of the pitfalls of this interpretation of autonomy from the people's point of view is that it bottles up the actors in a spatial location precisely in an era when their subsistence and cultural identity depend on mobility.[36] This formulation of autonomy may, therefore, not represent for the struggling groups a real alternative to neo-liberal globalization but rather replicate the top-down structure of existing political institutions without developing new leadership capacity at the local community level. At a further level, autonomy-as-decentralization in effect creates a new fourth level of government (alongside the federal, state, and municipal institutions) and actively constructs a new, dominant indigenous identity among the various indigenous groups that had formed part of the migrant stream settling in the region in question. The recognition of the benefits of being a member of the dominant group then advances faster among its leadership than the creation of consensus within its diverse base. On the one hand, it, therefore, suffers from tendencies toward 'boss' politics (or *cacicazgo*, as it is termed in Latin America) and creates resentment among the less privileged elements of the autonomy movement. The charges of 'selling out' to the Indian state that have been periodically raised within an autonomy movement against the dominant group by more 'radical' elements—be it in the case of the United Liberation Front of Assam (ULFA) or the NNC and later the Nationalist Socialist Council of Nagaland (NSCN)—bear testimony to this. On the other hand, it enables the state to affirm its dubious axiom that struggles for autonomy and justice are in essence intergroup struggles for parity and accordingly the state can then play up the resentment within an autonomous region and without (between two autonomous councils, say). This has recently been evident in the slightly removed but intimately related context of the Gorkhaland movement in Darjeeling.[37]

The second snare that the neo-liberal state sets up for autonomy movements relates to resource allocation. The same neo-liberal ideology that 'frees' individuals to fend for themselves in the market can also spin off unprofitable state functions and services that used to be part of the citizenship compact. The market paradigm privatizes gains while socializing costs and risks. Thus, social sectors and regions may be cut loose as newly autonomous without any hold on state resources, free to compete with each other for a share of the shrinking pie. As a result, recognition of autonomous spaces in the polity turns out to be a new mechanism for division and co-optation.[38] As a wider range of groups compete for scarcer state resources, they become vulnerable to clientelistic local politicians and, for that matter, to paternalistic NGOs moving into the breach. In the scramble for resources, in the north-east it has been seen that when a state government can step in, establish firm control expressed through political will, and try to guide the market forces to some extent, the territorial autonomy model works. Tripura is a case in point.[39] However, where it cannot (that is to say the rest of the north-east) market forces wreak havoc on autonomy movements. Developed basically in recent history as what can be called an economy of 'a market along the foothills', which bears the characteristics of an extraction economy around coal and limestone, and a plantation economy around tea and timber, the entire scenario in the north-east represents today what Ranabir Samaddar has termed following Dietmar Rothermund as 'an enclave economy'.[40] The neo-liberal strategy is designed to pry open this 'enclave' and integrate it with world market. As such, one important mode of social governance in the north-east has been to encourage what can be called at best 'marketization of economic relations' and at worst 'crony capitalism' in the region.

There are three more developments strengthening this economic thrust: first, the strategy of opening up the north-east to the greater commercial interests that connect India to Southeast Asia, a strategy known as the 'Look East' policy;[41] second, the opening of villages and far-flung areas through new institutions, namely schools, colleges, banks, offices, communication networks; and third, the already-alluded policy of encouraging homelands resulting in communal strife, anti-migrant measures, and ethnic policing. The neo-liberal model recognizes the pluralism of ethnic identities as long as those identities do not become the basis for collective organization around substantive rights. Paradoxically, this divisive policy has had the positive impact of ending the insularity of the north-east somewhat. However, the situation is also marked by a tense apprehension that unrest may erupt again, for, as Samaddar says, 'while peace has returned, governance has failed to ensure justice'.[42] The situation is nonetheless not unremittingly hopeless. To quote Samaddar at length:

> If it is true that what we face here [the north-east] is a situation of aporia, a cycle of production of nativity-linkages-marketization-immigration-nationalism-ethnicity-violence-law-linkages-marketization-immigration-nativity-nationalism … it is also true that it is contention [and not market forces alone] that prises open the situation again and again. Precisely the collective politics that in its moments of frenzy makes immigration the most contentious issue in the life of a nation, also exhibits factors or aspects that make the dialogic quest for justice continue.[43]

In other words, what Hale for a different context has termed 'managed neo-liberal multiculturalism'[44] may have worked so far in the north-east—and seems to be working well too. The same state that oversees economic liberalization and privatization is establishing itself as the arbiter of the boundary between individual and group rights, carefully circumscribing the latter to exclude challenges to class-based inequalities. Autonomy defined as mere disengagement has left autonomous communities cut off from resources and unprotected from the forces of the global market and, further, autonomy defined as simply cultural pluralism has fallen into the neoliberal 'multiculturalism trap' of atomizing communities, substituting formal 'equality' for the power to establish collective identities and demand substantive rights and in many cases engendering xenophobia. Yet, it is in this tenebrous situation (of collective politics as xenophobic outburst against perceived 'immigrants') that new linkages are being forged which, in Samaddar's powerful enunciation, in time would overcome the ignominious circumstances of its birth and spearhead the 'dialogic quest for justice'.

Peacemakers in the North-east: Women and Other 'New' Subjects

To recapitulate, it had been argued that the forces of globalization and concurrent social governance that affect class relations are experienced and resisted through at least another locally relevant 'identity' than ethnicity—gender. The argument here, predictably, is not that women are resplendent symbols of peace who stay away from supporting the male members of their communities when they are embroiled in violent actions. In her book *Battle Cries and Lullabies*, Linda Grant DePauw has powerfully depicted the various roles women play in situations of conflict. Covering millennia and spanning the globe in its scope, DePauw's study depicts women both and equally as victims and as warriors; as nurses, spies, sex workers, and wives and mothers of soldiers; as warrior queens leading armies into battle, and as baggage carriers marching in the rear.[45] However, it may be argued that such participation does not in any way diminish the marginalization of women. In fact, oftentimes such participation is enforced by patriarchal injunction: women of the Bantu-speaking Kisii tribe in southwestern Kenya, for instance, are enjoined by patriarchal requirements to scream to announce the beginning of a war with, say, the Kipsigis, the Maasai or any other hostile Nilotic community. Failure to do this is punished by divorce by their husbands. However, the 'double marginalization of women' in conflict situation, as Paula Banerjee terms it[46]—first, because they are willy-nilly party to the insurgent group claiming autonomy and second, because they are under the cosh of the same group's patriarchy—does not entirely extinguish their agency. At least in the case of Nagaland in the north-east, appeals have been made with some degree of success to favour political, dialogic and non-military solutions. In other words, the neo-liberal state has been able to enlist the support of Naga women to work for peace with some amount of success. In spite of their cooperation with the state as peacebuilders, however, women have often been able to dodge the governmental 'snares' that were discussed in the previous section and have paved the way for dynamic collective political action of the non-belligerent kind.

To quote at length from the work of Paula Banerjee and Ishita Dey who finished their fieldwork in Nagaland in early 2012:

> [W]omen ... through lived experiences of conflict started working for peace [in the north-east]. In their activism for peace they acquired a legitimacy to enter the space for political decision-making that was denied to them. In their commitment for peace, they motivated their society to

observe a ceasefire. The state found in them an unusual ally and could see their far-reaching influence in society. When the state decided to move away from their mode of conflict with the Naga people it reinvented its indispensability by championing the cause of women. It was around the same time that women's activism was going through a generational change. Younger women leaders decided to innovate with new agenda for women and brought in the question of women's rights. In this they found much of the traditional leadership allied against them. They found the state keen to ally with their cause in its role as an arbiter.[47]

The mutual coming together of Naga women and the government of Nagaland, Banerjee and Dey argue, is reflected in the activism for a Women's Reservation Bill. The women used all government institutions to further the cause for peace, justice and equity.[48] However, the astute authors are apprehensive: 'This coming together was timely although the alliance is bound to be fragile. Both the sides are giving lip service to this alliance to further their own interest. However, for now this alliance has proved transformative for gender roles in society, helping the cause of peace, stability and justice.'[49]

They conclude their collaborative study, with the following penetrating aperçu: 'It remains to be seen whether this alliance can in any way be liberating for Naga society as a whole; otherwise it will soon become redundant'.[50]

Women in autonomy movements present a peculiar conundrum. On the one hand, they have to identify with the 'autonomous' identity the group promotes and fights for. On the other hand, they are constantly acutely faced with the fact that 'autonomy' after all has long been coded as masculine and is associated with masculine ideal. This is true, despite autonomy being something which women have often called for in their own rights. As Jessica Benjamin argues, while we are formally committed to equality, 'gender polarity underlies such familiar dualisms as autonomy and dependency'.[51] In claiming autonomy, therefore, female agents collapse this dubious binarism between autonomy and dependency because, as Carol Gilligan persuasively argues, 'for women, identity has as much to do with intimacy as with separation'.[52] The trajectory is thus less about individualization and independence than towards ultimately balancing and harmonizing an agent's interests with those of others.

This movement towards harmonization is most effectively mediated by women actors. Nagaland is, Banerjee and Dey may concur, a case in point. At another level, it also announces the arrival of a 'new' subject—whose 'newness' does not consist in merely having a different biological sex, but in the performance of gender roles in a way that rearticulates the standard modes of interacting with (and counteracting) the state.

The role played by women, in Nagaland at least, poses the issue of a certain kind of public ethics of self-government growing out of the dynamics of subject-formation through conflict governance. That is to say, that conflict can be analysed as a historically singular mode of experience, whereby the 'objects' of conflict governance are transformed into 'subjects' through certain specific procedures, such as the procedure of building peace, or the attempts at peace at micro-levels, and through the contradictory process of securitization. Yet, we must understand that subject-formation is not a one-sided process. Each phase of 'conflict resolution', so to speak, produces in turn another phase, precisely because the governmental policies of suppression not only stokes fear and loathing but also produces a revised subjectivity that takes stock of the strengths and weaknesses of the 'adversary'. Besides the women in Nagaland, there are also the instances of the recent peasant mobilizations in Assam by Krishak Mukti Sangram Samiti led by Akhil Gogoi and others and the environmental movements in the entire region that we must take note of. These new movements, Sanjay Barbora insists, gives us a picture—however indistinct—of that new kind of subjectivity.[53] Therefore, the result of the operation of new governing techniques is not one that produces passive, depoliticized subjects—Foucauldian docile bodies, if you will—although such indeed may be the original purpose of social governance. The subject of conflict is, in this sense, irreducibly obstreperous. It can only partially be made the economic subject, and it is important to bear in mind that the economic subject and the subject of rights have different relationships with political power. Their autonomies are of different, often incompatible natures. The problem of 'government of peace', like any other self-styled mode of good governance, is that it will have to deal with different subjects.

The situation that presents itself in the Northeast bears the hopeful mark of this dynamic principle of heterogeneity.

Notes

* The quote is from William Shakespeare's *Romeo and Juliet*, Act 1, Scene 1.
I am heavily indebted to the Calcutta Research Group, in general, and Prof. Ranabir Samaddar and Prof. Paula Banerjee, in particular, for providing me the opportunity and encouragement to write this piece.

1. *Big Noise Tactical Media, 2000*; http://www.bignoisefilms.org/films/features/90-zapatista (last accessed 25 October 2013).
2. See, for instance, Samir K. Das, 'Peace by Governance or Governing Peace? A Case Study of the United Liberation Front of Assam (ULFA)', *Policies and Practices 50*, Mahanirban Calcutta Research Group, July 2012; Ranabir Samaddar, 'Government of Peace', *Policies and Practices 53*, Mahanirban Calcutta Research Group, October 2012; Paula Banerjee and Ishita Dey, 'Women, Conflict and Governance in Nagaland', *Policies and Practices 51*, Mahanirban Calcutta Research Group, July 2012; Sajal Nag, 'A Gigantic Panopticon: Counter-Insurgency and Modes of Disciplining and Punishment in Northeast India', *Policies and Practices 46*, Mahanirban Calcutta Research Group, March 2012.
3. Subir Bhaumik describes a slightly different case in Tripura, one of the seven states of the north-east. Though pacification has been an important part of the government counter-insurgency toolkit here, the reason why the state has not gravitated towards what has been termed 'durable disorder' for the rest of the north-east is twofold: first, the political will of—and the decades-long, relatively corruption-free government provided by—the Communist Part of India (Marxist)-led Left Front and, second, economic development tied to the boom in rubber plantation. Bhaumik, however, appends a caveat to this interpretation. He says this Bengali-dominated state's 'success in economic development and in providing relatively corruption-free governance will be undermined by festering ethnic rancour that may explode into bouts of anomic violence anytime soon' if vigorous initiative is not taken to restore 'tribal lands and rights' and to undo 'the marginalization of the indigenous peoples by some innovative socio-political engineering'. Subir Bhaumik, 'Tripura:

Ethnic Conflict, Militancy and Counterinsurgency', *Policies and Practices 52*, Mahanirban Calcutta Research Group, August 2012, p. 1. The point about the political will and good governance of the Left Front government has also been made by Jayanta Bhattacharya in 'Political Will and the Success of Aadhaar in Tripura', in Atig Ghosh, ed., *Branding the Migrant: Arguments of Rights, Welfare and Security*, Kolkata: Frontpage, 2013. For economic development as a tool of counterinsurgency and the boom in rubber plantation, see Bhaumik, 'Tripura', especially pp. 8-9 and also Ratna Bharali Talukdar, 'Tripura Taps the Rubber Economy', *India Together*, 22 October 2007, http://www.indiatogether.org/2007/oct/eco-rubber.htm (last accessed 25 October 2013). A case for Tripura's exceptionalism is also made by Ranabir Samaddar, 'Government of Peace', pp. 17-18. 'Durable disorder' is the principal motif of Sanjib Baruah's influential work *Durable Disorder: Understanding the Politics of Northeast India*, New Delhi: Oxford University Press, 2005.

4. Das, 'Peace by Governance or Governing Peace?', op. cit., p. 3.
5. One of the seven states of the north-east. The other six states are: Arunachal Pradesh, Manipur, Meghalaya, Mizoram, Nagaland, and Tripura. Lately, Sikkim, too, is being considered as a state—the eighth state—of the north-east.
6. 'Assam violence: Four more bodies found, toll rises to 77', IBN, 8 August 2012; http://ibnlive.in.com/generalnewsfeed/news/assam-violence-four-more-bodies-found-toll-rises-to-77/1038364.html (last accessed 25 October 2013.)
7. K. Sandeep, Balchand Joshi and Sushanta Talukdar, 'Crack down on ring leaders, Centre tells Assam', *The Hindu*, 25 July 2012, http://www.thehindu.com/news/national/article3683459.ece (last accessed 25 October 2013); & 'India's PM promises help to riot victims', *Al Jazeera*, 28 July 2012 http://www.aljazeera.com/news/asia/2012/07/2012728152819365333.html (last accessed 25 October 2013).
8. 'He [Patel] stood for the transformation of India into a major industrial power, which he thought could be achieved only by a strong, centralized state.' In Paul R. Brass, 'Patel, Vallabhbhai Jhaverbhai (1875/6-1950)', *Oxford Dictionary of National Biography*, New Delhi: Oxford University Press, 2004; http://www.oxforddnb.com/view/article/35403 (last accessed 25 October 2013).
9. To get an idea of the money and projects involved, see the official site of DoNER: http://mdoner.gov.in/
10. The North Eastern Council (NEC) is the nodal agency for the eco-

nomic and social development of the North-Eastern Region which consists of the eight states of Arunachal Pradesh, Assam, Manipur, Meghalaya, Mizoram, Nagaland, Tripura and Sikkim (The North-Eastern Council [Amendment] Act, 2002, inter alia, added Sikkim as the eighth member-State of the Council). The NEC was constituted in 1971 by an Act of Parliament. The official NEC site has the following to say by way of publicity: 'Over the last thirty five years, NEC has been instrumental in setting in motion a new economic endeavour aimed at removing the basic handicaps that stood in the way of normal development of the region and has ushered in an era of new hope in this backward area full of great potentialities.' http://necouncil.nic.in (last accessed on 25 October 2013).

11. For comprehensive information on the AFSPA, see the Report of the National Campaign Committee against Militarization and Repeal of the Armed Forces (Special Powers) Act: 'Where Peacekeepers have Declared War: Report on Violations of Democratic Rights by Security Forces and the Impact of the Armed Forces (Special Powers) Act on Civilian Life in the Seven States of the Northeast', New Delhi, 1997; also, see Paula Banerjee, 'Communities, Gender and the Border: A Legal Narrative on India's Northeast', in Kalpana Kannabiran and Ranbir Singh (eds.), *Challenging the Rules of Law: Colonialism, Criminology and Human Rights in India*, New Delhi: Sage, 2008, pp. 257-80.
12. Samaddar, 'Government of Peace', op. cit., p. 1.
13. Ibid.
14. For an overview, see the chapters in Gerardo Otero (ed.), *Mexico in Transition: Neoliberal Globalism, the State, and Civil Society*, London: Zed Books, 2004. Also see, Heather L. Williams, *Social Movements and Economic Transition: Markets and Distributive Conflict in Mexico,* New York: Cambridge University Press, 2001.
15. Text of the 'Marshall Plan' speech at Harvard University, 5 June 1947 available at the Organization for Economic Cooperation and Development (OECD) website: http://www.oecd.org/general/themarshallplanspeechatharvarduniversity5june1947.htm (last accessed 25 October 2013); for a detailed and influential history of the Plan, see Michael J. Hogan, *The Marshall Plan: America, Britain and the Reconstruction of Western Europe, 1947-52*, New York: Cambridge University Press, 1989.
16. The aid would have amounted to US$ 148 billion at inflation-adjusted rates in 2013; http://www.usinflationcalculator.com/ (last accessed 25 October 2013).

17. Werner Abelshauser, for one, in a review of West Germany's economy from 1945 to 1951, found that 'foreign aid was not crucial in starting the recovery or in keeping it going' (Werner Abelshauser, 'West German Economic Recovery, 1945-51: A Reassessment', *The Three Banks Review*, 135, 1982, p. 52). Economist Tyler Cowen found that the economic recoveries of France, Italy, and Belgium also predated the flow of US aid. (Tyler Cowen, 'The Marshall Plan: Myths and Realities', in Doug Bandow (ed.), *US Aid to the Developing World: A Free Market Agenda*, Washington: Heritage Foundation, 1985, pp. 61-74). In any case, economic scholarship since the 1990s has been more hostile to idea of foreign aid itself. Alesina and Weder write that foreign aid is primarily used wastefully and self-servingly by government officials, and ends up increasing governmental corruption (Alberto Alesina and Beatrice Weder, 'Do Corrupt Governments Receive Less Foreign Aid?', *American Economic Review* 92 (4), September 2002, pp. 1126-37). This policy of promoting corrupt government can then be attributed back to the initial impetus of the Marshall Plan (Jeffrey Tucker, 'The Marshall Plan Myth', *The Free Market* 15 (9): September 1997; http://mises.org/freemarket_detail.aspx?control=120 (last accessed 25 October 2013).
19. Historians such as Walter LaFeber have argued that the Plan was US economic imperialism and directed at gaining control over Western Europe. See, for instance, William F. LaFeber, *America, Russia and the Cold War, 1945-75 (America in Crisis)*, 3d edn., New York: John Wiley & Sons Inc, 1976.
20. If the Marshall Plan had imperial designs, it cloaked them in tall talks of generosity. This has been often lampooned in popular culture. In 'Wee Small Hours' (Episode 9, Season 3, Mad Men), Conrad Hilton tells Don Draper the hotel chain's expansion plan is to bring America to the world, whether they like it or not, and even to the moon. The reason for it is 'Generosity: Like the Marshall Plan'.
21. See, for example, Mark Aarons and John Loftus, *Unholy Trinity: The Vatican, The Nazis, and the Swiss Bankers*, New York: St. Martin's Press, 1991 (revd., 1998); Christopher Simpson, *Blowback: The First Full Account of America's Recruitment of Nazis and Its Disastrous Effect on the Cold War, Our Domestic and Foreign Policy*, New York: Grove/Atlantic, 1988; Michael Phayer, Pius XII, the Holocaust, and the Cold War, Indianapolis: Indiana University Press, 2008.
21. 'History of the Italian Rat Line' (10 April 1950), document signed by 'IB Operating Officer', Paul E. Lyon, 430th Counter Intelligence

Corps (CIC), Headquarters of the US Forces in Austria, http://archive.is/wzv2u (last accessed 25 October 2013); also see: Richard Breitman, Norman J.W. Goda, Timothy Naftali and Robert Wolfe, *US Intelligence and the Nazis*, Cambridge: Cambridge University Press, 2005 and, more recently, John Loftus, *America's Nazi Secret: An Insider's History*, Waterwille: Trine Day, 2010.

22. Noam Chomsky, *The Umbrella of US Power: The Universal Declaration of Human Rights and the Contradictions of US Policy*, Series editor: Greg Ruggiero, New York: Seven Stories Press, 1999, p. 9.
23. Michel Foucault, *Birth of Biopolitics: Lectures at the Collège de France, 1978-79*, ed. Michel Sennelart, Picador/Palgrave Macmillan: New York, 2008, p. 4.
24. The same kind of argument has been made for México and Latin America by, respectively, Jonathan Fox, 'The Difficult Transition from Clientelism to Citizenship: Lessons from Mexico', in Douglas A. Chalmers et al., eds., *The New Politics of Inequality in Latin America: Rethinking Participation and Representation,* New York: Oxford University Press, 1997, and Susan Eva Eckstein and Timothy P. Wickham-Crowley, *Struggles for Social Rights in Latin America, New York: Routledge*, 2003.
25. For corroborating experiences from other parts of the world, see June C. Nash, *Mayan Visions: The Quest for Autonomy in an Age of Globalization*, New York: Routledge, 2001; Deborah J. Yashar, *Contesting Citizenship in Latin America: The Rise of Indigenous Movements and the Post-liberal Challenge*, Cambridge: Cambridge University Press, 2005.
26. Judith Adler Hellman, 'The Study of New Social Movements in Latin America and the Question of Autonomy', in Arturo Escobar and Sonia E. Alvarez, eds., *The Making of Social Movements in Latin America: Identity, Strategy and Democracy*, Boulder: Westview Press, 1992, pp. 52-61.
27. Joysankar Hazarika, *Geopolitics of North-East India: A Strategical Study*, New Delhi: Gyan Publishng House, 1996, p. 74.
28. Samaddar, 'Government of Peace', op. cit., p. 10.
29. B. Datta Ray and S.P. Agrawal, eds., *Reorganization of Northeast India since 1947*, New Delhi: Concept Publishing, 1996.
30. Ibid.; also find the text of the Act at http://indiankanoon.org/doc/318384/ (last accessed 25 October 2013).
31. Nag, 'A Gigantic Panopticon', op. cit.
32. On the miserable condition of these 'cluster villages' planned by the Tripura police chief, B.L. Vohra, see 'Tripura Tribal Rehab

Plan Goes Awry', *The Telegraph*, 1 October 2005, http://www.telegraphindia.com/1051001/asp/northeast/story_5304499.asp (last accessed 25 October 2013); also see Archana Prasad, 'Forestry and Tribal Development: A Background Note for Tripura State Human Development Report', 2004-5, http://planningtripura.nic.in/THDR/backgroundreport/Forestry%20&%20Tribal%20Development.pdf (last accessed 25 October 2013).

33. Sujata Dutta Hazarika, 'Conflict and Development: Implications for Democracy and Governance', in Ranabir Samaddar and Suhit K. Sen, eds., *New Subjects and New Governance in India*, New Delhi: Routledge, 2012, pp. 211-44; also, Sujata Dutta Hazarika, 'Examining Autonomy: The 73rd Constitutional Amendment in Assam', *Policies and Practices 8*, Mahanirban Calcutta Research Group, 2005.
34. Sanjay Barbora, 'Autonomy in the Northeast: The Frontiers of Centralized Politics', and Subir Bhaumik and Jayanta Bhattacharya, 'Autonomy in the Northeast: The Hills of Tripura and Mizoram', in Ranabir Samaddar, ed., *The Politics of Autonomy: Indian Experiences*, New Delhi: Sage, 2005, pp. 196-241.
35. For a discussion on peace accords and their socio-political function, see Ranabir Samaddar, Chap. 6: 'Governing Through Peace Accords', in *The Politics of Dialogue: Geopolitical Histories of War and Peace in South Asia,* Aldershot: Ashgate, 2004; Samir K. Das, 'Nobody's Communiqué: Ethnic Accords in Northeastern India', in Ranabir Samaddar and Helkmut Reifeld, eds., *Peace as Process: Reconciliation and Conflict Resolution in South Asia*, New Delhi: Manohar, 2001, pp. 231-52; for a brief account, see Samaddar, 'Government of Peace', op. cit., pp. 6-11.
36. A similar argument for Ecuador has been made by Rudi Colloredo-Mansfeld, 'Autonomy and Interdependence in Native Movements: Towards a Pragmatic Politics in the Ecuadorian Andes', *Identities: Global Studies in Culture and Power*, 9 (2) 2002, pp. 173-95.
37. See the entire 'Ei Muhurte' page of *Ei Samay*, 27 October 2013 and especially the article 'Meghmukto Paharh' [Cloudless Hills] on the same page by Amal Sarkar.

    The Gorkhaland Territorial Administration is a semi-autonomous administrative body of the Nepali-speaking Gorkha ethnic group of the Darjeeling hills that was created in 2011.
38. Again to get a non-Indian perspective, see George A. Collier, 'The New Politics of Exclusion: Antecedents to the Rebellion in Mexico', *Dialectical Anthropology* 19 (1) 1994, pp. 1-44.

39. For Tripura's exceptionalism, see n. 3.
40. Samaddar, 'Government of Peace', op. cit., p. 14; Dietmar Rothermund's conceptualization in *An Economic History of India: from Pre-Colonial Times to 1991*, New York: Routledge, 1993 (this is the updated version; the original was published in 1988).
41. Baruah, Sanjib, 'Between South and Southeast Asia: Northeast India and the Look East Policy', CENISEAS Paper 4, Guwahati Centre for Northeast India, South and Southeast Asia Studies, 2004; Also, Samir K. Das, 'India's Look East Policy: Imagining a New Geography of India's Northeast', *India Quarterly*, 66 (4), December 2010, pp. 343-58.
42. Samaddar, 'Government of Peace', op. cit., p. 13.
43. Ibid.
44. Charles R. Hale, 'Does Multiculturalism Menace? Governance, Cultural Rights, and the Politics of Identity in Guatemala', *Journal of Latin American Studies* 34 (3) 2002, pp. 485-524
45. DePauw, Linda Grant, *Battle Cries and Lullabies: Women in War from Prehistory to the Present*, Norman: University of Oklahoma Press, 2000.
46. Speaking about displaced women, Paula Banerjee writes, 'Displaced women are often doubly marginalized since state policies are weighted against them both because they are women and also because often they are members of minority ethnic, religious and linguistic groups.' This argument neatly fits the case of women in conflict too.

    Paula Banerjee, 'Resisting Erasure: Women IDPs in South Asia', in Paula Banerjee, Sabyasachi Basu Ray Chaudhury, Samir Kumar Das and Bishnu Adhikari, eds., *Internal Displacement in South Asia: The Relevance of the UN's Guiding Principles*, New Delhi: Sage, 2005, p. 305.

    More relevant to our present context is the following statement she makes: 'In situations where the state is not an actor, the majority group imitates state behaviour thereby victimizing women as in the massacres by Bodo militants.'
47. Banerjee and Dey, 'Women, Conflict and Governance in Nagaland', op. cit., p. 23.
48. For the activism around the Bill, see: 'SC directs Nagaland Govt. to respond on 33% women quota', *The Morung Express*, 20 November 2012, http://www.morungexpress.com/frontpage/88603.html (last accessed 25 October 2013).
49. Banerjee and Dey, 'Women, Conflict and Governance in Nagaland', op. cit., p. 23.

50. Ibid., pp. 23-4.
51. Jessica Benjamin, *The Bonds of Love: Psychoanalysis, Feminism, and the Problem of Domination*, New York: Pantheon Books, 1988, p. 7.
52. Carol Gilligan, *In a Different Voice: Psychological Theory and Women's Development*, Cambridge, Mass.: Harvard University Press, 1982, p. 98.
53. Barbora, Sanjay, 'Assam's New Voice of Dissent', *Economic and Political Weekly,* XLVI (28), 9 July 2011, pp. 19-22; Udayon Misra, 'A New Edge to People's Protest in Assam', *Economic and Political Weekly*, XLVI (28), 9 July 2011, pp. 16-18.

CHAPTER 14

Parama

A Journey from Society to 'Self'

Manjima Chatterjee

The portrayal of women in Indian films, in general, and Bengali films, in particular, has traversed a path which has often posed questions at her, demanding answers about her integrity, responsibility, morality as well as her exposure to the outer world. The films of colonial India as well as films produced after independence portrayed women through the same sociological mirror. However, this stereotype portrayal of women characters in films was reviewed in the 1980s by a galaxy of women directors like Sai Paranjpye, Kalpana Lajmi, Aruna Raje, Prema Karanth, Mira Nair and others who were all educated, urban and progressive and were ready to deal with these issues which were so long considered a taboo in Indian films. Their women take their identity from the position they occupy in relation to certain commonly held attitudes about love, marriage or motherhood. Even if they are rarely allowed any possibility of personal transcendence, one often finds characters whose deviance from a gender-determined norm is so pronounced, that they have the effect of denying and challenging their supposed or desired norm. Moreover, once the matters of women's sexuality and women's role have been brought into prominence, they acted as a potential threat to destabilize the position of their male counterpart. Aparna Sen's *Parama* perfectly fits into this genre of films, where the societal notions of a woman's role were revisited to finally initiate her on a journey to her own 'self'.

Aparna Sen's *Parama*, released in 1985, was a much discussed film not only for its quite unusual depiction of a sexual relationship between a married woman and a much younger man at that time. But the director actually addresses a whole gamut of feminist concerns like marriage, sexuality and motherhood. Yet, the film does not overtly stamp the female protagonist as a celluloid feminist in the sense of taking an active part in women's movement or belonging to some women's organization. Initially, one finds Parama, the central character of the film, blissfully oblivious about her specific needs as a woman and stays cocooned in a so-called happy marriage. As the film unravels one finds her to be reacting against the life of twentieth century with acute sensitivity, which is infinitely adaptable and supple to catch the tones, the light and shade of experience of a so-called urban, upper-middle-class married woman. From a tiny, marginalized shell Parama emerges as a person dignified and empowered, ready to make her own choice.

Parama, the Bengali word, means many things—the best, the unique, over and above everything extremely feminine. Parama is a devoted housewife who lives in an urban, affluent middle class family in Calcutta. In her marriage Parama appears to be content in many roles—as a wife, mother, daughter-in-law, sister-in-law, etc. In the first few frames of the film, she is seen to be performing her religious and familial duties by constantly moving and smiling, trying her best to cater to the need of each and everyone in the house and earning praises from her mother-in-law who says, 'Chhotobou has her eye on everything'. The idol of Durga at the background re-instates her as powerful, omnipresent and as benevolent as the goddess herself. She is an ultimate performer who performs consciously or unconsciously, for the comfort and amusement of her so-called urban, elitist, middle-class family. Thus, her housework is directly related to her prioritized position in her family.

Parama, thus, is in complete control of the domestic scene. She has control over the housekeeping, paying of the servants, shopping, etc. She can even visit a friend but only after a nod from her mother-in-law. However, the woman to whom Parama can relate most is Sheela, her childhood friend. A visit to Sheela's home is probably her only breathing space and for this she does not hesitate to bribe her mother-in-law with the latter's favourite *mochar ghanto* (a typical Bengali delicacy). On her visit to Sheela's place, she comes to know about her friends' activities outside the domestic sphere. Sheela, herself a divorcee, is passionate to the cause of spastic children, while some of her other friends are variously preoccupied outside their domestic sphere. One finds, for the first time, Parama surprised and bewildered when she thinks that she does not even have the time to play the *sitar*, which was one of her childhood passions. Even if she is aware of the fact that innumerable demands are being made on her without really taking into consideration of her own needs and desires, she apparently does not show it. In Indian society socializing of girls are so complete that most women feel that they are socially, emotionally and politically unfulfilled and incomplete without a marriage. Like most middle class Indian married women, Parama too finds her role of a mother, wife, and daughter-in-law to be extremely satisfying and derives a sense of empowerment through such gender specific roles. Thus, when her teenage daughter Esha, a budding feminist herself, talks about womens' liberation and even rebukes her mother for her parasitic existence ('Second hand *bneche gele*, through bapi') 'You lived a second-hand life, through Bapi', Parama is a little surprised and defends traditional Indian values and man's role in the outer world. Even when she is asked about her name, it is her daughter Esha who steps in and promptly announces her name as 'Parama Chowdhury' and she has no other option but to accept it gracefully.

Parama does not seem to be a person who is troubled with her sex life either. She is extremely passive during sexual intercourse with Bhaskar, her husband, and both of them engage in mundane conversations, like her husband's business deal or planning to buy a new flat at Ballygunge, then an upcoming posh area in south Calcutta. She seems to be totally indifferent and dispassionate about the whole episode; neither enjoys it nor abhors it. She parts her legs in a habitual reflex just as she does any other household duties. Sexuality in terms of sexual liberation and sexual identity did not surface in the social discourse of the majority of middle-class

Indian household at that time. Social and gender identities were comparatively easily discussed and talked about but sexual issues were still a taboo. *Parama* is certainly an exception in this context.

Thus, nothing disturbs Parama. As days, months, years roll by, there is no rupture in her acceptance of her own self, which is of an urban woman functioning within a patriarchy that pretends to be democratic and gender neutral. Things, however, take a different turn when Rahul, a friend of Bhaskar's nephew, a diasporic Bengali, comes to visit Parama's family in Calcutta to shoot the traditional way of celebrating the Durga Puja, the largest festival of the Bengalis. He is fascinated by Parama's typical Indian feminine beauty as he takes random shots of Parama decked up in white *garad saree* with wide, red border. The camera zooms in to click her beaming face with a huge dot of vermilion on her forehead. Rahul almost inevitably chooses Parama to feature as an ideal Bengali housewife in his next photo feature. Parama's initial hesitance to be featured is ignored by her husband who does not even think it necessary to take her consent. He gives a go-ahead signal over the phone, though not before asking his mother. Both of them take pride in the fact that Parama has been chosen as a subject for modelling. Bhaskar sees no threat in this young, liberal, Westernized male being in close proximity with his wife. Rahul, a renowned photographer, is more highlighted as 'Babu's friend' within the family, Babu being almost like a son to Parama. Never in his wildest nightmares could Bhaskar imagine his wife transgressing the patriarchal social boundaries.

As Rahul's camera captures the intense physical beauty of Parama, taking intimate shots of her *alta*-adorned feet or tight close-up of her beautiful face from different angle, his mind's eye starts rolling. During the modelling sessions, Parama's initial discomfiture with her body is overlooked by Rahul who gets on with his job quite seriously. As he looks through his camera, he is satisfied enough to comment on what he sees 'devastating'. A comment, which is probably directed at the object through the lens and not Parama as a woman, nevertheless boosts the confidence of a middle-aged married woman, with three children. He discovers a woman who is traditional, unindividualistic and most significantly not conscious about her own self. He tries to reorient her by convincing her to change her lifestyle, priorities and ambition. Rahul's question, 'what do you do all day, what do you think about?' leads her into a space previously unknown to her. A visit to her ancestral house during the photo shoot reminds her about her girlhood, early sexual desires, her insane aunt and most enigmatically a long forgotten plant. The name of the plant eludes her as her own identity does. All of these memories snowballed into a sudden surge of emotional and sexual outburst. She steps out of convention—bound marriage and expresses her sexuality freely. Thus, with the tune of *sitar* and visuals of saplings in the background and with the first kiss to Rahul, she crosses over the *lakshmanrekha* of society. She, for the first time, starts to 'live dangerously' as suggested by Rahul. The flight of the pigeons, which temporarily restores her sanity, is probably also her first flight to individuality. Though Parama initially is completely shocked at her own reaction, later this new sense of sexual identity gives her a breathing space so long unknown. Rahul's liberality, virility and, over and above everything, complete lack of predictability makes him, extremely enigmatic in the eyes of Parama. They dream of a journey across America in a caravan, where Parama would give sitar recitals at different small towns while Rahul would go on with his photo shoot. The journey would map out 'an itinerary which is not only geographical but psychological and for Parama, emotionally liberating as well'.[1] Parama, for most of the time of her married life was forced to stay within the nucleus of her family. This forced post-colonial modern isolated existence not only restricted her physical movement but also killed her emotional needs and priorities, in striking contrast to her free, imaginative self of her pre-marital days. For fulfilling her needs she is primarily dependent on either her husband or her children who are unavailable for a greater part of the day. Thus, the family, which should have played the role of protector, is often seen as a perpetrator of her oppressions. Rarely Indian women belonging to a middle-class household have the chance or courage to break the shackles of her claustrophobic existence.

However, both men in Parama's life, her husband Bhaskar Chowdhury and the lover, Rahul, are gradually relegated to the background after they have served as two catalytic agents though in completely two different ways towards her self-realization. It is as if Rahul's question whether Parama would be able to find the lost sapling of her childhood, that goads on Parama to a rediscovery of her own self. She starts relinquishing some of her familial duties which were so important to her earlier, only to discover newer patterns of life which may yield greater satisfaction like practising a monsoon *raga* with her *sitar* or trying to retrieve a lost sapling from her childhood memory. She is so engrossed in this fascinating process that even Rahul's departure fails to make a mark on her outer world. Parama performs mechanically, yet her morose appearance shows clearly her intense mental torment. Parama's psyche is torn between her insensitive husband and a bohemian lover. She, thus, religiously waters the young sapling, a gift from Rahul. She is almost in love with it and treats it as an extension of her inner self and in the process keeps her sanity intact. She quietly revolts against the isolation that a married woman is forced to bear with by shunning all the shackles of the so-called urban, self-contained, nuclear family which cages her. She is no longer dependent on Bhaskar or her children to fulfil her social and emotional needs. Now she even shudders to think about having a sexual relationship with her husband. Thus, a consciousness of 'self', comprising her new perception of her mind and body began to take shape in the inner world of Parama. It is here that for the first time Parama reacts to her own needs and desires in contrast to her earlier self which had been that of a performer constantly performing in order to please others. She starts writing letters to Rahul and as if enters into a dialogue with her own self. She muses over the lack of concern her family shows in matters related to her. That she can write love letters and letters can arrive for her too would be a thing hard to imagine.

However, real crisis emanates when Rahul sends a copy of the *Life* magazine with Parama's sensuous photographs in it. They were inadvertently found out by her husband, thus exposing her affair with Rahul. Adultery, which is mostly regarded as a male prerogative, shook the inner fabric of this so-called urban, progressive, middle class household and immediately laid bare all its hypocrisies and double-standards. Parama who fails to live up to the societal notion of moral standards, or to conform to the idea of chastity, which runs like a constant thread in all man-woman relationship, is branded as a whore. Thus, the earlier goddess, queen of the household at one stroke is reduced to a prostitute. The over-shooter is completely alienated and isolated by her family members, robbed of her roles as a loving wife, mother and daughter-in-law. In a desperate attempt she even asks Bhaskar to forgive her. Bhaskar, whose own moral intention seems quite dubious at times, especially in his interaction with his lady secretary, has no feeling of guilt. His earlier assertion that he knew how far his wife can go gets shattered and the hurt male ego immediately reacts and completely rejects her plea. A casual fling of the husband with a secretary is acceptable and even overlooked by the society but the portrayal of a semi-nude house-wife was unthinkable to a middle class 'bhadralok' mind. The benevolent protector, here the husband, thus in no time becomes the oppressor. For once Parama even holds Rahul responsible for this situation. But Sheela keeps her firmly rooted to the reality reminding her of Rahul's individuality and bohemianism and in a way making her more vulnerable. Robbed of her self-esteem and self-dignity, Parama slits her wrist in an attempt to commit suicide.

The woman who now emerges out of the ashes of the old one is a completely transformed individual. 'The suicide attempt is therefore, a positive catharsis in Parama's life.... It is the first step towards the dramatic metamorphosis that follows'.[2] Parama, thus in a white *saree*, her beautiful tresses chopped off, distinctly reminds us of Sudha, her adulterous aunt who was branded as deviant, distressed and so psychic. Sudha *pishi* appears thrice in Parama's nightmare. Significantly, in one of these, she is found to be peeping from behind the bars of the window in her room, urging Parama to unlock the door and set her free. Thus, in *Parama*, we find repeatedly women are socially ostracized for freely expressing their emotional and sexual desires. These nightmares are, thus subconscious efforts on Parama's part to come out of the shackles of her own marital prison. Parama, however, refuses to step into her hapless aunt's shoes. At the hospital, she is found to be staring vaguely without a fixed gaze. A distorted close-up of all family members appears on the screen. After a few moments Parama, who is completely dissociated from her surroundings, turns her head away. Her husband is ready to forgive and forget. Her son, daughter, all her relatives—they want her back home, safe in her familial roles, because after all she had suffered immensely for her 'mistake'. Now it is time to take her in but not before a round of psychological counselling. The screenplay reads here[3]:

Dr. Dasgupta: (Off voice) Listen, you have passed through such a trauma—physical and mental, so there has to be a reaction. But surely you want to get back to your earlier space (place?). Don't you?

Parama: What is that place?

There is a big close-up of Parama's eyes. Doctor's voice is heard. The camera pans from Parama's bedroom, kids' room, her mother-in-law's room, the living and dining room, the kitchen and store and finally rests on the bunch of house-keys.

Doctor: (Off voice) Tell me don't you want to get back to your earlier roles of the lady of the house, the wife, the mother—don't you want to live life as before? Your husband, your children, your mother-in-law, your household. . . .

There is a close-up of the doctor.

Doctor: You must be your own, older self amidst all your family members and relations.

There is a big close-up of Parama.

Parama: Why?

Close-up of the doctor.

Bhaskar: (in a tired voice) . . . I don't want to think about it. You also try to forget.

Doctor: That is why you need a psychiatrist so that you can come out of this mental agony . . . this feeling of guilt.

Parama: (Big close-up) But I don't have any sense of guilt!

This assertion endorses once and for all Parama's utterly changed psyche and an unexpected sense of freedom. The new lease of life strips her of the initial sense of guilt of having an adulterous affair, however, absurd it may seem to her family members. She becomes absolutely firm and resolute and decides to return home but on her own terms. This new found individuality not only makes her bold enough to speak out her mind as she starts writing diary, but also gives her the courage to flip through the pages of her favourite issue of *Life* magazine without feeling ashamed any more. Once again, the person she can connect to is Sheela who had been beside her through thick and thin. Sheela, without being overtly feminist, throughout the film had not only been a pillar of strength for Parama but is also inspirational for her to make her own choice and owe its responsibility. So, it is almost natural that Parama would ask Sheela at this crucial juncture to find her a job even if that means working as a sales person at 'Khadi' earning Rs. 600. Her decision baffles her husband to whom she replies that it will still be her own money. This is in sharp contrast to the earlier housewife who was doled out a handsome allowance and happily considered her husband's money to be her own. Thus, it is not merely a question of Parama's financial independence but also opens up an alternative social, economic and political space for her future life. Her white *saree*, the traditional attire of an Indian widow, her disinterested look at her family and her complete lack of interest in Rahul too, transports her to a world where she does not need a man anymore. She totally rejects the idea of slipping back into the same socially acceptable roles; she had internalized at the beginning of the film. It is here for the first time she remembers the name of the long forgotten plant which had so long eluded her since her early womanhood. Parama lovingly stares at the young sapling of *Shyam Kanchan* which Sheela brought for her in the nursing home. The plant stands in sharp contrast to the conscious arrangement of flowers in the vase that her family brings for her in the nursing home. The blooming sapling restates the fact that Parama had already started inhabiting a new breathing space, hitherto unknown to her. It is going to be a fresh start as she is re-united with at least one of her family members, her daughter Esha. The latter, though initially rejected her mother, now comes forward and holds her hand. She salutes her mother's inner strength and probably feels vulnerable for the first time in this new found situation. Though the end of the film is somewhat lucid and open and one is not sure whether Parama would go back to her domestic space, yet she successfully re-constructs the traditional paradigm of marriage and at the same time ventures out into a woman's space.

Marriage is ideally thought of as a relationship between two equal partners based on love and companionship. Sociological research over several decades, however, shows that marital relationships often fail to live up to this ideal. Gender inequalities, which normally characterize the most personal relationships, have to be understood as inseparable from the broader inequalities and cultural lacuna in which this relationships are embedded. The priorities of women, envisaged in different societal roles, are overlooked, uncared for and most dangerously taken for granted in patriarchal social understanding. Bhaskar, Parama's husband, thus fails to realize that a generous allowance, social security and healthy children can not satisfy all the needs of a woman. Thus, any deviance is seen as a potential threat to patriarchy which either tries to brand it as something undesirable or tries to absorb it within its framework and reorient it. *Parama*, thus, cinematically reveals to what extent a woman might be pushed in order to discover herself. Deviant behaviour for one may be perfectly rational for the other in extreme circumstances.

Notes

1. Shoma A. Chatterjee, *Parama and Other Outsiders: The Cinema of Aparna Sen*, Calcutta: Paramita Publications, 2002, p. 94.
2. Shoma A. Chatterjee, *Subject: Cinema, Object: Woman: A Study of the Portrayal of Women in Indian Cinema*, Calcutta: Paramita Publications, 1998, pp. 215-16.
3. Screenplay of *Parama* by Aparna Sen (in Bengali), *Bibhab: Cinema-r Eksho Bachhor (Bibhab: 100th Year of Cinema)*, Special Issue on Screenplay, no. 63, Calcutta, 1402 BS (1995), pp. 395-6 [translated by the author]:
   Dr. Dasgupta: (off voice) Shunun, shunun—Etobaro ekta durghatana-r modhye diye gelen to apni. Sharirik manasik. Tar ekta reaction achhei. Nijer jaigai abar phire aste hobe na apnake?
   Parama: Se jaigata ki?
   (Parama-r chokher birat close-up. Daktar katha bolchhe—Parama-r chokher samne Parama-r shobar ghar bhese othe—ekghat theke onyo ghar—chheleder ghar, thammar ghar, bosbar ghar, khaoar ghar, rannaghar, store sob fanka ghargulo Parama-r chokher samne bhese othe porpor. Rannagharer derajer opor pore royechhe Parama-r chabir gochha.)
   Dakatar: (off voice) Apni-i bolun na. Grihini hisebe, stree hisebe, ma hisebe—abar ager moto kore banchte hobe na apnake? Apnar swami,

apnar chhelemeye, apnar shasuri, apnar sangsar...
Parama: (off voice) Amar rannaghar, amar bhanrar, amar chabir gochha—
(Daktar-er close up)
Daktar: Apnar atmiyoswajon, poribarer sakoler modhye apnake abar ager moton hote hobe.
(Parama-r big close-up)
Parama: Keno?
(Daktar-er close-up)
Bhaskar: (Klanto hoye bole) Ja hoye gachhe, hoye gachhe. Amra se sob ar mone rakhte chai na. Tumio bhule jao.
(Dakta-er close-up)
Daktar: Sei jonyoi bolchhi manasik chikitsar darker jate ei niye apnar je aparadhbodh—seta apni katiye uthte paren.
(Parama-r big close-up)
Parama: Kintu amar to kono aparadhbodh nei.

Contributors

ACHINTYA KUMAR DUTTA is Professor of History, Burdwan University, Burdwan. He has worked extensively on the history of health and medicine in colonial India.

AMITAVA CHATTERJEE's research interest includes the history of sports in the colonial period. He is an Assistant Professor, Kazi Nazrul University, Asansol.

ARABINDA SAMANTA is Retd. Professor of History, Burdwan University, Burdwan. His research interest lies in the history of health and medicine in colonial India.

ARPITA SEN is Associate Professor of History in Visva-Bharati, Santiniketan. She has been working on the Indian National Movement, history of the North-East and missionary history.

ATIG GHOSH is Assistant Professor of History in Visva-Bharati, Santiniketan. He is member and honorary research fellow of the Calcutta Research Group. His research interest lies in contemporary politics, conflict resolutions and peace building in South-East Asia.

BIPASHA RAHA is Professor and Head of Department of History in Visva-Bharati, Santiniketan. Her research interest lies in the socio-economic history of colonial India.

MADHUMITA MONDAL has been working on the history of gender in colonial India for a very long time. She teaches in Kulti High School (H.S.) in Kulti, West Bengal.

MANJIMA CHATTERJEE is Assistant Professor of English in Sri Chaitanya College, Habra, West Bengal. She has worked extensively on Partition of India, feminist issues and Indian films.

NAINA BANERJEE is Assistant Professor of History in Asansol Girls' College, Asansol. Before that she had taught in Bolpur College for more than a decade. She has worked extensively on the coal industry in Bengal.

SAJAL NAG is Professor of History, Assam University, Silchar. He has published extensively on the history of the north-east India.

SUBHAYU CHATTOPADHYAY is Assistant Professor of History in Visva-Bharati, Santiniketan. He has been working on the history of science and socio-cultural history in colonial India.

SUJATA MUKHERJEE is Professor of History, Rabindra Bharati University, Kolkata. She has been working on the history of health, medicine and environment in the colonial period for a very long time.

SUPTI RAHA is Associate Professor of History in Rishi Bankim College, Naihati, West Bengal. She has been working on artisans in Bengal in the colonial period.

SWATI GANGULY is Associate Professor in the Department of English and Other Modern European Languages, Visva-Bharati, Santiniketan. She has worked extensively on Renaissance culture and theatre, feminism and Rabindranath Tagore.

Index